Your Pregnancy
week by week

Other books by Glade B. Curtis, M.D., and Judith Schuler, M.S.

Your Baby's First Year Week by Week
Your Pregnancy: Every Woman's Guide
Your Pregnancy after 35
Your Pregnancy Questions & Answers
Your Pregnancy Recovery Guide

Your Pregnancy
week by week

Fourth Edition

Glade B. Curtis, M.D., OB/GYN

Judith Schuler, M.S.

PERSEUS
PUBLISHING

Copyright © 2000 by Glade B. Curtis and Judith Schuler

Library of Congress Cataloging -in-Publication Data
Curtis, Glade B.
  Your Pregnancy Week by Week / Glade B. Curtis & Judith Schuler. -- 4th ed.
  p.cm.
  Includes index.
  ISBN 1-5551-256-3 (hardcover) -- ISBN 1-55561-260-1 (pbk.)
  1. Pregnancy. 2. Fetus--Growth. 1. Schuler, Judith. II. Title

RG525.C92 2000
618.2'4--dc21   00-034817

Perseus Publishing is a member of the Perseus Books Group.
Find us on the World Wide Web at http://www.perseuspublishing.com

Perseus Publishing books are available at special discounts for bulk purchases in the United States by corporations, institutions, and other organizations. For more information, please contact the Special Markets Department at the Perseus Books Group, 11 Cambridge Center, Cambridge, MA 02142, or call (800) 255-1514 or (617) 252-5298, or e-mail j.mccrary@perseusbooks.com.

Photos on pages 1, 31 and 47 from Lifestyles Today photo CD © 1998 PhotoDisc, Inc. All photos except the above from New Family photo CD © 2000 EyeWire, Inc.

Text design by Gary Smith
Illustration: Leslie Sinclair
Technical Illustration: David Fischer
Cover Design: Lynn Bishop

EBA   04 03 02—20 19 18 17 16 15

About the Fourth Edition

Dr. Glade Curtis may be the most beloved obstetrician in the world. Hundreds of thousands of his pregnancy books are in print in many editions, in the United States, Europe and Asia. Dr. Curtis's success is based on his commitment to providing the most up-to-date information about pregnancy. Drawing on his experience as a practicing obstetrician and the help of co-author Judith Schuler, Dr. Curtis has again met that commitment in this completely revised edition of *Your Pregnancy Week by Week*.

The unique week-by-week format helps women from before they conceive their baby until they give birth. Read this book straight through when you buy it, then reread chapters as the weeks pass—one for each week throughout your entire pregnancy. Learn how your baby is developing and review changes in your own body as they happen. In a timely way, read about lab tests you may take, how your actions affect your baby and any possible complications you may be facing. These essential facts are easy to absorb at the right time. Check the index if you are looking for a specific topic.

This edition is more reader-friendly in design, with the following new features:

- nutrition information in each week to help you feel your best and to provide your baby with what it needs to grow and to develop
- dad tips: from helping mom to helping himself be more involved in the pregnancy
- more boxes, charts and checklists, with cross-references to topics that matter specifically to you
- spreads on important topics, such as exercise, prenatal classes and more

Having a baby is an exciting event in your life. There's a lot to learn and a lot to look forward to. With this new edition of *Your Pregnancy Week by Week*, you'll be prepared for all the big and little changes coming your way.

About the Authors

Glade B. Curtis, M.D., is board-certified by the American College of Obstetricians and Gynecologists. He is in private practice in obstetrics, gynecology and infertility in Sandy, Utah.

One of Dr. Curtis's goals as a doctor is to provide patients with many types of information about gynecological and obstetrical conditions they may have, problems they may encounter and procedures they may undergo. In pursuit of that goal, he has written several books especially for pregnant women, including *Your Pregnancy Questions & Answers, Your Pregnancy after 35, Your Pregnancy: Every Woman's Guide* and *Your Pregnancy Recovery Guide.* His latest book deals with baby's development after birth and is titled *Your Baby's First Year Week by Week.*

Dr. Curtis is a graduate of the University of Utah and the University of Rochester School of Medicine and Dentistry in New York. He was an intern, resident and chief resident in Obstetrics and Gynecology at the University of Rochester Strong Memorial Hospital.

Judith Schuler, M.S., has worked with Dr. Glade Curtis for over 18 years, as his co-author and editor. They have collaborated together on nine books dealing with pregnancy, women's health and children's health. Ms. Schuler earned a Master of Science degree in Family Studies from the University of Arizona in Tucson.

Before becoming an editor for HPBooks, where she and Dr. Curtis first began working together, Ms. Schuler taught at the university level in California and Arizona. She has one son. She divides her time between Tucson, Arizona, and Laramie, Wyoming.

Acknowledgments

Glade B. Curtis. In this, the fourth edition of *Your Pregnancy Week by Week,* I have continued to draw upon the many questions from discussions with my patients and their partners, and my professional colleagues. Nearly every day brings new insights and greater understanding of the joy and anticipation of impending parenthood. I rejoice in my patients' happiness and thank all of them for allowing me to be part of this miraculous process.

Credit must also be given to my understanding and generous wife, Debbie, and our family, who support me in a profession that requires much of them. Beyond that commitment, they have supported and encouraged me to pursue the challenge of this project. And my parents have always offered their love and support.

Judi Schuler continues to be a fresh source of energy and enthusiasm. I appreciate her commitment to excellence and accuracy. Special thanks to Elizabeth Warner, M.D., and Marcia Vavich, R.N., for reviewing the text and to Kathy Michael for her valuable help.

Judith Schuler. I wish to thank my parents, Bob and Kay Gordon, and my son, Ian, for their love and continued support. It is very important to me. And special thanks to Bob Rucinski for helping me in so many ways—for your professionalism, your expertise and your encouragement and support.

Contents

Preparing for Pregnancy

Nothing compares with the miracle and magic of pregnancy. It is your chance to be involved in life's creative process. Planning ahead for this experience can improve your chances of doing well yourself and of having a healthy baby.

You can have an effect on one of the most important factors in your baby's health—your lifestyle. By planning ahead, you can ensure you and your baby are exposed to good things and avoid harmful things during your pregnancy.

By the time most women realize they are pregnant, they are 1 to 2 months into their pregnancy. By the time they see their doctor, they are 2 or 3 months along. The first 12 weeks of pregnancy are extremely important because this is when the baby forms its major organ systems. Many important things can happen before you realize you are pregnant or before you see your doctor. Getting in shape for pregnancy means physical and mental preparation.

Pregnancy is a condition, not an illness; a pregnant woman is not sick. However, you will experience major changes during the course of your pregnancy. Having good general health before pregnancy can help you deal with the physical and emotional stresses of pregnancy, labor and delivery. It can help you prepare to take care of a newborn baby.

Your General Health

There has been an explosion of technology, new medications, medical advances and medical treatments in recent years. Through these advances, we have learned that your health at the beginning

Preparing for Pregnancy

The following are important actions to take before you get pregnant.

- Achieve your ideal weight.
- Start a regular exercise program if you haven't already.
- Schedule medical tests, such as X-rays.
- Schedule vaccinations, such as MMR (measles, mumps, rubella).
- Consider how pregnancy fits into your future plans (education, career, travel).
- If you smoke, stop now.
- If you use drugs or alcohol, stop now.

The above actions are much harder to take during a pregnancy. Deal with these issues before pregnancy, know you are healthy, and you won't have to worry about the risks they may pose while you're pregnant. It makes sense to continue birth control until you've achieved the above.

of pregnancy and during pregnancy can have a major effect on you and your developing baby.

In the past, the emphasis was on being healthy while pregnant. Today, most doctors suggest looking at pregnancy as lasting 12 months instead of just 9 months. This includes at least a 3-month period of preparation. Preparing your body with good general health can help you prepare for a healthy pregnancy and a healthy baby.

Seeking Medical Advice

Seeing a doctor before you get pregnant is good preparation for pregnancy. Also consider choosing someone to take care of you during your pregnancy. Arrange for a checkup and discuss your plans with your doctor before you get pregnant. Then you will know that when you do get pregnant, you are in the best possible health.

You may have a medical condition that requires attention before pregnancy. If you don't take care of it before trying to conceive, it may affect your ability to get pregnant. You may need to change medications you are taking, or you may need to make lifestyle changes.

Tests for You

A general physical exam before you get pregnant helps ensure you won't have to deal with new medical problems during pregnancy. A Pap smear and a breast exam should be included in this physical. Lab tests to consider before pregnancy include tests for rubella, blood type and Rh-factor. If you are 35 or older, a mammogram is also a good idea.

If you have been exposed to HIV or hepatitis, have your caregiver conduct tests for these. If you have a family history of other medical problems, such as diabetes, ask your caregiver whether you should have any tests to rule them out. If you have other chronic medical problems, such as anemia or recurrent miscarriages, your healthcare provider may suggest other specific tests.

X-rays and Other Imaging Tests

When you are scheduled to have any test involving radiation, including dental work, ask for a pregnancy test first. Tests that involve radiation include X-rays, CT scans and MRIs. Use reliable contraception before these tests to make sure you are not pregnant. If you schedule these tests right after the end of your period, you can be sure you are not pregnant. If you must receive a series of these tests, continue to use contraception. (See Week 14.)

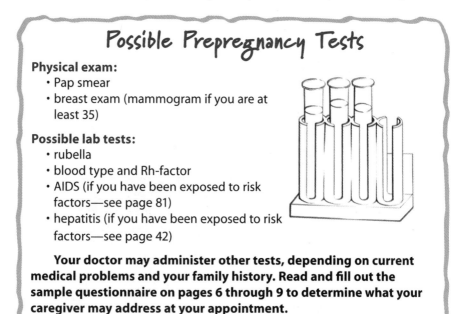

Possible Prepregnancy Tests

Physical exam:
- Pap smear
- breast exam (mammogram if you are at least 35)

Possible lab tests:
- rubella
- blood type and Rh-factor
- AIDS (if you have been exposed to risk factors—see page 81)
- hepatitis (if you have been exposed to risk factors—see page 42)

Your doctor may administer other tests, depending on current medical problems and your family history. Read and fill out the sample questionnaire on pages 6 through 9 to determine what your caregiver may address at your appointment.

Medical History

A prepregnancy visit with your doctor is the best time to discuss your medical history and any problems you may have had in other pregnancies. Ask your healthcare provider what you can do to eliminate or to decrease chances of the same problems recurring in your next pregnancy. This includes dealing with ectopic pregnancy, miscarriage, previous C-sections (Cesarean deliveries) or other complications.

This is also a good time to talk about exposure to and problems with sexually transmitted diseases or other infections. If you have had major surgery or any female surgery in the past, discuss it now. If you are being treated for other medical problems, discuss them with your healthcare provider. Make plans to be taking medications that are safe during your pregnancy *before* you try to get pregnant.

Before going to see the doctor, read and fill out the questionnaire starting on page 6. This questionnaire may be similar to the one you will fill out at your appointment, including medical history, current health, risk factors and so on. Cross-references guide you to further information in this book. For example, if you have diabetes, the page reference next to "Diabetes" refers you to more information on the condition and how it may affect pregnancy.

A Visit with the Doctor

I've had new patients come in who are pregnant and tell me they had a series of X-rays during the first or second month of pregnancy. I saw Susan for her first prenatal visit when she was 8 weeks pregnant. She told me she'd had a series of X-rays for some bowel problems 3 weeks before, and she was worried about radiation exposure. There wasn't much I could tell her. It's difficult to determine whether a test will harm a pregnancy. It's much better to know you aren't pregnant before these tests are done.

Discontinuing Contraception

It's important to continue using some form of contraception until you are ready to get pregnant. If you are in the middle of treatment for a medical problem or if you are undergoing tests, finish the course of treatment or tests before trying to conceive. (If you're not using some form of birth control, you're basically trying to get pregnant.) After discontinuing your regular contraceptive, use some other birth-control method until your periods become normal. You can choose from condoms, spermicides, the sponge or a diaphragm.

Birth-Control Pills
Most doctors recommend you have two or three normal periods after you stop taking birth-control pills before you get pregnant. If you get pregnant immediately after stopping oral contraceptives, it may be difficult to determine when you conceived. This can make it harder to determine your due date. This may not seem important now, but it will be very important to you during pregnancy and at the end of your pregnancy.

IUDs
If you have an IUD (intrauterine device), you must have it removed before you try to conceive. If you have any sign of infection with an IUD, take care of it before trying to get pregnant. The best time to remove an IUD is during a menstrual period.

Norplant®
If you use Norplant, you should have at least two or three normal menstrual cycles after it is removed before trying to get pregnant. It may take a few months for your periods to return to normal after Norplant is removed. If you get pregnant immediately after removing Norplant, it may be difficult to determine when you got pregnant and what your due date is.

Depo Provera®
Depo provera, a hormone injection used for birth control, should be discontinued for at least 3 to 6 months before trying to conceive. Wait until you have had at least two or three normal periods.

Sample OB/GYN Questionnaire

In addition to your name, address, phone number and insurance information, your healthcare provider will need information about your health and lifestyle. If you fill it out before you go to your first appointment, you'll have time to think about what you need to know or are unsure of. Read the pages listed next to each question for more information about that particular issue.

Do you think you are currently pregnant? ❑ yes ❑ no ❑ unsure

Health History
Genetic
Check if any of the following apply to you or *anyone in your family.* See the page listed next to each condition for information on that condition and how it relates to pregnancy.

❑ Birth defects (see pages 17, 164)
❑ Cystic fibrosis (see page 17)
❑ Down syndrome (see pages 17, 19, 125, 164, 171)
❑ Hemophilia (see pages 17, 164)
❑ Huntington's chorea
❑ Hydrocephalus (see pages 125, 184)
❑ Muscular dystrophy (see page 17)
❑ Sickle cell trait/disease (see pages 17, 164, 210)
❑ Spina bifida/anencephaly (see pages 17, 156, 164)
❑ Tay-Sachs (see page 17)
❑ Thalassemia (see page 212)
❑ Other: _____

Medical
❑ Anemia (see pages 10, 210)
❑ Asthma (see pages 10, 261)
❑ Blood disease/transfusion (see page 193)
❑ Cancer (see pages 11, 138, 158, 277)

❑ Cardiac (heart) disease (see page 13)
❑ Diabetes mellitus (see pages 11, 220)
❑ Drug allergy
List drugs you are allergic to:

_____
_____
_____

❑ Gastrointestinal disease
❑ HIV (see page 81)
❑ Hypertension (high blood pressure) (see pages 13, 287)
❑ Kidney and bladder problems (see pages 11, 181)
❑ Liver disease
❑ Lung disease
❑ Lupus (see pages 13, 255)
❑ Organ transplant
❑ Psychiatric disease
❑ Seizure disorder (see pages 12, 243)
❑ Stroke
❑ Surgeries
❑ Thyroid disease (see pages 14, 236)
❑ Venous thrombosis/pulmonary embolism (see page 199)
❑ Other: _____

Obstetric Risk Factors (Pregnancy History)
Check if any of the following applied to you (not your family) during a previous pregnancy. See the page listed next to each risk factor for further information.

❑ Abortion
❑ Abruption (see page 301)
❑ Age 35 or older at time of delivery (see page 18)
❑ Antibody sensitization
❑ Fetal distress in labor (see pages 296, 345)
❑ Fetus or infant had a birth defect
❑ Incompetent cervix (see page 229)
❑ Infant admitted to NICU
❑ Infant heavier than 9 pounds at birth
❑ Infant with IUGR (see page 281)
❑ Multiple gestation (see page 292)
❑ Placenta previa (see page 325)
❑ Poly/oligohydramnios (see page 227)
❑ Pre-eclampsia (see page 288)
❑ Previous Cesarean section (see page 331) Uterine incision type: _____
❑ Prior preterm birth (37 weeks or less) (see page 266)
❑ Recurrent urinary-tract infection (see pages 11, 181)
❑ Stillbirth/neonatal death (see page 94)
❑ Other: _____

Risk Factors for Preterm Birth
Check if any of the following applies to you. See the page listed next to each risk factor for more information on that factor.

❑ 2 or more abortions requiring D&C (see pages 94, 111, 229)
❑ African American
❑ DES exposure
❑ Drug abuse (including alcohol) (see pages 23, 40, 60)
❑ History of sexually transmitted diseases (see pages 26, 78)
❑ Known uterine malformation

❑ Older than 35 years old (see page 18)
❑ Previous uterine surgery
❑ Prior preterm birth (37 weeks or less) (see page 266)
❑ Psychosocial/physical abuse
❑ Smoking (see pages 24, 38)
❑ Weight: less than 55 kg (121 lbs)
❑ Younger than 18 years old
❑ Other: _____

Other Children
Fill in the following information about other children you have, starting with the oldest.

1. Name: _____

Birthdate: _____

Birth hospital and city: _____
_____

Sex: _____

Weight at birth: _____

Gestational age at birth: _____

Maternal age: _____

Labor length: _____

Anesthesia used: _____

Delivery type: _____

Maternal problems: _____

Newborn problems: _____

2. Name: _____

Birthdate: _____

Birth hospital and city: _____

Sex: _____

Weight at birth: _____

Gestational age at birth: _____

Maternal age: _____

(continued)

Labor length: _____

Anesthesia used: _____

Delivery type: _____

Maternal problems: _____

Newborn problems:_____

Medications

Please list all medications you currently take, recently stopped taking or plan to take:

Medication: _____

Dosage:_____

Start date:_____

Stop date (if any):_____

Medication: _____

Dosage:_____

Start date:_____

Stop date (if any):_____

Medication: _____

Dosage:_____

Start date:_____

Stop date (if any):_____

Do you regularly take any over-the-counter medications, vitamins, minerals, herbs or other supplements? Please list them below.

_____

_____

_____

_____

_____

_____

Lifestyle

• Do you use tobacco? (see pages 24, 38)_____

• How much alcohol do you drink per week? (see pages 24, 40, 59, 62) _

_____

_____

• Do you take any drugs that aren't prescribed for you? (see pages 23, 60)_____

• If yes, what kind(s)? _____

_____

• How often? _____

• How much caffeine do you ingest per day (including chocolate, coffee, soda, caffeinated tea)? (see pages 62, 141) _____

• Are you currently trying to lose weight? (see page 20)

_____

• Are you currently trying to gain weight? (see page 20)

_____

• How often do you exercise?

_____

• What kind of exercise? (see page 50)

_____

• What do you do for a living? (see pages 25, 139)

_____

• Are you exposed to any chemicals in the workplace? (see pages 25, 64)

_____

• Do you lift heavy objects or stand for long periods of time? (see pages 25, 141)_____

- What kind of contraception are you currently using, if any? (see pages 5, 69)_____

_____

- What was the date of the start of your last period? _____

- Have you ever been tested for any sexually transmitted diseases (STDs)? (see pages 26, 78) _____

- If so, when and what were the results? _____

_____

- If not, have you ever placed yourself at risk for an STD? (see pages 26, 78)_____

- Has your partner been tested for any STDs? _____

- If so, when and what were the results? _____

_____

- If not, has he ever placed himself at risk for an STD?

_____

- Have you ever been tested for HIV? (see page 81) _____

- If so, when and what were the results? _____

- If not, have you ever risked exposure to HIV? (see page 81)

_____

- Has your partner ever been tested for HIV? _____

- If so, when and what were the results? _____

_____

- If not, has he ever risked exposure to HIV?_____

Please list any medical tests (including X-rays, CT scans, MRIs and anything else involving radiation) you've had in the past 6 months:

Test:_____

Date: _____

Test:_____

Date: _____

Test:_____

Date: _____

Do you plan to take any medical tests in the near future?

When?_____

Why? _____

Please list any vaccinations you've had in the past 6 months:

Vac.:_____

Date: _____

Vac.:_____

Date: _____

Vac.:_____

Date: _____

Do you plan to have any vaccinations in the near future?

When?_____

Why? _____

Please list any questions or concerns you have about your current or future pregnancy:

_____

_____

_____

Current Medical Problems

Before you become pregnant, examine your lifestyle, diet, physical
activity and any chronic medical problems you have, such as high
blood pressure or diabetes. You may require extra care before
and during pregnancy. Tell your healthcare provider about any
medications you currently take. Discuss any tests you may be
planning to have, such as X-rays, and cover all medical problems
you are being treated for. It's easier to answer questions about these
problems, their treatment and their complications before you get
pregnant rather than after you are pregnant.

Anemia

Anemia means you do not have enough hemoglobin to carry
oxygen to your body's cells. Symptoms include weakness, fatigue,
shortness of breath and pale skin. *It is possible to develop anemia
during pregnancy even if you are not anemic before you get pregnant!*
While you are pregnant, the baby makes great demands on your
body for iron and iron stores. If you have low iron levels at the
beginning of pregnancy, pregnancy can tip the balance and make
you anemic. Ask for a CBC (complete blood count) as a part of your
prepregnancy physical.

    If you have a family history of anemia (such as sickle cell anemia
or thalassemia), discuss these with your healthcare provider *before*
you get pregnant. (See Week 22 for more information on different
types of anemia.) If you take hydroxurea to treat your sickle cell
disease, discuss with your caregiver whether you should continue
using it while trying to conceive. We do not know whether this
medication is safe during pregnancy.

Asthma

Asthma affects about 1% of all pregnant women. Half of those
women with asthma see no change in their condition during
pregnancy. For about 25%, asthma improves, and for about another
25%, the condition worsens.

    Most asthma medications are safe to take during
pregnancy, but talk to your healthcare provider about taking
any medication. Most people with asthma know what triggers
attacks. While you're trying to get pregnant and during pregnancy,

be especially careful to avoid things that trigger attacks. Try to get asthma under good control before trying to become pregnant. (Read more about how asthma affects pregnancy in Week 28.)

Bladder or Kidney Problems

Bladder infections, commonly called *urinary-tract infections* or *UTIs*, may occur more often during pregnancy. If a urinary-tract infection is not treated, it can cause an inflammation of the kidneys, called *pyelonephritis.*

Urinary-tract infections and pyelonephritis are associated with premature delivery. If you have a history of pyelonephritis or repeated urinary-tract infections, you should be evaluated before you begin pregnancy.

Kidney stones may also create problems during pregnancy. Because they cause pain, it may be difficult to differentiate between kidney stones and other problems that can occur during pregnancy. Kidney stones can also cause an increased chance of urinary-tract infections and pyelonephritis.

If you have had kidney or bladder surgery or major kidney problems or if you know your kidney function is less than normal, tell your healthcare provider. It may be necessary to evaluate your kidney function with tests before you become pregnant.

If you have had an occasional bladder infection, don't be alarmed. Your caregiver will decide whether further testing is necessary before you become pregnant. (See Week 18 for more information.)

Cancer

If you have had any type of cancer in the past, tell your healthcare provider when planning your pregnancy or as soon as you discover you are pregnant. He or she may need to make decisions about individualized care for you during this pregnancy. (See Week 30 for more information about cancer and pregnancy.)

Diabetes

Diabetes is a medical problem that can have serious effects during pregnancy. Historically, women with diabetes have had problems with pregnancy, but with good control, a diabetic woman today is usually able to have a healthy pregnancy.

If you have diabetes, it may be harder for you to become pregnant. It can also increase the chance of miscarriage, stillbirth and birth defects. These risks can be decreased by good control of blood sugar during pregnancy.

If your diabetes is not controlled, the combination of pregnancy and diabetes can be dangerous for you and your baby. Many of the problems and damage caused by diabetes occur during the first trimester (the first 13 weeks of pregnancy); poor control, however, can affect the entire pregnancy.

Pregnancy may affect diabetes by increasing your body's need for insulin. Insulin makes it possible for the body to use sugar. Most doctors recommend you have diabetes under good control for at least 2 to 3 months before pregnancy begins. Having your diabetes under control may require checking your blood sugar several times a day.

If you have a family history of diabetes or suspect you might have diabetes, have it checked before getting pregnant. This will help you lower your risks of miscarriage and other problems. If you haven't had diabetes before and develop it during pregnancy, it is called *gestational diabetes.* (See Week 23.)

Epilepsy and Seizures

Epilepsy includes several different problems. There are different kinds of seizures, called *grand mal* and *petit mal* seizures. A mother-to-be with epilepsy has a 1 in 30 chance of having a baby with a seizure disorder. Babies also have a higher chance of birth defects, perhaps related to medications taken for epilepsy during pregnancy.

If you take medication for epilepsy, it is important to consult your healthcare provider before you become pregnant. Discuss the amounts and the types of medication you take. Some medications are safe during pregnancy. Most doctors will have you switch to phenobarbital during the time you are trying to conceive and while you are pregnant.

Seizures can be dangerous to the mother and fetus. It is important for you to take your medication regularly and as prescribed by your caregiver. Do not decrease or discontinue any medication on your own!

Heart Disease

During pregnancy, the workload on your heart increases by about 50%. If you have any kind of heart condition, tell your healthcare provider about it before you get pregnant. Some heart problems, such as *mitral-valve prolapse*, may be serious during pregnancy and may require antibiotics at the time of delivery. Other heart problems, such as *congenital* heart problems, may seriously affect your health. Your healthcare provider may advise against pregnancy in these cases. Consult your caregiver about any heart condition so it can be dealt with before you become pregnant.

Hypertension

Hypertension, or high blood pressure, can cause problems for a pregnant woman and her unborn baby. For the woman, these problems may include kidney damage, stroke or headaches. For a developing baby, high blood pressure in a mother-to-be can cause decreased blood flow to the placenta, resulting in a smaller baby or intrauterine-growth retardation (IUGR).

If you have high blood pressure before pregnancy, you must closely monitor your blood pressure during pregnancy. Your healthcare provider may ask you to see an internist who will help you control your blood pressure.

Some high-blood-pressure medications are safe to take during pregnancy; others are not. *Do not stop or decrease any medication on your own!* This can be dangerous. If you're planning a pregnancy, ask your healthcare provider about the medication you take for high blood pressure and its safety during conception and pregnancy.

Lupus

Systemic lupus erythematosus (SLE) is an autoimmune disease. This means you produce antibodies to your own organs, which may destroy or damage those organs and their function. Lupus can affect many parts of the body, including joints, kidneys, lungs and the heart.

This problem can be difficult to diagnose. Lupus occurs in about 1 in 700 women between 15 and 64 years of age. In black women, it occurs once in 254 women. Lupus is found more often in women than in men, especially between the ages of 20 and 40.

There is no cure for lupus at present. Treatment is individual and usually involves taking steroids. It is best not to become pregnant while you are experiencing a flare-up. There is an increased risk of miscarriage and stillbirths in women with lupus, which requires extra care during pregnancy.

Babies born to women with lupus may have a rash, heart block and heart defects. These babies may be born prematurely or experience intrauterine-growth retardation. Consult your healthcare provider before you become pregnant if you have lupus. (See Week 27 for more information on lupus in pregnancy.)

Migraine Headaches

About 15 to 20% of all pregnant women suffer from migraine headaches. Many women notice an improvement in their headaches while they are pregnant. If you must take medication for headaches during pregnancy, check with your healthcare provider ahead of time so you'll know whether the one you take is safe to use.

> **Many women notice an improvement in their headaches while they are pregnant.**

Thyroid Problems

Thyroid problems can appear as either too much or too little thyroid hormone. Too much thyroid hormone, *hyperthyroidism,* results in a faster metabolism; it is usually caused by Graves' disease. The problem is often treated by surgery or medication to reduce the amount of thyroid hormone in your system. If left untreated during pregnancy, there is a higher risk of premature delivery and low birthweight. If treatment is necessary during pregnancy, there are safe medications you can take.

Too little thyroid hormone, *hypothyroidism,* is usually caused by autoimmune problems; the thyroid gland is damaged by your own antibodies. Doctors treat this problem with thyroid hormones. If left untreated, you may suffer from infertility or have a miscarriage.

If you have either thyroid problem, you should be tested before pregnancy to determine the correct amount of medication for you. Pregnancy can change medication requirements, so you will also need to be checked during pregnancy.

Other Problems

Many other specific chronic illnesses can affect a pregnancy. If you have any chronic problem or take any medication on a regular basis, talk it over with your caregiver.

Current Medications

It's important for you and your caregiver to consider the possibility of pregnancy each time you are given a prescription or told to take a medication. When you are pregnant, everything changes with regard to medications.

Medications that are safe when you are not pregnant may have harmful effects when you are pregnant. Whether a medication is safe during pregnancy is not always known. Ask your doctor before changing any medication. (Some effects of medications and chemicals are discussed in Week 4.)

Most organ development in the baby occurs in the first trimester. This is an important time to avoid exposing your baby to unnecessary medications. You'll feel better and do better during pregnancy if you have medication use under control before you try to get pregnant.

Some medications are intended for short-term use, such as antibiotics for infections. Others are for chronic or long-lasting problems, such as high blood pressure or diabetes. Some medications are OK to take while you are pregnant and might even help make your pregnancy successful. Other medications may not be safe to take during pregnancy. See the box below for some general medication guidelines to keep in mind and page 61 for information about specific medications and their safety during pregnancy.

Vaccinations

The same rule applies to vaccinations as to X-ray tests—when you have a vaccination, use reliable contraception. Some vaccines are safe during pregnancy; some are not. A good rule of thumb is to complete vaccinations at least 3 months before trying to get pregnant. Vaccinations are usually most harmful to a pregnancy in the first trimester.

A good rule of thumb is to complete vaccinations at least 3 months before trying to get pregnant.

Pregnancy and Medications

During pregnancy, play it safe. Some general guidelines for medication use while you are trying to get pregnant include the following.

- Do not stop birth control unless you want to be pregnant.

- Take prescriptions exactly as they are prescribed.

- Notify your doctor if you think you might be pregnant or if you are not using birth control when a medication is prescribed.

- Do not self-treat or use medications you were given in the past for other problems.

- Never use someone else's medications.

- If you are unsure about using a medication, ask your healthcare provider *before* you use it!

Genetic Counseling

If you're planning your first pregnancy, you are probably not considering genetic counseling. However, there may be circumstances in which genetic counseling could help you and your partner make informed decisions about childbearing.

Genetic counseling is an information session between you and your partner and a genetic counselor or group of counselors. Any information you share with or receive from a genetic counselor is confidential. It may involve one visit or several visits. Genetic

counseling is available at most major universities. Your physician can advise you.

Through genetic counseling, you and your partner hope to understand the possibilities or probabilities of what might affect your ability to get pregnant or your future offspring. The information you receive is not precise. Counselors may speak in terms of "chances" or "odds of a problem."

A genetic counselor will not make a decision for you. He or she will provide information on tests you might take and what the results of those tests may indicate. When speaking with a genetic counselor, don't hide information you feel is embarrassing or hard to talk about. It is important to give him or her as much information as possible.

Ask your healthcare provider if you should seek genetic counseling. Most couples who need genetic counseling do not find this out until after they have a child born with a birth defect. You might consider genetic counseling if any of the following apply to you.

- You will be at least 35 years old at the time of delivery.
- You have delivered a child with a birth defect.
- You or your partner has a birth defect.
- You or your partner has a family history of Down syndrome, mental retardation, cystic fibrosis, spina bifida, muscular dystrophy, bleeding disorders, skeletal or bone problems, dwarfism, epilepsy, congenital heart defects or blindness.
- You or your partner has a family history of inherited deafness (prenatal testing can identify congenital deafness caused by the Connexin-26 gene and allow the opportunity to manage the problem immediately).
- You and your partner are related (consanguinity).
- You have had recurrent miscarriages (usually three or more).
- You *and* your partner are descended from Ashkenazi Jews (risk of Tay-Sachs disease or Canavan's disease).
- You or your partner are African American (risk of sickle cell anemia).
- Your partner is at least 40 years old. (Medical information shows a father in his forties may have an increased chance of fathering a child with a birth defect. See page 19 for more information.)

Some of the information you need may be difficult to gather, especially if you or your partner was adopted. You may know little or nothing of your family's medical history. Discuss this with your doctor before you become pregnant. If you learn the chances of problems before getting pregnant, you won't be forced to make difficult choices after becoming pregnant. The primary goal in genetic counseling is the same as other goals in pregnancy—early diagnosis and prevention of problems.

Pregnancy after 30

More women are choosing to marry after they have established their career, and more couples are choosing to start their families at a later age. Today, physicians are seeing more older first-time mothers, and more of these mothers are having safe and healthy pregnancies than women their age did in the past.

We have found that an older woman considering pregnancy has two major concerns. She wants to know how the pregnancy will affect her and how her age will affect her pregnancy. There is a slight increase in the possibility of complications for the mother and baby when the mother is older. You may also want to read our book *Your Pregnancy after 30,* which focuses primarily on pregnancy in older women.

A pregnant woman older than 30 may be more likely to face increased risks of the following:

- a baby born with Down syndrome
- high blood pressure
- pre-eclampsia
- Cesarean delivery
- multiple births
- placental abruption
- bleeding and other complications
- premature labor
- pelvic pressure or pelvic pain

An older pregnant woman must also deal with problems a younger woman might not face. A broad simplification of this is that it is easier to be pregnant when you are 20 than it is when you are 40. Chances are, by age 40 you have a job or other children making demands on your time. You may find it harder to rest, exercise and eat right.

Maternal problems with increasing age include most of the chronic illnesses that tend to appear as age increases. High blood pressure is one of the more common pregnancy complications in women over 35 (see Week 31). There is also a higher incidence of pre-eclampsia (see Week 31). Older women who give birth have a slightly higher risk of abnormalities and problems, including premature labor, pelvic pressure and pelvic pain.

The chance of diabetes, as well as complications of diabetes, increases with age. Researchers cite figures showing that twice as many women over age 35 have complications with diabetes. In the past, hypertension (high blood pressure) and diabetes were major complications in any pregnancy. With today's advances, we can manage these complications of pregnancy quite well.

Down Syndrome

Through medical research, we know older women are at higher risk of giving birth to a child with Down syndrome, although many of these pregnancies end in miscarriage or stillbirth. Various tests are offered to an older woman during pregnancy to determine whether a baby will have Down syndrome. It is the most common chromosomal defect detected by amniocentesis. (See Week 16 for more information on amniocentesis.)

The risk of delivering a baby with Down syndrome increases as you get older. Look at the following statistics:

- at age 25 the risk is 1 in 1,300 births
- at 30 it is 1 in 965 births
- at 35 it is 1 in 365 births
- at 40 it is 1 in 109 births
- at 45 it is 1 in 32 births
- at 49 it is 1 in 12 births

But there is also a positive way to look at these statistics. If you're 45, you have a 97% chance of *not* having a baby with Down syndrome. If you're 49, you have a 92% chance of delivering a child without Down syndrome. If you are concerned about the risk of Down syndrome because of your age or family history, discuss it with your healthcare provider.

Father's Age

Research shows a father's age may also be important. Chromosomal abnormalities that cause birth defects occur more often in older women and in men over 40. Men over 55 have twice the normal risk of fathering a child with Down syndrome. The chance of chromosomal problems increases with the increase in the age of the father. Some researchers recommend that men father their children before age 40. However, there is still some controversy about this.

Your General Health

Important questions to consider before getting pregnant when you are older include those about your general health. Are you fit for pregnancy? If you are an older woman, you can maximize your chances of having a successful pregnancy by being as healthy as possible *before* you become pregnant.

Most researchers recommend a baseline mammogram be done at age 35. Have this test before you become pregnant. Paying attention to general recommendations for your diet and your health care are also important in preparing for pregnancy.

Your Nutrition before Pregnancy

Most people feel better and work better when they eat a well-balanced diet. Planning and following a good diet before pregnancy

ensures that your developing fetus receives good nutrition during the first few weeks or months of pregnancy.

Usually a woman takes good care of herself once she knows she is pregnant. By planning ahead, you will guarantee that your baby has a healthy environment for the entire 9 months of pregnancy, not for just the 6 or 7 months after you discover you truly are pregnant. When you make your nutrition plan, you are preparing the environment in which your baby will be conceived and will develop and grow.

Weight Management

Before trying to get pregnant, pay attention to your weight; you don't want to be too overweight or too underweight. Either condition can make pregnancy more difficult for you.

Do *not* diet during pregnancy or while you are trying to conceive! Don't take diet pills unless you're using reliable contraception. Consult your doctor *before* you try to get pregnant if you are considering a special diet for weight reduction or weight gain. Dieting may cause temporary

> **Do *not* diet during pregnancy or while you are trying to conceive!**

deficiencies in vitamins and minerals that both you and your developing baby need.

Be Careful with Vitamins, Minerals and Herbs

Don't self-medicate with large amounts or unusual combinations of vitamins, minerals or herbs. You *can* overdo it. Certain vitamins, such as vitamin A, can cause birth defects if used in excessive amounts.

As a general rule, stop all extra supplementation at least 3 months before pregnancy. Eat a well-balanced diet and take one

> **The key to good nutrition is balance.**

multivitamin or one prenatal vitamin a day. Most doctors are happy to prescribe prenatal vitamins if you are planning a pregnancy.

Folic Acid

Folic acid is a B vitamin (B_9) that can contribute to a healthy pregnancy. If a mother-to-be takes 0.4mg (400 micrograms) of folic acid each day, starting 3 or 4 months *before* pregnancy begins, it may protect her developing baby against various birth defects of the spine and brain, called *neural-tube defects.*

One of these defects, *spina bifida,* afflicts nearly 4,000 babies born in the United States every year. It develops in the first few weeks of pregnancy. Studies have shown that about 75% of all cases can be prevented if a mother-to-be takes folic acid. As you plan your pregnancy, ask your physician about supplementation.

In 1998, the U.S. government ordered that some grain products, such as flour, breakfast cereals and pasta, be fortified with folic acid. It is found in many other foods, too. A varied diet can help you reach your goal. Many common foods contain folic acid:

asparagus • avocados • bananas • black beans • broccoli • citrus fruits and juices • egg yolks • fortified breads and cereals • green beans • leafy green vegetables • lentils • liver • peas • plantains • spinach • strawberries • tuna • wheat germ • yogurt

Begin Good Eating Habits

Often, a woman carries her prepregnancy eating habits into her pregnancy. Many women eat on the run and pay little attention to what they eat most of the day. Before pregnancy, you may be able to get away with this. However, because of the increased demands on you and the requirements of your developing baby, this won't work when you do become pregnant.

The key to good nutrition is balance. Eat a balanced diet. Going to extremes with vitamins or fad diets can be harmful to you and your developing baby. It could even make you feel run-down during pregnancy.

Specific Considerations

Specific factors to consider before getting pregnant include whether you follow a vegetarian diet, the amount of exercise you do, whether you skip meals, your diet plan (are you trying to lose or gain weight?) and any special dietary needs you might have.

> ## Can You Help Avoid Morning Sickness in Pregnancy?
>
> **A recent study showed that women who ate high amounts of saturated fat—the kind found in cheese and red meat—in the year *before* they got pregnant had a higher risk of suffering severe morning sickness during pregnancy. If you're planning a pregnancy, you may want to cut down on these foods.**

If you eat a special diet because of medical problems, consult your doctor about it. Much information is available through your doctor or your local hospital about good diets and healthful nutrition.

Many diets go to extremes that you may be able to tolerate, but these extremes can be harmful to a developing baby. It is important to discuss dieting with your doctor ahead of time. You don't want to find out when you are 8 weeks pregnant that you are malnourished because of dieting.

Exercise before Pregnancy

Exercise is good for you—before you become pregnant and during pregnancy. Benefits may include weight control, a feeling of well-being and increased stamina or endurance, which will become important later in pregnancy.

Begin exercising regularly before you become pregnant. Making adjustments in your lifestyle to include regular exercise will benefit you now and make it easier to stay in shape throughout pregnancy.

Exercise can be carried to extremes, however, which can cause problems. While you are trying to get pregnant, avoid intense training. Don't try to increase your exercise program. This is not a good time to play competitive sports that involve pushing yourself to the maximum.

It's important to find exercise you enjoy and will continue on a regular basis, in any kind of weather. Concentrate on improving strength in your lower back and abdominal muscles to help during your pregnancy.

Tip for Prepregnancy

Even though you know you aren't pregnant, treat your body as if you were during this preparation period. When you do get pregnant, you'll be on the right track for eating, exercising and avoiding harmful substances.

If you have concerns about exercise before or during pregnancy, discuss them with your doctor. Exercise you tolerate well and easily before pregnancy may be difficult for you during pregnancy.

The American College of Obstetricians and Gynecologists (ACOG) has proposed guidelines for exercise before pregnancy and during pregnancy. Many hospitals and health clubs or spas have exercise programs for pregnant women. ACOG has videotapes available on exercising during pregnancy and after pregnancy. Ask your caregiver how to obtain these tapes or the guidelines. See pages 50 through 52 for more detailed information about exercise, including guidelines, suggestions and possible problems.

The best approach to exercise is a balanced one. Regular exercise that is enjoyable helps you feel better and enjoy your pregnancy more. It will also provide your developing baby with a healthy environment.

Substance Use before Pregnancy

In the past, little was understood about drug or alcohol abuse, and not a lot could be done to help a person with these problems. Today healthcare providers are able to give suggestions and provide care for those who use or abuse drugs, alcohol or other substances. Don't be embarrassed to confide in your doctor about substance use. Your doctor's concern is for you and your developing baby.

We have learned much about drug and alcohol use and the effect on pregnancy in recent years. We now believe the safest approach to drug or alcohol use during pregnancy is *no use at all*.

It makes sense to solve these problems before pregnancy. By the time you realize you're pregnant, you may already be 8 or

Don't be embarrassed to confide in your doctor about substance use. Your doctor's concern is for you and your developing baby.

10 weeks along. Your developing baby goes through some of its most important stages in the first 13 weeks of pregnancy. You might use drugs and not realize you are pregnant. Few women would take these substances if they knew they were pregnant. Stop using any substance you don't need at least 3 months before trying to conceive!

Research continues, showing that use of drugs or alcohol during pregnancy may affect a child's IQ, attention span and learning ability. To date, no safe level of these substances has been determined.

Drug use before pregnancy is serious business. Fortunately, there is help for those who use drugs. Get help before you become pregnant. Preparing for pregnancy may be a good reason for you and your partner to change your lifestyle.

Common Substances of Abuse

Tobacco

We have known for a long time that smoking affects fetal development. Mothers who smoke during pregnancy are more likely to have low-birthweight babies or babies with intrauterine-growth retardation. Ask for help to stop smoking before you become pregnant. Your caregiver should be receptive to this request. (See page 39 for tips on quitting.)

Alcohol

In the past, some believed a small amount of alcohol during pregnancy was OK. Today, we believe no amount of alcohol is safe to drink during pregnancy. Alcohol crosses the placenta and directly affects your baby. Heavy drinking during pregnancy can cause fetal alcohol syndrome (FAS) or fetal alcohol exposure (FAE), discussed in Weeks 1&2.

Cocaine

Cocaine has been shown to affect the baby throughout pregnancy, not just during the first trimester. If you use cocaine during the first 12 weeks of pregnancy, you run a higher risk of miscarriage. Cocaine can also cause severe deformities in a fetus. The type of defect it causes depends on the point at which cocaine is used in the pregnancy.

Infants born to mothers who use cocaine during pregnancy have been found to have long-term mental deficiencies. Sudden infant death syndrome (SIDS) is also more common in these babies. Many babies born to women who use cocaine are stillborn.

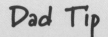

Dad Tip

If your partner is making lifestyle changes to prepare for pregnancy, such as giving up smoking or not drinking alcohol, support her in her efforts. Quit these habits with her if you share them.

Cocaine affects the mother, too. It is a stimulant and increases the user's heart rate and blood pressure. Women who use the drug during pregnancy have a higher rate of placental abruption, the premature separation of the placenta from the uterus.

In some parts of the United States, more than 10% of all pregnant women use cocaine at some time during their pregnancy. Stop using cocaine before you stop using birth control. Damage to the embryo (later the fetus) can occur as early as 3 days after conception!

Marijuana

Marijuana (and hashish) is dangerous during pregnancy because it crosses the placenta and enters the baby's system. It can have long-lasting effects on babies exposed before birth. Research has shown that a mother's marijuana use during pregnancy can affect cognitive function, decision-making ability and planning ability in her child. Use can also affect a child's verbal reasoning and memory.

Work and Pregnancy

You may need to consider your job when you plan a pregnancy. Many women do not know they are pregnant until the early stages of the pregnancy are already behind them. It's wise to plan ahead. Learn about things you are exposed to at work.

Some jobs might be considered harmful during pregnancy. Some substances you might be exposed to at work, such as chemicals, inhalants, radiation or solvents, could be a problem during pregnancy. Much of this chapter has discussed your lifestyle and how you take care of yourself. It is important to consider things you are exposed to at work as part of your lifestyle. Continue reliable contraception until you know the environment at work is safe.

Other important work-related considerations are the types of benefits or insurance coverage you have and your company's maternity-leave program. Most programs allow some time off work. It makes sense to check into this before getting pregnant. With the expense of medical care and having a baby, it could cost you several thousand dollars if you don't plan ahead.

Women who stand for long periods have smaller babies. If you have had a premature delivery in the past or if you have had an incompetent cervix, a job that requires you to stand a great deal may not be the wisest choice for you during pregnancy. Talk to your doctor about your work situation.

Sexually Transmitted Diseases

Infections or diseases passed from one person to another by sexual contact are called *sexually transmitted diseases* (STDs). These infections can affect your ability to get pregnant and can harm your developing baby. The type of contraception you use may have an effect on the likelihood of your contracting an STD. Condoms and spermicides can lower the risk of getting an STD. You are more likely to get a sexually transmitted disease if you have more than one sexual partner.

Pelvic Inflammatory Disease

Some STD infections can cause *pelvic inflammatory disease* (PID). PID is serious because it can spread from the vagina and cervix through the uterus and involve the Fallopian tubes and ovaries. The result can be scarring and blockage of the tubes, making it difficult or impossible for you to become pregnant or making you more susceptible to an ectopic pregnancy (see Week 5).

Protecting Yourself from STDs

Part of planning and preparing for pregnancy includes protecting yourself against STDs.

- Use a condom (regardless of what other type of contraception you might be using).
- Limit the number of sexual partners you have.
- Have sexual contact only with those you are sure do not have multiple sexual partners.

Ask for treatment if you think you have a sexually transmitted disease. Get tested if you have any remote chance of having an STD, even if you haven't had any symptoms.

Prepregnancy Journal

Weight

My current weight: _____   My ideal weight: _____

Nutrition

My healthful eating plan: _____

_____

_____

Eating habits to change: _____

_____

_____

_____

Medical tests

What tests and vaccinations do I need now or over the next year?

_____

_____

I've scheduled them for the following dates:

_____

_____

I've scheduled my prepregnancy checkup for the following date:

_____

Concerns and questions to discuss with the doctor at my checkup:

_____

_____

_____

_____

_____

Substances
Before I get pregnant, I need to quit or cut down on

O Smoking   O Drinking

O Drugs (including everyday drugs, such as caffeine)

O Other: _____

How my life will change after pregnancy (consider education, career, travel, goals and so on):

_____

_____

_____

_____

_____

_____

Notes

If you've just found out you're pregnant, you might want to begin by reading the previous chapter.

Weeks 1 & 2

Pregnancy Begins

This is an exciting time for you—having a baby growing and developing inside you is an incredible experience! This book will help you understand and enjoy your pregnancy. You will learn what is going on in your body and how your baby is growing and changing.

One focus of this book is to help you see how your actions and activities affect your health and well-being and that of your growing baby. If you're aware of how a particular test at a particular time, such as an X-ray, will affect the growing baby, you may decide on another course of action. If you understand how taking a certain drug can harm your baby or cause long-lasting effects, you may decide not to use it. If you know a poor diet can cause heartburn or nausea in you or delayed growth in your baby, you may choose to eat nutritiously. If you are aware of how much your actions affect your pregnancy, you may be able to choose wisely, free yourself from worry and enjoy your pregnancy more.

Material in this book is divided into weeks of pregnancy. Illustrations help you see clearly how you and your baby are changing and growing each week. General topics each week cover areas of special concern as well as how big your baby is, how big you are and how your actions affect your baby.

The information in this book is *not* meant to take the place of any discussion with your healthcare provider. Be sure you discuss any and all concerns with him or her. Use this material as a starting place in your dialogue. It may help you put your concerns or interests into words.

Signs and Symptoms of Pregnancy

Many signs and symptoms indicate a pregnancy, but most may also point to some other cause. Have any of the following symptoms checked out by your healthcare provider.

Sign or symptom of pregnancy	Other possible causes for the symptom
Missed menstrual period	extreme change in weight (gain or loss), stress, fatigue, hormonal problems, stopping birth control, breastfeeding, anxiety
Nausea, with or without vomiting	stomach disorder, food poisoning, stress
Fatigue	stress, depression, the common cold or flu, anemia
Breast changes and breast tenderness	hormonal imbalance, starting birth-control pills, menstruation about to begin
Frequent urination	diabetes, urinary-tract infection, excessive diuretic consumption (such as coffee)

What will you notice first? It's different for every woman. When your expected menstrual period does not begin, it may be the first sign of pregnancy.

When Is Your Baby Due?

The beginning of a pregnancy is actually figured from the beginning of your last menstrual period. That means, for your doctor's computational purposes, you are pregnant 2 weeks before you actually conceive! This can be confusing, so let's examine it more closely. Refer to the due date calendar starting on page 393 for help calculating your own due date.

Figuring Your Due Date

Most women don't know the exact date of conception, but they are usually aware of the beginning of their last period. This is the point from which a pregnancy is dated. A due date is important in pregnancy because it helps your doctor determine when to perform certain tests or procedures. It also helps estimate the baby's growth and may indicate whether you are overdue. For most women, the fertile time of the month (ovulation) is around the middle of their monthly cycle, or about 2 weeks before the beginning of their next period.

Pregnancy lasts about 280 days, or 40 weeks, from the beginning of the last menstrual period. You can calculate your due date by counting 280 days from the first day of bleeding of your last period. Or count back 3 months from the date of your last period and add 7 days. This also gives you the approximate date of delivery. For example, if your last period began on February 20, your due date is November 27.

Calculating a pregnancy this way gives the gestational age (menstrual age). This is how most doctors and nurses keep track of time during pregnancy. It is different from ovulatory age (fertilization age), which is 2 weeks shorter and dates from the actual conception.

Many people count the time during pregnancy using weeks. It's really the easiest way. But it can be confusing to remember to begin counting from when your period starts and that you don't become pregnant until about 2 weeks later. For example, if your doctor says you're 10 weeks pregnant (from your last period), conception occurred 8 weeks ago.

You may hear references to your stage of pregnancy by trimester. *Trimesters* divide pregnancy into three periods, each about 13 weeks long. This helps group together developmental stages.

Definitions of Time

Gestational age (menstrual age): Begins from the first day of your last period, which is actually about 2 weeks before you conceive. This is the age most doctors use to discuss your pregnancy. Average length of pregnancy: 40 weeks.

Ovulatory age (fertilization age): Begins the day you conceive. Average length of pregnancy: 38 weeks.

Trimester: Each trimester lasts about 13 weeks. There are three trimesters in a pregnancy.

Lunar months: 28 days. A pregnancy lasts an average of 10 lunar months.

For example, your baby's body structure is largely formed and his or her organ systems develop during the first trimester. Most miscarriages occur during the first trimester. During the third trimester, most maternal problems with pregnancy-induced hypertension or pre-eclampsia occur.

> **Think of your due date as a goal—a time to look forward to and to prepare for.**

You may even hear about lunar months, referring to a complete cycle of the moon, which is 28 days. Because pregnancy is 280 days from the beginning of your period to your due date, pregnancy lasts 10 lunar months.

40-Week Timetable

In this book, pregnancy is based on a 40-week timetable. Using this method, you actually become pregnant during the third week. Details of your pregnancy are discussed week by week beginning with Week 3. Your due date is the end of the 40th week.

Each weekly discussion includes the actual age of your growing baby. For example, in the Week 8 chapter you'll see the following:

Week 8 (gestational age)
Age of Fetus—6 Weeks (fertilization age)

In this way, you'll know how old your developing baby is at any point in pregnancy.

It's important to understand a due date is only an *estimate,* not an *exact date.* Only 1 out of 20 women delivers on her due date. It's a mistake to count on a particular day (your due date or an earlier date). You may see that day come and go and still not have your baby. Think of your due date as a goal—a time to look forward to and to prepare for. It's helpful to know you're making progress. Understanding how time is recorded during pregnancy helps.

No matter how you count the time of your pregnancy, it's going to last as long as it's going to last. But a miracle is happening—a living human being is growing and developing inside you! Enjoy this wonderful time in your life.

Your Menstrual Cycle

Menstruation is the normal periodic discharge of blood, mucus and cellular debris from the cavity of the uterus. The usual interval for menstruation is 28 days, but this can vary widely and still be considered normal. The duration and amount of menstrual flow can also vary; the usual duration is 4 to 6 days.

Two important cycles actually occur at the same time—the *ovarian cycle* and the *endometrial cycle*. The ovarian cycle provides an egg for fertilization. The endometrial cycle provides a suitable site for implantation of the fertilized egg inside your uterus. Because endometrial changes are regulated by hormones made in the ovary, the two cycles are intimately related.

The ovarian cycle produces an egg (ovum) for fertilization. There are about 2 million eggs in a newborn girl at birth. This decreases to about 400,000 in girls just before puberty. The maximum number of eggs is actually present *before* birth. When a female fetus is about 5 months old (4 months before birth), she has about 6.8 million eggs.

Some women (about 25%) experience lower abdominal pain or discomfort on or about the day of ovulation, called *mittelschmerz*. It is believed to be caused by irritation from fluid or blood from the follicle when it ruptures. The presence or absence of this symptom is not considered proof that ovulation did or did not occur.

> **Tip for Weeks 1&2**
>
> Over-the-counter pregnancy tests are reliable and can be positive (indicate pregnancy) as early as 10 days after conception.

Your Health Affects Your Pregnancy

Your good health is one of the most important factors in your pregnancy. Good nutrition, proper exercise, sufficient rest and attention to how you care for yourself all affect your pregnancy. Throughout this book, we provide information about medications you may take, medical tests you may need, over-the-counter substances you might use and many other areas that may concern you. This information is necessary for you to be aware of how your actions affect your health and the health of your developing baby.

The health care you receive can also affect your pregnancy and how well you tolerate being pregnant. Good health care is important to the development and well-being of your baby.

Your Healthcare Provider

You have many choices when it comes time to choose your healthcare provider. An *obstetrician* is a doctor who specializes in the care of pregnant women, including delivering babies. Obstetricians are M.D.s (medical doctors who have graduated from an accredited medical school and have fulfilled the requirements for a medical license) or D.O.s (doctors of osteopathic medicine who have graduated from an accredited school of osteopathic medicine and have fulfilled the requirements for a medical license). Both have completed further training after medical school (residency).

Obstetricians who specialize in high-risk pregnancies are *perinatologists*. Few women require a perinatologist (1 out of 10). Ask your doctor if you need to see a specialist, if you're concerned about past health problems. Some women choose a *family practitioner* because he or she is the family doctor. In some cases, an obstetrician may not be available because a community is small or in a remote area. The family practitioner often serves as your internist, obstetrician/gynecologist and pediatrician. Many family practitioners are experienced at delivering babies. If problems arise, a family practitioner may need to refer you to an obstetrician for your prenatal care. This may also be the case if a Cesarean section is required for delivery of your baby.

Pregnant women sometimes choose *certified nurse-midwives* for their care. A certified nurse-midwife is a trained professional who delivers low-risk uncomplicated pregnancies. These professionals are registered nurses with additional training and certification in nurse-midwifery. They require the immediate availability of a physician, in case complications arise.

Communication Is Important

It's important to be able to communicate well with your healthcare provider. Pregnancy and delivery are individual experiences. You need to be able to ask your doctor any questions you have, such as those below.

- What about natural childbirth? Do you believe in it?
- Are there routines you perform on every patient? Does everyone get an enema, fetal monitoring or more?

- Who covers patient care for you when you are away?
- Are there other doctors I will meet or who will take care of me?

Express your concerns and talk about whatever is important to you. Your healthcare provider has experience involving hundreds or thousands of deliveries and is drawing on this for your well-being. Your caregiver has to consider what is best for you and your baby, while he or she tries to honor any "special" requests you may have. Don't be afraid to ask any question; your doctor has probably already heard it. It may be that a request is unwise or risky for you, but it's important to ask about it ahead of time. If a request is possible, you can plan for it together, barring unforeseen developments.

Finding the Right Caregiver for You
How do you find someone who "fits the bill"? If you already have an obstetrician you're happy with, you may be all set. If you don't, call your local medical society. Ask for references to professionals who are taking new patients for pregnancy.

An added credential is *board certification*. Not all doctors who deliver babies are board-certified. It is not a requirement. Board certification means your doctor has put in extra time preparing for and taking exams to qualify him or her to care for pregnant women and to deliver their babies.

Board certification is administered by the American Board of Obstetrics and Gynecology, under the direction of the American College of Obstetricians and Gynecologists. If your doctor has passed his or her boards, it is often indicated by the initials *F.A.C.O.G.* after the doctor's name. This means he or she is a Fellow of the American

What about the Hospital?

When you pick a healthcare provider, you usually also pick a hospital. Keep the following in mind when choosing where to have your baby.

- Is the facility close by?
- What are the policies regarding your partner and his participation?
- Can he be present if you have a Cesarean section?
- Can you have an epidural?
- Is it a birthing center (if that's what you want)?
- Does your HMO (health maintenance organization) or your insurance cover the doctor *and* the hospital?

College of Obstetricians and Gynecologists. Your local medical society can also give you this information.

There are other ways to find a caregiver you'll be happy with. Ask friends who have recently had a baby about their experiences. Ask the opinion of a labor-delivery nurse at your local hospital. Various publications, such as the *Directory of Medical Specialties* or the *Directory of the American Medical Association,* are available at most U. S. libraries. In Canada, refer to the *Canadian Medical Directory.* Another doctor, such as a pediatrician or internist, may also provide a reference.

How Your Actions Affect Your Baby's Development

It's never too early to start thinking about how your activities and actions can affect your growing baby. Many substances you normally use may have adverse effects on the baby you carry. These substances include drugs, tobacco, alcohol and caffeine. Below is a discussion on cigarette smoking and alcohol use. (See pages 60 and 62 for information on drug abuse.) Any of these activities can harm a developing baby.

Cigarette Smoking
Smoking cigarettes has harmful effects on a pregnancy. A pregnant woman who smokes 20 cigarettes a day (one pack) inhales tobacco smoke more than 11,000 times during an average pregnancy!

Tobacco smoke contains many harmful substances, such as nicotine, carbon monoxide, hydrogen cyanide, tars, resins and some cancer-causing agents (carcinogens). These substances may be responsible singly or together for damaging your developing baby.

Nicoderm® Patch and Nicorette® Gum

Many studies have shown the harmful effects of cigarette smoking during pregnancy. The *specific* effects of Nicoderm and Nicorette on fetal development are unknown. However, if you are pregnant, researchers advise avoiding both of these stop-smoking systems.

Tips for Stopping Smoking

- List things you can do instead of smoking, especially activities that involve using your hands, such as puzzles or needlework.
- List things you'd like to buy for yourself or your baby. Set aside the money you normally spend on cigarettes to buy these items.
- Identify all of your "triggers"—what brings on an urge to smoke. Make plans to avoid them or to handle them differently.
- Instead of smoking after meals, brush your teeth, wash dishes, go for a walk.
- If you always smoke while driving, clean your car inside and out and use an air freshener. Sing along with the radio or a cassette tape. Take a bus or carpool for a while.
- Drink lots of water.

Scientific evidence has shown smoking during pregnancy increases the risk of fetal death or fetal damage. Smoking interferes with a woman's absorption of vitamins B and C and folic acid. Lack of folic acid can result in neural-tube defects and increases the risk of pregnancy-related complications in a mother-to-be.

For more than 20 years, we have known infants born to mothers who smoke weigh less by about 7 ounces (200g). That is why cigarette packages carry a warning to women about smoking during pregnancy. Decreased birthweight is directly related to the number of cigarettes the expectant mother smoked. These effects don't appear in her other babies if the mother doesn't smoke with other pregnancies. There is a direct relationship between smoking and impaired fetal growth.

Children born to mothers who smoked during pregnancy have been observed to have lower IQ scores and increased incidence of reading disorders compared with children of nonsmokers. The incidence of minimal-brain-dysfunction syndrome (hyperactivity) has also been reported to be higher among children of mothers who smoked during pregnancy.

Cigarette smoking during pregnancy increases the risk of miscarriage and fetal death or death of a baby soon after birth. The risk is also directly related to the number of cigarettes the pregnant woman smokes. The risk may increase as much as 35% in a woman who smokes more than one pack of cigarettes a day.

Smoking also increases the incidence of serious complications in a mother-to-be. An example of this is placental abruption, discussed in detail in Week 33. The risk of developing placental abruption increases by almost 25% in moderate smokers and more than 65% in heavy smokers.

Placenta previa (discussed in Week 35) also occurs more frequently among smokers. The rate of occurrence increases by 25% in moderate smokers and 90% in heavy smokers.

Known or suspected harmful effects to general health from smoking are numerous and include increased risk of many illnesses:

- pulmonary diseases, such as chronic bronchitis, emphysema and cancer
- cardiovascular diseases, including ischemic heart disease, peripheral vascular disease or arteriosclerosis
- bladder cancer
- peptic-ulcer disease

In addition, smokers have a mortality rate 30 to 80% higher than nonsmokers.

What can you do? The answer sounds simple but isn't—quit smoking (see the box on page 39). In more realistic terms, a woman who smokes during pregnancy will benefit from reducing or stopping cigarette use before or during pregnancy—and so will her developing baby. Some studies indicate that a nonsmoker and her unborn baby exposed to secondary smoke (cigarette smoke in the environment) are exposed to nicotine and other harmful substances. Perhaps pregnancy can serve as good motivation for everyone in the family to stop smoking!

Alcohol Use

Alcohol use by a pregnant woman carries risk. Moderate drinking has been linked to an increased chance of miscarriage. Excessive alcohol consumption during pregnancy often results in fetal abnormalities. Chronic use of alcohol in pregnancy can lead to abnormal fetal development called *fetal alcohol syndrome (FAS)*.

FAS is characterized by growth retardation before and after birth, and defects in limbs, the heart and facial characteristics of children. Facial characteristics are recognizable—the nose is upturned and short, the upper jawbone is flat and the eyes look "different." An FAS child may also have behavioral problems.

FAS children often have impaired speech, and their fine and gross motor functions are impaired. The perinatal (time before, during and immediately after birth) mortality rate is 15 to 20%.

Most studies indicate women would have to drink four to five drinks a day for FAS to occur. But mild abnormalities have been associated with two drinks a day (1 ounce of alcohol). These milder defects are the result of *fetal alcohol exposure* (FAE), a condition that can result from very little alcohol. This has led many researchers to conclude there is *no safe level of alcohol consumption* during pregnancy. For this reason, all alcoholic beverages in the United States carry warning labels similar to those on cigarette packages. The warning advises women to avoid alcohol during pregnancy because of the possibility of fetal problems, including fetal alcohol exposure and fetal alcohol syndrome.

Taking drugs with alcohol increases the chances of damage to a baby. Analgesics, antidepressants and anticonvulsants cause the most concern. Some researchers have suggested the father's heavy alcohol consumption before conception may also result in fetal alcohol syndrome. Alcohol intake by the father has been cited as one possible cause of intrauterine-growth retardation.

As a precaution, be very careful about over-the-counter cough and cold remedies you may use. Many contain alcohol—some as much as 25%!

Some women want to know if they can drink socially. There is a great deal of disagreement about it because there is no known safe level of alcohol consumption during pregnancy. Why take chances? For the health and well-being of your developing baby, abstain from alcohol during pregnancy. Responsibility for preventing these problems rests squarely on your shoulders!

Alcohol in Cooking

Most pregnant women know they should avoid alcohol during pregnancy, but what about recipes that call for alcohol? A good rule of thumb is it's probably OK to eat a food that contains alcohol if it has been baked or simmered for at least 1 hour. Cooking for that length of time cooks out most of the alcohol content.

Your Nutrition

If your weight is normal before pregnancy, you need to increase
your caloric intake during pregnancy. During the first trimester
(first 13 weeks), you should eat a total of about 2,200 calories a day.

During the second and third trimesters,
you probably need an additional 300
calories each day.

Extra calories provide the energy your
body needs for you and your growing
baby. Your baby uses the energy to create
and to store protein, fat and carbohydrates. It needs energy for fetal
body processes to function. The extra calories also support changes
your body is going through. Your uterus increases in size and your
blood volume increases by about 50%.

You can meet most of your nutritional needs by eating a well-
balanced, varied diet. The *quality* of your calories is important, too.
If a food grows in the ground or on a tree (meaning it's fresh), it's
probably better for you than if it comes out of a box or can.

Be cautious about adding the extra 300 calories to your nutrition
plan—it doesn't mean doubling your portions. A medium apple and
a cup of low-fat yogurt add up to 300 calories!

You Should Also Know

Hepatitis in Pregnancy

Hepatitis is a viral infection of the liver. It is one of the most
serious infections that can occur during pregnancy. Hepatitis B
is responsible for nearly half the
cases of hepatitis in the United
States. It is transmitted by sexual
contact or reuse of hypodermic
needles.

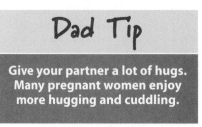

Dad Tip

Give your partner a lot of hugs.
Many pregnant women enjoy
more hugging and cuddling.

Those at risk for contracting
hepatitis B include people with a
history of intravenous drug use, a history of sexually transmitted
diseases or exposure to people or blood products that contain
hepatitis B. The B type can be transmitted to the developing fetus
of a pregnant woman.

Hepatitis symptoms include the following:

- nausea
- flulike symptoms
- jaundice (yellow skin)
- dark urine
- pain in or around the liver or upper-right abdomen

Hepatitis B is diagnosed by blood tests. In most areas, women are tested for hepatitis B at the beginning of pregnancy. If you test positive, your baby may receive *immune globulin* (antibodies to fight hepatitis) following delivery. It is now recommended that all newborns receive hepatitis vaccine shortly after birth. Ask your pediatrician if this vaccine is available in your area.

Although this book is designed to take you through your pregnancy by examining one week at a time, you may seek specific information. Because the book cannot include *everything* you need *before* you know you're looking for it, check the index, beginning on page 413, for a particular topic. For example, if you're searching for information early in your pregnancy on ways to snack healthfully, check the index for various page references. We may not cover the subject until a later week.

First Trimester Journal

Exercise

My plan for starting or continuing an exercise program (aerobic and strengthening):

_____

_____

_____

_____

Kinds of exercise I might enjoy during pregnancy:

_____

_____

When I can find time to exercise: _____

_____

Concerns and questions for the doctor at my next checkup:

_____

_____

_____

_____

Chart Your Pregnancy Weight Gain

Week	Weight at Each Prenatal Appointment	Weight Gain
4	_____	_____
8	_____	_____
12	_____	_____
16	_____	_____
20	_____	_____
24	_____	_____
28	_____	_____
32	_____	_____
34	_____	_____
36	_____	_____
37	_____	_____
38	_____	_____
39	_____	_____
40	_____	_____

Total pregnancy weight gain: _____

Notes

If you've just found out you're pregnant, you might want to begin by reading the previous chapters.

Week 3

Age of Fetus: 1 Week

How Big Is Your Baby?

The embryo growing inside you is very small. At this point, it is only a group of cells that are multiplying and growing rapidly. The embryo is the size of the head of a pin and would be visible to the naked eye if it weren't inside you. The group of cells doesn't look like a fetus or baby; it looks like the illustration on page 48. During this first week, the embryo is about 0.006 inch (0.150mm) long.

How Big Are You?

In this third week of pregnancy, you won't notice any changes. It's too soon! Few women know they have conceived. Remember, you haven't even missed a period yet.

How Your Baby Is Growing and Developing

A great deal is happening, even though your pregnancy is in its earliest stage. Ovaries lie free in your pelvis (or peritoneal cavity). They are close to the uterus and Fallopian tube. At the time of ovulation, the end of the tube (called the *fimbria*) lies close to the ovary. Some researchers believe this tube opening covers the area on the ovary where the egg (ovum) is released at the time of ovulation. The release site on the ovary is called the *stigma*.

During intercourse, an average of 0.06 to 0.15 ounce (2 to 5ml) of semen is deposited in the vagina. Each milliliter contains an average of 70 million sperm; each ejaculation contains 140 to 350 million sperm. Only about 200 sperm actually reach the egg in the tube. Fertilization is the joining together of one sperm and an egg.

Fertilization of the Egg

Fertilization is believed to occur in the middle part of the tube, called the *ampulla,* not inside the uterus. Sperm travel through the uterine cavity and out into the tube to meet the egg.

When the sperm and egg join, the sperm must pass through the outer layer of the ovum, the *corona radiata.* The sperm must then digest its way through another layer of the ovum, the *zona pellucida.* Although several sperm may penetrate the outer layers of the ovum, usually only one sperm enters the ovum and fertilizes it.

After the sperm penetrates the ovum, the sperm head attaches to its surface. The membranes of the sperm and ovum unite, enclosing them in the same membrane or sac. The ovum reacts to this contact with the sperm by making changes in the outer layers so no other sperm can enter.

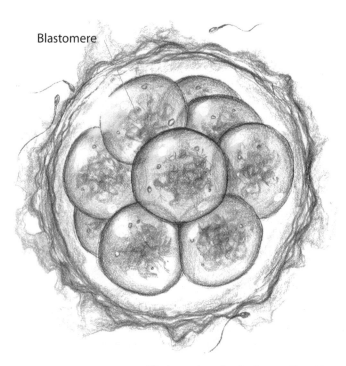

Blastomere

9-cell embryo 3 days after fertilization. The embryo is made up of many blastomeres; together they form a blastocyst.

Once the sperm gets inside the ovum, it loses its tail. The head of the sperm enlarges and is called the *male pronucleus;* the ovum is called the *female pronucleus.* The chromosomes of the male and female pronuclei intermingle. When this happens, extremely small bits of information and characteristics from each partner unite. This chromosomal information gives each of us our particular characteristics. The usual number of chromosomes in each human is 46. Each parent supplies 23 chromosomes. Your baby is a combination of chromosomal information from you and your partner.

Boy or Girl?

Your baby's sex is determined at the time of fertilization by the type of sperm (male or female) that fertilizes the egg. A Y-chromosome–bearing sperm produces a male, and an X-chromosome–bearing sperm produces a female.

Embryonic Development Begins

The developing ball of cells is called a *zygote.* The zygote passes through the uterine tube on its way to the uterus as the division of cells continues. These cells are called a *blastomere.* As the blastomere continues to divide, a solid ball of cells is formed, called a *morula.* The gradual accumulation of fluid within the morula results in the formation of a *blastocyst,* which is tiny.

During the next week, the blastocyst travels through the uterine tube to the cavity of the uterus (3 to 7 days after fertilization in the tube). The blastocyst lies free in the uterine cavity as it continues to grow and to develop. About a week after fertilization, it attaches to the uterine cavity (implantation). The cells burrow into the lining of the uterus.

Changes in You

Some women can tell when they ovulate. They may feel mild cramping or pain, or they may have an increased vaginal discharge. Occasionally at the time of implantation of the fertilized egg into the uterine cavity, a woman may notice a small amount of bleeding.

It's too early for you to notice many changes. Your breasts haven't started to enlarge and you aren't starting to "show." That lies ahead! (See the box on page 32 for more signs and symptoms of pregnancy.)

Exercise

Exercise is an important part of life for many women. The more we learn about health, the more the advantages of regular exercise become evident. Regular exercise may decrease your risk of developing several medical problems, including cardiovascular disease, osteoporosis (softening of bones), depression, premenstrual syndrome (PMS) and obesity.

There are many types of exercise to choose from before, during and after pregnancy. Each offers its own advantages. Aerobic exercise is very popular with women who want to keep in shape. Muscle-building exercises are becoming a popular way to tone and increase strength. Many women combine the two.

Aerobic Exercise

For cardiovascular fitness, aerobic exercise is the best. You must exercise at least 3 times a week at a sustained heart rate of 110 to 120 beats a minute, maintained for at least 15 continuous minutes. The rate of 110 to 120 beats a minute is an approximate target for people of different ages.

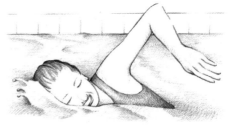

Good choices for aerobic exercise during pregnancy:

- brisk walking
- stationary bicycling
- swimming
- aerobic exercise designed especially for pregnant women

If you exercised aerobically before pregnancy, you can probably continue aerobic exercise at a somewhat lower rate. If you have any problems, such as bleeding or premature labor, you and your doctor will have to choose another program.

It is unwise to start a strenuous aerobic exercise program or to increase training during pregnancy. If you haven't been involved in

Target Heart Rates

Age (years)	Target heart rate (beats/minute)	Max. heart rate (beats/minute)
20	120–150	200
25	117–146	195
30	114–146	190
35	111–138	185
40	108–135	180
45	105–131	175
50	102–131	170

(U.S. Department of Health and Human Services)

regular, strenuous exercise before pregnancy, walking and swimming are probably about as involved as you should get with exercise.

Before you begin any exercise program, discuss it with your doctor. Together you can develop a program consistent with your current level of conditioning and your exercise habits.

> **If you haven't been involved in regular, strenuous exercise before pregnancy, walking and swimming are probably about as involved as you should get with exercise.**

Muscle Strength

Some women exercise for muscle strength. To strengthen a muscle, there has to be resistance against it. There are three different kinds of muscle contractions—*isotonic, isometric* and *isokinetic.*

- **Isotonic exercise** involves shortening the muscle as tension is developed, such as when you lift a weight.
- **Isometric exercise** causes the muscle to develop tension but doesn't change its length, such as when you push against a stationary wall.
- **Isokinetic exercise** occurs when the muscle moves at a constant speed, such as when you swim.

Cardiac and skeletal muscles cannot usually be strengthened at the same time. Strengthening skeletal muscles requires lifting heavy weights, but you can't lift these heavy weights long enough to strengthen the cardiac muscle.

Weight-bearing exercise is the most effective way of promoting increased bone density to help avoid osteoporosis. Other advantages of exercise include flexibility, coordination, improvement in mood and alertness. Stretching and warming up muscles before and after exercise help you improve flexibility and avoid injury.

Should You Exercise during Pregnancy?

As a pregnant woman, you are probably concerned about the risks of exercise. Can you or should you exercise when you're pregnant?

Pregnant women need cardiovascular fitness. Women who are physically fit are better able to perform the work of labor and delivery. Exercise during pregnancy is not without some risk, however. Risks to the developing baby can include any of the following:

- increased body temperature
- decreased blood flow to the uterus
- possible injury to the mother's abdominal area

You can exercise during pregnancy if you do it wisely. Avoid raising your body temperature above 102F (38.9C). Aerobic exercise can raise your body temperature higher than this, so be careful. A rise in body temperature can be increased by dehydration. Avoid prolonged aerobic exercise, particularly during hot weather.

While exercising aerobically, blood can be diverted to the exercising muscle or skin and away

(continued)

Possible Problems

Stop exercising and consult your healthcare provider if you experience any of the following:

- bleeding or loss of fluid from the vagina while exercising
- shortness of breath
- dizziness
- severe abdominal pain
- any other pain or discomfort

Consult your doctor and exercise only under supervision if you experience or know you have any of the following:

- irregular heartbeat
- high blood pressure
- diabetes
- thyroid disease
- anemia
- any other chronic medical problem

Consult your doctor about exercise if you have a history of

- three or more miscarriages
- an incompetent cervix
- intrauterine-growth retardation
- premature labor
- any abnormal bleeding during pregnancy

General Exercise Guidelines

- Before beginning any exercise program, consult your healthcare provider about past medical problems and past pregnancy problems.
- Begin any exercise program before you are pregnant.
- Begin exercising gradually. Start with 15-minute workout sessions, with 5-minute rest periods in between.
- Take your pulse every 15 minutes. Don't let it exceed 140 beats a minute. An easy way to calculate your pulse is to count the number of heartbeats by feeling the pulse in your neck or wrist for 15 seconds. Multiply by 4. If your pulse exceeds 140 beats a minute, rest until your pulse drops below 90.
- Allow enough time to warm up and to cool down.
- Wear comfortable clothing during exercise, including clothing that is warm enough or cool enough, and good, comfortable shoes.
- Do not get overheated.
- Exercise on a regular basis.
- Avoid risky sports, such as horseback riding or water skiing.
- Increase the number of calories you consume.
- When you're pregnant, be careful about getting up and lying down.
- After the fourth month of pregnancy (16 weeks), don't lie on your back while exercising. This can decrease blood flow to the uterus and placenta.
- When you finish exercising, lie on your left side for 15 to 20 minutes.

from other organs, such as the uterus, liver or kidneys. A lower workload during pregnancy is advised to avoid potential problems. Now is *not* the time to try to set new records or train for an upcoming marathon! During pregnancy, keep your pulse below 140 beats a minute.

How Your Actions Affect Your Baby's Development

Aspirin Use

Almost any medication taken during pregnancy can have some effect on your baby. This includes aspirin, a drug taken frequently for many reasons, either alone or in combination with other medications.

Tip for Week 3

Talk with your doctor before starting an exercise program during pregnancy. If you have been exercising, cut back your level of exercise to no more than 80% of your prepregnancy level.

Aspirin use can increase bleeding. Aspirin causes changes in the platelet function; platelets are important in blood clotting. This is particularly important to know if you are bleeding during pregnancy or if you are close to delivery at the end of your pregnancy. Small doses of aspirin may be acceptable during pregnancy; check with your physician.

Read labels on any medication you take to see if it contains aspirin. Avoid using aspirin or any products that contain aspirin during pregnancy unless you have discussed it first with your healthcare provider.

If you need a pain reliever or a medication to reduce fever, and you cannot reach your physician for advice, acetaminophen (Tylenol®) is one over-the-counter medication you can use for a short while with little fear of complications or problems for you or your baby. For further information about over-the-counter medication use during pregnancy, see Week 7.

Your Nutrition

Folic acid, also referred to as *folate, folacin* or *vitamin B₉*, is important to you during pregnancy. Recent studies indicate taking folic acid during pregnancy may help prevent or decrease the incidence of  *neural-tube defects,* which are defective closures of the neural tube during early pregnancy. Some of these defects include *spina bifida,* when the base of the spine remains open, exposing the spinal cord and nerves; *anencephaly,* congenital (present at birth) absence of the brain and spinal cord; and *encephalocele,* a protrusion of the brain through an opening in the skull.

A folic-acid deficiency can also result in anemia for a mother-to-be. Additional folic acid may be necessary with multiple fetuses or when the mother suffers from Crohn's disease or alcoholism.

A prenatal vitamin contains 0.8mg to 1mg of folic acid in each dose. This is usually sufficient for a woman with a normal pregnancy. Researchers believe spina bifida may be prevented if the mother-to-be takes 0.4mg of folic acid a day, beginning before pregnancy and continuing through the first 13 weeks. This is suggested for all pregnant women. A pregnant woman's body excretes four or five times the normal amount of folic acid. Because folic acid is not stored in the body for very long, it must be replaced every day.

> **Because folic acid is not stored in the body for very long, it must be replaced every day.**

Beginning in 1998, the U.S. government ordered that some grain products, including flour, breakfast cereals and pasta, be fortified with folic acid. Eating 1 cup of fortified breakfast cereal, with milk, and drinking a glass of orange juice supplies about half of your folic-acid requirement for one day. Folic acid is found in many other foods, too, such as fruits, legumes, brewer's yeast, soybeans, whole-grain products and dark, leafy vegetables. A well-balanced diet can help you reach your folic-acid-intake goal. See the list of foods that are good folic-acid sources on page 21.

You Should Also Know

Bleeding during Pregnancy
Bleeding during pregnancy causes concern. In the first trimester, bleeding can make you worry about the well-being of your baby and the possibility of a miscarriage. (We discuss miscarriage in Week 8.)

Bleeding during pregnancy is *not* unusual. Some researchers estimate that 1 in 5 pregnant women bleeds during the first trimester. Although it makes you worry about possible problems, not all women who bleed have a miscarriage.

Bleeding at the time of implantation is mentioned on page 49. This can occur as the blastocyst burrows into the uterine lining. At this point, you won't know you are pregnant because you haven't missed a period. If this happens, you may just think your period is starting early.

As your uterus grows, the placenta forms and vascular connections are made. Bleeding may occur at this time. Strenuous exercise or intercourse may also cause some bleeding. If this occurs, stop your activities and check with your healthcare provider, who will advise you what to do.

Dad Tip

Bring home flowers for no special occasion.

If bleeding causes your caregiver concern, he or she may order an ultrasound exam. Sometimes ultrasound can show a reason for bleeding, but during this early part of pregnancy, there may be no discernible reason for it.

Most doctors suggest resting, decreasing activity and avoiding intercourse when bleeding occurs. Surgery or medication are not helpful and are unlikely to make a difference. Call your doctor if you experience any bleeding. He or she will advise you what to do.

Benefits of Pregnancy

- Allergy and asthma sufferers may feel better during pregnancy because the natural steroids produced during pregnancy help reduce their symptoms.
- Pregnancy may help protect against breast cancer and ovarian cancer. The younger a woman is when she starts having babies, and the more pregnancies she has, the greater the benefit.
- Migraine headaches often disappear during the second and third trimesters of pregnancy.
- Menstrual cramps are a thing of the past during pregnancy. An added benefit—they may not return after your baby is born!
- Endometriosis (when endometrial tissue attaches to parts of the ovaries and other sites outside the uterus) causes pelvic pain, heavy bleeding and other problems during menstruation for some women. Pregnancy can stop the growth of endometriosis.

Notes

If you've just found out you're pregnant, you might want to begin by reading the previous chapters.

Week 4

How Big Is Your Baby?

Your developing baby is still tiny. Its size varies from 0.014 inch to about 0.04 inch (0.36mm to about 1mm) in length. One millimeter is half the size of a letter "o" on this page.

How Big Are You?

At this point, your pregnancy doesn't show at all. You haven't gained weight, and your figure hasn't changed. The illustration on page 58 gives you an idea of how small your baby is, so you can see why you won't notice any changes yet.

How Your Baby Is Growing and Developing

Fetal development is still in the very early stages, but many great changes are taking place! The implanted blastocyst is embedded more deeply into the lining of your uterus, and the amniotic cavity, which will be filled with amniotic fluid, is starting to form. The placenta, which plays an important role in hormone production and transport of oxygen and nutrients, is forming. Vascular networks that contain maternal blood are establishing.

Germ Layers
Different layers of cells are developing. These *germ layers* develop into specialized parts of your baby's body, such as various

57

organs. There are three germ layers—the *ectoderm, endoderm* and *mesoderm.*

The ectoderm will become the nervous system (including the brain), the skin and the hair. The endoderm develops into the lining of the gastrointestinal tract, the liver, pancreas and thyroid. From the mesoderm comes the skeleton, connective tissues, blood system, urogenital system and most of the muscles.

Changes in You

You are probably expecting a period around the end of this week. When it doesn't occur, pregnancy may be one of the first things you think of!

The Corpus Luteum

When you ovulate, the egg leaves the ovary. The area on the ovary where the egg comes from is called the *corpus luteum.* If you become pregnant, it is called the *corpus luteum of pregnancy.* The corpus luteum forms immediately after ovulation at the site of the ruptured follicle where the egg is released. It looks like a small sac of fluid on the ovary. It undergoes rapid blood-vessel development in preparation for producing hormones, such as progesterone, to support a pregnancy before the placenta takes over.

The importance of the corpus luteum is the subject of much debate. It is believed to be essential in the early weeks of pregnancy because it produces progesterone. The placenta takes over this function between 8 and 12 weeks of pregnancy. The

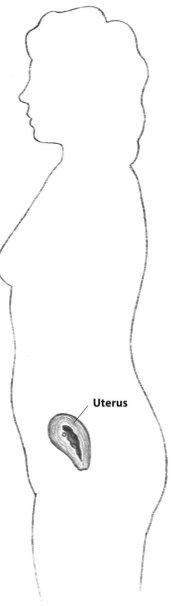

Uterus

pregnancy at around 4 weeks
(fetal age—2 weeks)

corpus luteum lasts until about the 6th month of pregnancy, when it shrinks, although normal corpus lutea have been found with full-term pregnancies. Successful pregnancies have also occurred when the corpus luteum was removed because of a ruptured cyst as early as the 20th day after a menstrual period or about the time of implantation.

How Your Actions Affect Your Baby's Development

During pregnancy, nearly all parents worry whether their baby will be perfect. Most parents worry unnecessarily. Major birth defects are apparent in only about 3% of all newborns at birth. Of those 3%, are causes of these abnormalities known? Could they have been prevented?

Abnormal Fetal Development
Teratology is the study of abnormal fetal development. An exact cause or reason for a birth defect is found in less than half of all cases. Obstetricians and other doctors providing care to pregnant women are often asked about substances *(teratogens)* that may be harmful. Researchers have been unable to prove the danger of some agents we believe are harmful. They *have* proved the harm of other agents.

Some agents cause major defects if exposure occurs at a specific, critical time in fetal development. But they may not be harmful at other times. Once the fetus has completed major development, usually by the 13th week, the effect of a certain substance may be only growth retardation or smaller organ size rather than large structural defects. One example is rubella. It can cause many anatomical defects, such as heart malformations, if the fetus is infected during the first trimester of pregnancy. A rubella infection occurring later is less serious.

Individual Response to Exposure
Individual responses to particular agents and to different doses of agents vary greatly. Alcohol is a good example. Large amounts appear to have no effect on some fetuses, while other fetuses may be harmed by low amounts.

Animal studies provide much of our information about possible harmful agents. This information can be helpful but cannot always be applied directly to humans. Other information comes from situations in which women were exposed who did not know they were pregnant or that a particular substance could be harmful. Information gathered from these instances is difficult to apply directly to a particular pregnancy.

A list of known teratogens and the effects they may have on an embryo or fetus appears on page 61. If you have taken any of these substances, discuss them as soon as possible with your healthcare provider for your peace of mind. If testing or follow-up is necessary, your doctor will advise you.

Tip for Week 4

Secondary smoke may harm a nonsmoking woman and her developing baby. Ask those who smoke to refrain from smoking around you during your pregnancy.

Drug Use and Abuse

Information about the effects of a specific drug on a human pregnancy comes from cases of exposure before the pregnancy is discovered. These case reports help researchers understand possible harmful effects but leave gaps in our knowledge. For this reason, it can be difficult or impossible to make exact statements about particular drugs and their effects. The following charts list possible effects of various legal and illegal drugs.

If you use drugs, be honest with your doctor. Ask questions about drugs and drug use. Tell your doctor about anything you take. The victim of drug use is your baby. A drug problem may have serious consequences that your healthcare provider can best deal with if he or she knows about your drug use in advance.

Effects of Various Substances on Fetal Development

Many substances can affect your baby's early development. Below are lists of common prescription drugs and other chemicals plus some drugs of abuse to help you see their effects on your baby. For further information on substance use, see page 23.

Common Prescription Drugs and Other Chemicals

Drug or Chemical	Effects on Your Baby
Androgens (male hormones)	ambiguous genital development (depends on dose given and when given)
Anticoagulants	bone and hand abnormalities, intrauterine-growth retardation, central-nervous-system and eye abnormalities
Antithyroid drugs (propylthiouracil, iodide, methimazole)	hypothyroidism, fetal goiter
Chemotherapeutic drugs (methotrexate, aminopterin)	increased risk of miscarriage
Diethylstilbestrol (DES)	abnormalities of female reproductive organs, female and male infertility
Isotretinoin (Accutane®)	increased miscarriage rate, nervous-system defects, facial defects, cleft palate
Lead	increased miscarriage and stillbirth rates
Lithium	congenital heart disease
Organic mercury	cerebral atrophy, mental retardation, spasticity, seizures, blindness
Phenytoin (Dilantin®)	intrauterine-growth retardation, mental retardation, microcephaly
Streptomycin	hearing loss, cranial-nerve damage
Tetracycline	hypoplasia of tooth enamel, discoloration of permanent teeth
Thalidomide	severe limb defects
Trimethadione	cleft lip, cleft palate, intrauterine-growth retardation, miscarriage
Valproic acid	neural-tube defects
X-ray therapy	microcephaly, mental retardation, leukemia

(Modified from A.C.O.G. Technical Bulletin #84, Teratology, February, 1985, American College of Obstetricians and Gynecologists)

Some Drugs of Abuse

Drug	Possible Effects on Your Baby
Alcohol	fetal abnormalities, fetal alcohol syndrome (FAS), fetal alcohol exposure (FAE), intrauterine-growth retardation
Barbiturates	possible birth defects, withdrawal symptoms, poor eating habits, seizures
Benzodiazepines including tranquilizing agents, such as diazepam (Valium®) and chlordiazepoxide (Librium®), along with newer agents	increased chance of congenital malformations
Caffeine	decreased birthweight, smaller head size, breathing problems, sleeplessness, irritability, jitters, poor calcium metabolism, intrauterine-growth retardation, mental retardation, microcephaly, various major malformations
Cocaine/crack	miscarriage, stillbirth, congenital defects, severe deformities in a fetus, long-term mental deficiencies, sudden infant death syndrome (SIDS)
Marijuana and hashish	attention deficit disorder (ADD), attention deficit hyperactivity disorder (ADHD), memory problems, impaired decision-making ability
Nicotine	miscarriage, stillbirth, neural-tube defects, low birthweight, lower IQ, reading disorders, minimal-brain-dysfunction syndrome (hyperactivity)
Opioids such as morphine, heroin, Demerol®	congenital abnormalities, premature birth, intrauterine-growth retardation, withdrawal symptoms in baby

Your Nutrition

You must be prepared to gain weight during your pregnancy. It's necessary for your health and the health of your developing baby. Getting on the scale and seeing your weight rise may be very hard for you. Acknowledge now that it's OK to gain weight. You don't have to let yourself go—you can control your weight by eating carefully and nutritiously. But you *need* to gain enough weight to meet the needs of your pregnancy.

Many years ago, women were not allowed to gain much weight—sometimes only 12 to 15 pounds for their entire pregnancy! Today, we know that restricting weight gain to this extent is not healthy for the baby or the mother-to-be.

Gain weight slowly. Don't let yourself go just because you're pregnant. You may be eating for two, but you don't have to eat twice as much!

You probably won't be able to eat all you want during pregnancy, unless you are one of the lucky women who doesn't have a problem with calories. Even then, you must pay strict attention to the foods

Health of the Baby's Father

Can the father's health and drug or alcohol use affect the health of the developing baby?

In recent years, more attention has been given to the father's contribution in pregnancy. We now believe if a father is over 40, it may increase the risk of Down syndrome, although there is not a great deal of evidence to support this theory. A father's drug habit at the time of conception may influence the outcome of a pregnancy. Evidence is scanty, but there does appear to be an effect. Why take the chance?

you choose, and eat healthfully. Eat nutritious foods. Avoid those with empty calories (lots of sugar and fat). Choose fresh fruits and vegetables. Avoid caffeine when possible. We discuss many of these subjects in later weeks.

Some Pollutants to Avoid during Pregnancy

Lead
The toxicity of lead has been known for centuries. In the past, most lead exposure came from the atmosphere. Today, exposure may come from many sources, including some gasoline (now regulated), water pipes, solders, storage batteries, construction materials, paints, dyes and wood preservatives.

Lead is easily transported across the placenta to the baby. Toxicity can occur as early as the 12th week of pregnancy, which could result in lead poisoning in the baby.

Avoid exposure to lead. If you might be exposed in your workplace, discuss it with your physician.

Mercury
Mercury has a long history as a potential poison to a pregnant woman. Reports of fish contaminated with mercury have been linked to cerebral palsy and microcephaly.

PCBs
Our environment has been significantly contaminated with polychlorinated biphenyls (PCBs). PCBs are mixtures of several chemical compounds.

Most fish, birds and humans now have measurable amounts of PCBs in their tissues. Some experts have suggested that pregnant women limit their intake of fish (to avoid exposure to mercury and PCBs), particularly if a woman is exposed to PCBs where she works.

Pesticides
Pesticides cover a large number of agents used to control unwanted plants and animals. Human exposure is common because pesticides are used extensively. Those of most concern contain several agents—DDT, chlordane, heptachlor, lindane and others.

You Should Also Know

Environmental Pollutants and Pregnancy

Some environmental pollutants may be harmful to a developing baby. Avoiding exposure to these pollutants is important for a mother-to-be. The box opposite provides information on specific pollutants.

What Can You Do?

There is a lack of clear information on the safety of many chemicals in our environment. The safest course of action is to avoid exposure when possible, whether by oral ingestion or through the air you breathe. It may not be possible to eliminate all contact with every possible chemical.

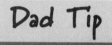

Dad Tip

Make it a habit to pull out your favorite pregnancy book, such as *Your Pregnancy Week by Week*, and read together about what is happening each week in your pregnancy.

If you know you will be around various chemicals, wash your hands well before eating. Not smoking cigarettes also helps.

One reassuring fact is that most of the chemicals tested have produced illness in the mother-to-be before damage to her growing baby occurred. An environment that is healthful for you will be healthful for your developing baby.

Notes

If you've just found out you're pregnant, you might want to begin by reading the previous chapters.

Week 5

Age of Fetus: 3 Weeks

How Big Is Your Baby?

Your developing baby hasn't grown a great deal. It's about 0.05 inch (1.25mm) long.

How Big Are You?

At this point, there are still no big changes in you. Even if you are aware you're pregnant, it will be a while before others notice your changing figure.

How Your Baby Is Growing and Developing

As early as this week, a plate that will later become the heart has developed. The central nervous system (brain and spinal cord) and muscle and bone formation are beginning to take shape. During this time, your baby's skeleton is also starting to form.

Changes in You

Many changes are occurring now. You may be aware of some of them; others will be evident only after some kind of test.

Pregnancy Tests
Pregnancy tests have become more sensitive, which makes early diagnosis of pregnancy more common. Tests detect the presence

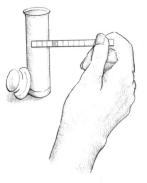

of *human chorionic gonadotropin* (HCG), a hormone of early pregnancy. A pregnancy test can be positive even before you have missed a period! Many tests can provide positive results (pregnant) 10 days after conception. But it's usually best to wait until you have missed a period before investing money and emotional energy in pregnancy tests, whether done at a hospital, in a clinic or at home.

Most home tests range in price from $12 to $30. They vary in how effective they are in helping you "diagnose" your pregnancy. Many hospitals or clinics offer free pregnancy testing, which can save you some money.

Nausea and Vomiting

An early symptom of pregnancy for some women is nausea, with or without vomiting. This is often called *morning sickness,* whether it occurs in the morning or later in the day. It usually starts early and improves throughout the day as you become active. Morning sickness can begin around the 6th week of pregnancy and usually improves by the end of the first trimester (around 13 weeks).

Many women have nausea. It doesn't usually cause enough trouble to require medical attention. However, a condition called *hyperemesis gravidarum* (severe nausea and vomiting) causes a great deal of vomiting, which results in loss of nutrients and fluid. The pregnant woman is often treated in the hospital with intravenous fluids and medications. Hypnosis has also been used successfully in treating the problem.

There is no completely successful treatment for the normal nausea and vomiting of pregnancy. Currently, there are no approved medications to treat the problem. This is an extremely important period in the development of your baby. Don't expose your unborn baby to medication, herbs, over-the-counter treatments or any other "remedies" for nausea that are not known to be safe during pregnancy. Discuss ways to deal with nausea with your healthcare provider.

If morning sickness causes you to be absent from your job, you may be interested to know that the Family and Medical Leave Act (FMLA) states you do *not* need a doctor's note verifying the problem. Nausea and vomiting of pregnancy is classified as a "chronic condition" and may require you to be out occasionally, but you don't need a doctor's treatment.

Other Changes You May Notice

In early pregnancy, you may need to urinate frequently. It can continue during most of your pregnancy and become particularly annoying near delivery, as your uterus enlarges and puts pressure on your bladder.

You may notice changes in your breasts. Tingling or soreness in the breasts or nipples is common. You may also see a darkening of the areola or an elevation of the glands around the nipple. (See Week 13 for more information on how your breasts are affected by pregnancy.)

Another early symptom of pregnancy is tiring easily. This common symptom may continue throughout pregnancy. Be sure to

If you experience fatigue, avoid sugar and caffeine; either can make the problem worse.

take your prenatal vitamins and any other medications prescribed by your healthcare provider, and get enough rest. If you experience fatigue, avoid sugar and caffeine; either can make the problem worse.

How Your Actions Affect Your Baby's Development

When Should You Visit the Doctor?

One of the first questions you may ask yourself when you suspect you're pregnant is, "When should I see my doctor?"

Good prenatal care is necessary to the health of the baby and mother-to-be. Make an appointment to see your physician as soon as you are reasonably sure you're pregnant. This could be as early as a few days after a missed period.

Getting Pregnant while Using Birth Control

If you have been using some type of birth control, tell your healthcare provider. No method is 100% effective. Occasionally a method fails, even oral contraceptives. If you are sure you're pregnant, stop taking the pill and see your healthcare provider as soon as possible. Don't become overly alarmed if this happens to you; talk to your caregiver about it.

Pregnancy can also occur with an intrauterine device (IUD) in place. If this happens, see your healthcare provider immediately. Discuss whether the IUD should be removed or left in place. In most cases, an attempt is made to remove the IUD. If left in place, the risk of miscarriage increases slightly.

Spermicides alone, or with a condom, sponge or diaphragm, may be in use when pregnancy occurs. They have not been shown to be harmful to a developing baby.

Your Nutrition

As discussed previously, you may have to deal with nausea and vomiting during pregnancy. Not every woman suffers from it, but many women do. The same hormone—HCG (human chorionic gonadotropin)—that makes a home pregnancy test change color causes morning sickness. If you suffer this discomfort, you may be happy to know that HCG levels taper off near the end of the first trimester, so your nausea and vomiting should improve then. If you experience morning sickness, try some of these suggestions.

- Eat small meals frequently to keep your stomach from being overfull.
- Drink lots of fluid.
- Find out what foods, smells or situations make you nauseated. Avoid them when possible.
- Avoid coffee because it stimulates stomach acid.
- A high-protein snack before bed may help stabilize blood sugar.
- Sometimes a high-carbohydrate snack before bed helps.
- Ask your partner to make you some dry toast in the morning before you get up; eat it in bed. Or keep crackers or cereal near the bed so you can nibble on them before you get up in the morning. They all help absorb stomach acid.
- Keep your bedroom cool at night and air it out often. Cool, fresh air may help you feel better.
- Get out of bed slowly.
- If you take an iron supplement, take it an hour before meals or 2 hours after a meal.

- Nibble on raw ginger or pour boiling water over it and sip the "tea."
- Salty foods help some women with nausea.
- Lemonade and watermelon may help alleviate symptoms.

Weight Gain during Pregnancy

The amount of weight women gain during pregnancy varies greatly. It may actually range from weight loss to a total gain of 50 pounds or more.

We know complications arise at the extremes of these weight changes. Because of this, it's difficult to set one figure as an "ideal" weight gain during pregnancy. How much weight you gain is affected by your weight before you became pregnant. Many quote a weight-gain figure of $2/3$ of a pound (10 ounces) a week until 20 weeks, then 1 pound a week from 20 to 40 weeks.

Average Pregnancy Weight Gain

Body Type	Acceptable Gain (pounds)
Underweight	28 to 40
Normal weight	25 to 35
Overweight	15 to 25

Other researchers have suggested weight-gain amounts acceptable for underweight, normal weight and overweight women. See the box above.

If you have any questions about your weight gain during pregnancy, discuss them with your physician. He or she will advise you on how much weight you should gain during pregnancy.

Dieting during pregnancy is not a wise idea, but that doesn't mean you shouldn't watch your caloric intake. You should! It's important for your baby to get proper nutrition from the foods you eat. Choose your foods for the nutrition they provide for you and your growing baby.

You Should Also Know

Ectopic Pregnancy

As described in Weeks 1 & 2, fertilization occurs in the Fallopian tube. The fertilized egg travels through the tube to the uterus, where it implants on the cavity wall. An *ectopic pregnancy* occurs when the egg implants outside the uterine cavity, usually in the tube itself. Ninety-five percent of all ectopic pregnancies occur in the tube (hence the term *tubal pregnancy*). Other possible sites of implantation are the ovary, cervix or other places in the abdomen. The illustration below shows some possible locations of an ectopic pregnancy.

Ectopic pregnancy occurs in 1 of every 100 pregnancies. Chances of an ectopic pregnancy increase with damage to the Fallopian tubes from pelvic inflammatory disease (PID); from other infections, such as a ruptured appendix; or from abdominal surgery. If you have had a previous ectopic pregnancy, there is a 12% chance of recurrence. Use of an intrauterine device (IUD) also increases the chance of ectopic pregnancy.

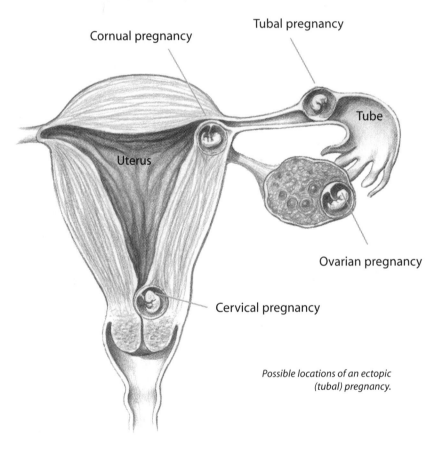

Possible locations of an ectopic (tubal) pregnancy.

Symptoms of an Ectopic Pregnancy
Symptoms include vaginal bleeding, pain in the abdomen and other signs, such as tender breasts or nausea. However, it may be difficult

for your healthcare provider to diagnose an ectopic pregnancy because many of these symptoms can be present in a normal pregnancy.

Diagnosing Ectopic Pregnancy

To test for an ectopic pregnancy, human chorionic gonadotropin (HCG), a hormone produced during pregnancy, is measured. The test is called a *quantitative HCG*. The level of HCG increases rapidly in a normal pregnancy and doubles in value about every 2 days. If HCG levels do not increase as they should, an abnormal pregnancy is suspected. In the case of an ectopic pregnancy, the woman may have a high HCG level with no sign of a pregnancy inside the uterus.

Ultrasound testing is also helpful in diagnosing an ectopic pregnancy. (We discuss ultrasound in detail in Week 11.) A tubal pregnancy may be visible in the tube during ultrasound examination. Doctors may see blood in the abdomen from rupture and bleeding or a mass in the area of the Fallopian tube or the ovary.

Our ability to diagnose an ectopic pregnancy has improved with use of *laparoscopy*. Tiny incisions are made in the area of the bellybutton and in the lower-abdominal area. Doctors view the inside of the abdomen and the pelvic organs with a small instrument (called a *laparascope*). They can see an ectopic pregnancy if one is present.

An attempt is made to diagnose a tubal pregnancy before it ruptures and damages the tube, which could make it necessary to remove the entire tube. Early diagnosis also attempts to avoid the risk of internal bleeding from a ruptured, bleeding tube.

Most ectopic pregnancies are detected around 6 to 8 weeks of pregnancy. The key in early diagnosis involves communication between you and your doctor about symptoms and their severity.

Treatment for Ectopic Pregnancy

With an ectopic pregnancy, the doctor's goal is to remove the pregnancy while preserving fertility. Surgical treatment requires general anesthesia, laparoscopy or laparotomy (a larger incision and no scope), and recovery from surgery. In many instances, it is necessary to

Tip for Week 5

Precaution! Be careful about using over-the-counter cough and cold remedies. Many contain alcohol—some as much as 25%!

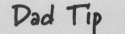

Dad Tip

Clean or vacuum the house without being asked.

remove the Fallopian tube, which affects future fertility.

A new, nonsurgical treatment of an unruptured ectopic pregnancy involves the use of a cancer drug, methotrexate. Methotrexate is given by an I.V. in the hospital or outpatient clinic. Methotrexate is *cytotoxic;* it terminates the pregnancy. HCG levels should decrease after this treatment, which indicates the pregnancy has been terminated. Symptoms should improve.

What Sex Will Your Baby Be?

You can guess the sex of your child as well as your doctor—often better! As we've mentioned, the sex of your baby is determined when the egg is fertilized by the sperm.

Many couples ask for ways to "get a boy" or "get a girl" before they try to get pregnant. In a few cases, sperm separation is used. Male and female sperm are separated, and artificial insemination deposits the selected sperm in the woman. It's not a foolproof method, and it is expensive. This procedure may be done when there is a sex-specific problem, such as a family history of hemophilia.

If you've just found out you're pregnant, you might want to begin by reading the previous chapters.

Week 6

How Big Is Your Baby?

The crown-to-rump length of your growing baby is 0.08 to 0.16 inch (2 to 4mm). *Crown-to-rump* is the sitting height or distance from the top of the baby's head to its rump or buttocks. This measurement is used more often than crown-to-heel length because the baby's legs are usually bent, making that determination difficult.

Occasionally, with the proper equipment, a heartbeat can be seen on ultrasound by the 6th week. Ultrasound is discussed in detail in Week 11.

How Big Are You?

You may have gained a few pounds by now. If you have been nauseated and not eating well, you may have lost weight. You have been pregnant for 1 month, which is enough time to notice some changes in your body. If this is your first pregnancy, your abdomen may not have changed much. Or you may notice your clothes are getting a little tighter around the waist. You may be gaining weight in your legs or other places, such as your breasts.

If you have a pelvic exam, your healthcare provider can usually feel your uterus and note some change in its size.

How Your Baby Is Growing and Developing

This is the beginning of the embryonic period (from week 6 to week 10 of pregnancy, or from week 4 to week 8 of fetal development).

It is a period of extremely important development in your baby! At this time, the embryo is most susceptible to factors that can interfere with its development. Most malformations originate during this critical period.

As the illustration on page 77 shows, the result of this growth is a body form showing the head and tail area. Around this time, the neural groove closes and early brain chambers form. The eyes are also forming. Limb buds appear. The heart tubes fuse and heart contractions begin. This can be seen on ultrasound.

Changes in You

Heartburn

Heartburn discomfort *(pyrosis)* is one of the most common complaints of pregnancy. It may begin early, although generally it becomes more severe later in pregnancy. It is usually caused by the backing up *(reflux)* of gastric and duodenal contents into the esophagus. This occurs more frequently during pregnancy for two reasons—food moves more slowly through the intestines, and the stomach is compressed by the uterus as it enlarges and moves up into the abdomen.

Symptoms are not severe for most women. Eat small, frequent meals and avoid some positions, such as bending over or lying flat. One sure way to get heartburn is to eat a large meal, then lie down! (This is true for anyone, not just pregnant women.)

Some antacids provide considerable relief, including aluminum hydroxide, magnesium trisilicate and magnesium hydroxide (Amphojel®, Gelusil®, Milk of Magnesia® and Maalox®). Follow your caregiver's advice or the instructions on the package relating to pregnancy. Don't overdo taking antacids! Avoid sodium bicarbonate because it contains excessive amounts of sodium that may cause you to retain water.

Constipation

Your bowel habits will probably change during pregnancy. Most women notice some constipation, often accompanied by irregular bowel movements. Hemorrhoids may occur more often (see Week 14).

You can help avoid constipation problems during pregnancy. Increase your fluid intake. Exercise also helps. Many doctors suggest

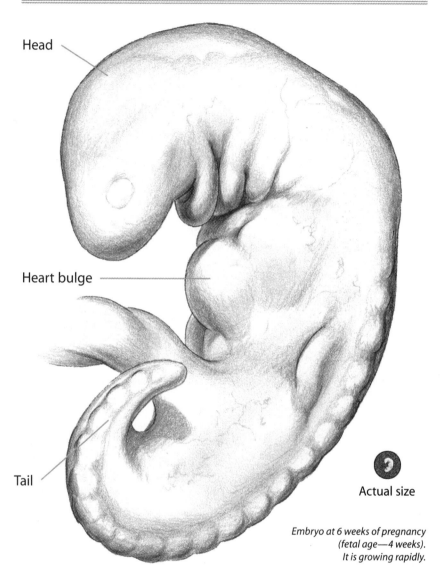

Head

Heart bulge

Tail

Actual size

*Embryo at 6 weeks of pregnancy
(fetal age—4 weeks).
It is growing rapidly.*

a mild laxative, such as Milk of Magnesia or prune juice, if you have problems. Certain foods, such as bran and prunes, can increase the bulk in your diet, which may relieve constipation.

Do not use laxatives, other than those mentioned, without your healthcare provider's OK. If constipation is a continuing problem, discuss treatment with your doctor. Try not to strain when you have a bowel movement. Straining can lead to hemorrhoids.

A Visit with the Doctor

Cissy, pregnant for the first time, was having trouble sleeping because of stomach problems. She and her husband Robbie often ate out after work. We talked about not eating late or lying down soon after eating. I suggested five or six small meals a day might be a better plan for her. I also advised her that occasionally using antacids was OK.

Try to find foods (and amounts of foods) that don't give you heartburn, but don't go overboard. If you find chocolate malts don't cause you problems, for example, don't have one at every meal!

How Your Actions Affect Your Baby's Development

During pregnancy, a sexually transmitted disease (STD) can harm your growing baby. Take care of any STD as soon as possible.

Genital Herpes Simplex Infection

Usually a herpes infection during pregnancy is a reinfection, not a primary infection. Infection in the mother is associated with higher risks of premature delivery and low-birthweight infants. We believe an infant can be infected when traveling through the birth canal. When membranes rupture, the infection may also travel upward to the uterus.

There is no safe treatment during pregnancy for genital herpes. When a woman has an active herpes infection late in pregnancy, a Cesarean section is done to deliver the baby.

Monilial Vulvovaginitis

Monilial (yeast) infections are more common in pregnant women than in nonpregnant women. They have no major negative effect on pregnancy, but they may cause you discomfort and anxiety.

Yeast infections are sometimes harder to control when you're pregnant. They may require frequent retreatment or longer treatment (10 to 14 days instead of 3 to 7 days). Creams used for treatment are usually safe during pregnancy. Your partner does not need to be treated.

A newborn infant can get thrush after passing through a birth canal infected with monilial vulvovaginitis. Treatment with nystatin is effective. Avoid the use of fluconazole (Diflucan®); it may not be safe to use during pregnancy.

Trichomonal Vaginitis
This infection has no major effects on pregnancy. However, a problem in treatment may arise because some doctors believe metronidazole, the drug of choice, shouldn't be taken in the first trimester of pregnancy. Most healthcare providers will prescribe metronidazole for a bad infection after the first trimester.

Condylomata Acuminatum
This condition is commonly called *venereal warts*. If you have extensive venereal warts, a Cesarean delivery may be necessary to avoid heavy bleeding.

Warty skin tags often enlarge during pregnancy. In rare instances, they have blocked the vagina at the time of delivery. Infants have also been known to get *laryngeal papillomas* (small benign tumors on the vocal cords) after delivery.

Gonorrhea
Gonorrhea presents risks to a woman and her partner, and to her baby when it passes through the birth canal. The baby may contract *gonorrheal ophthalmia*, a severe eye infection. Eyedrops are used in newborns to prevent this problem. Other infections may also result. Gonorrheal infections in the mother are easily treated with penicillin or other medications that are safe to use during pregnancy.

Syphilis
Detection of a syphilis infection is important for you, your partner and your infant. Fortunately this rare infection is also treatable. If you notice any open sore on your genitals during pregnancy, have your healthcare provider check it out. Syphilis can be treated effectively with penicillin and other medications that are safe in pregnancy.

Chlamydia
You may have heard or read about *Chlamydia*. It is a common sexually transmitted disease (STD); between 3- and 5-million people are infected every year. It may be difficult to determine if you have a

chlamydial infection because you may not have symptoms. Infection is caused by a germ that invades certain types of healthy cells. Infection may be passed through sexual activity, including oral sex.

Between 20 and 40% of all sexually active women have probably been exposed to *Chlamydia* at some time. Infection can cause serious problems if left untreated, but these problems can be avoided with treatment.

Chlamydia is most likely to occur in young people who have more than one sexual partner. It may also occur in women who have other sexually transmitted diseases. Some doctors believe *Chlamydia* occurs more commonly in women who take oral contraceptives. Barrier methods of contraception, such as diaphragms and condoms used with spermicides, may offer protection from infection.

Tip for Week 6

If you have questions between your prenatal visits, call and ask your healthcare provider or a nurse in the office. It's OK to call; as a matter of fact, your doctor wants you to call and get correct medical information. You'll probably feel more comfortable when your questions are answered.

One of the most significant complications of *Chlamydia* is pelvic inflammatory disease (PID), a severe infection of the upper genital organs involving the uterus, the Fallopian tubes and even the ovaries. There may be pelvic pain, or there may be no symptoms at all. PID can result from an untreated infection that spreads throughout the pelvic area.

Chlamydia is one of the main causes of PID. If a PID infection is prolonged or recurrent, the reproductive organs, Fallopian tubes and uterus may be damaged, with formation of adhesions. Surgery may be required to repair them. If tubes are damaged, scar tissue can increase the risk of ectopic or tubal pregnancy.

Chlamydia in Pregnancy

During pregnancy, a mother-to-be can pass the infection to her baby as it comes through the birth canal and vagina. The baby has a 20 to 50% chance of getting *Chlamydia* if the mother has it. It may cause an eye infection, but that is easily treated. Complications that are more serious include pneumonia, which may require hospitalization of the baby.

Research has shown that chlamydial infection may be linked to ectopic pregnancy. One study showed 70% of the women they studied who had an ectopic pregnancy also had *Chlamydia*. If a woman is trying to get pregnant, she may want to be screened for this STD, which can be treated easily.

Testing for Chlamydia
Chlamydia can be detected by a cell culture, but as we've said, more than half of those infected have no symptoms. Symptoms that may appear include burning or itching in the genital area, discharge from the vagina, painful or frequent urination, or pain in the pelvic area. Men may also experience symptoms. Rapid diagnostic tests can be done in the doctor's office. They can provide a result quickly, possibly even before you go home.

Chlamydia is usually treated with tetracycline, but this drug should not be given to a pregnant woman. During pregnancy, erythromycin may be the drug of choice. After treatment, your healthcare provider may want to do another culture to make sure the infection is gone. If you're concerned about a possible chlamydial infection, discuss it with your healthcare provider. He or she will advise you.

HIV and AIDS
Women make up one of the fastest growing groups infected with the *human immunodeficiency virus* (HIV). Most affected women are of childbearing age.

HIV is the causative agent of *acquired immune deficiency syndrome* (AIDS). The exact number of people infected with HIV is unknown. Currently it is estimated that up to 2 million people in the United States alone may be infected. The AIDS epidemic among women has grown to 15% of all reported cases.

Infection with HIV can lead to a progressive debilitation of the immune system, which is AIDS. This can leave the individual susceptible to and unable to fight against various infections.

Women at greatest risk include current or former intravenous drug users and women whose sexual partners have used drugs intravenously or engaged in bisexual activities. Women with sexually transmitted diseases, those who engage in prostitution or those who received blood transfusions before screening began are also at higher risk. If you are unsure about your risk, seek counseling about testing for the AIDS virus.

A Visit with the Doctor

When Helen came to see me for an HIV test, she wasn't pregnant but was planning a pregnancy in the next 6 months. I told her having the HIV test *before* she got pregnant was a good idea. She could be reassured she was not HIV-positive when she got pregnant. She was relieved to receive negative test results and she began her pregnancy with greater peace of mind.

A woman infected with HIV may not have symptoms. There may be a period of weeks or months when tests do not reveal the presence of the virus. In most cases, antibodies can be detected 6 to 12 weeks after exposure. In some cases, this latent period can be as long as 18 months. Once the test is positive, a person may remain without symptoms for a variable amount of time. For every patient with AIDS, there are 20 to 30 infected individuals who have no symptoms.

There is no evidence of transmission through casual contact with water, food or environmental surfaces. There is no evidence the virus can be transmitted with RhoGAM®. (See Week 16.) A mother can pass HIV to her baby before birth or during its birth.

Pregnancy may hide some AIDS symptoms, which makes the disease harder to discover. Because the illness can be a serious threat to an unborn child, counseling and psychological support are critical.

There is some positive news for women who suffer from AIDS. We know that if a woman is in the early course of the illness, she can usually have an uneventful pregnancy, labor and delivery. Her baby has a risk of being infected during pregnancy, birth or breastfeeding. However, research shows that the risk of a woman infected with HIV passing the virus to her baby can now be greatly reduced and nearly eliminated. If she takes AZT during pregnancy and has a Cesarean delivery, she reduces the risk of passing the virus to about 2%!

Testing for AIDS

Testing comprises two tests—the ELISA test and the Western Blot test. The ELISA is a screening test. If positive, it should be confirmed by the Western Blot test. Both tests involve testing blood to measure antibodies to the virus, not the virus itself. No test should be considered positive until the Western Blot test is done. It is believed to be more than 99% sensitive and specific.

Your Nutrition

To get the nutrition you need during your pregnancy, you must be selective in your food choices. You *cannot* eat whatever you want. Eating the right foods, in the correct amounts, takes planning. Eat foods high in vitamins and  minerals, especially iron, calcium, magnesium, folic acid and zinc. You also need fiber and fluids to help alleviate any constipation problems.

 Below is a list of the various food groups, and amounts from each, that you need *every* day. Ways to get enough of each food group are discussed in the following weeks. Check out each weekly discussion for nutrition tips for you.

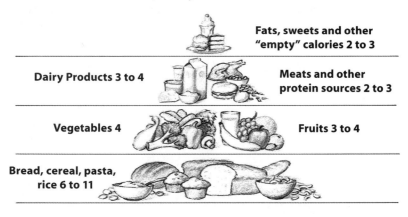

Fats, sweets and other "empty" calories 2 to 3

Dairy Products 3 to 4

Meats and other protein sources 2 to 3

Vegetables 4

Fruits 3 to 4

Bread, cereal, pasta, rice 6 to 11

You Should Also Know

Your First Visit to the Doctor
Your first visit to your healthcare provider may be your longest visit. There's a lot to accomplish. If you saw your caregiver before you got pregnant, you may have already discussed some of your concerns.

 Feel free to ask questions to get an idea of how this person will relate to you and your needs. This factor is important as your pregnancy progresses. During pregnancy, there should be an exchange of ideas. Consider what your doctor suggests and

> During pregnancy, there should be an exchange of ideas. Consider what your doctor suggests and why.

why. It's important to share your feelings and ideas. You also need to remember that your doctor has experience that can be valuable to you during pregnancy.

What Will Happen?

What should you expect at this first visit? First, your healthcare provider will ask for a history of your medical health. (To prepare, read and fill out the questionnaire on pages 6 through 9.) This includes general medical problems and any problems relating to your gynecological and obstetrical history. Your caregiver will ask about your periods and recent birth-control methods. If you've had an abortion or a miscarriage, tell your healthcare provider. If you've been in the hospital for surgery or for some other reason, it's important information. If you have old medical records, bring them with you.

Your caregiver needs to know about any medication you take or any medication you are allergic to. Your family's medical history may also be important, such as the occurrence of diabetes or other chronic illness. Your healthcare provider will perform a physical exam, including a pelvic exam and Pap smear. This exam determines if your uterus is the appropriate size for how far along you are in your pregnancy.

Dad Tip

Bring home her favorite dinner or cook it yourself.

Laboratory tests may be done at this first visit or on a subsequent visit. If you have questions, ask them. If you think you may have a high-risk pregnancy, discuss it with your doctor.

In most cases, you will be asked to return every 4 weeks for the first 7 months, then every 2 weeks until the last month, then every week. If problems arise, you may be scheduled for more frequent visits.

If you've just found out you're pregnant, you might want to begin by reading the previous chapters.

Week 7

How Big Is Your Baby?

Your baby has an incredible growth spurt this week! At the beginning of the 7th week, the crown-to-rump length of your growing baby is 0.16 to 0.2 inch (4 to 5mm). This is about the size of a BB pellet. By the end of the week, your baby has more than doubled in size, to 0.44 to 0.52 inch (11 to 13mm).

How Big Are You?

Although you are probably quite anxious to show the world you're pregnant, there still may be little change. Changes will come soon, though.

How Your Baby Is Growing and Developing

Leg buds are beginning to appear as short fins. As you can see on page 86, arm buds have grown longer; they have divided into a hand segment and an arm-shoulder segment. The hand and foot have a digital plate where the fingers and toes will develop.

The heart bulges from the body. By this time, it has divided into right and left heart chambers. The primary *bronchi* are present; bronchi are air passages in the lungs. The cerebral hemispheres, which make up the brain, are also growing. Eyes and nostrils are developing.

Intestines are developing, and the appendix is present. The pancreas, which produces the hormone insulin, is also present. Part of the intestine bulges into the umbilical cord. Later in your baby's development, it will return to the abdomen.

Changes in You

Changes are occurring gradually. You still probably won't "show," and people won't be able to tell you're pregnant unless you tell them. You may be gaining weight throughout your body, but you should have gained only a couple of pounds this early in your pregnancy.

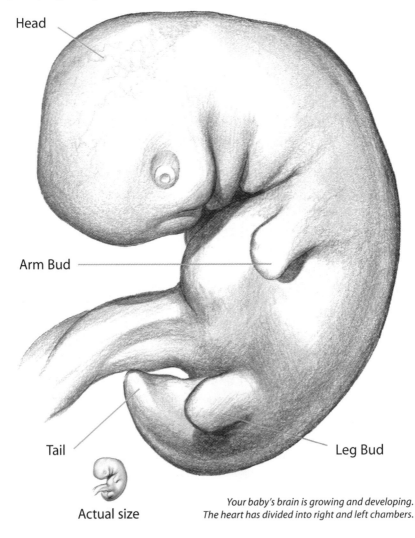

Head

Arm Bud

Tail

Leg Bud

Actual size

Your baby's brain is growing and developing.
The heart has divided into right and left chambers.

If you haven't gained weight or if you have lost a couple of pounds, it isn't unusual. It will go the other direction in the weeks to come. You may still experience morning sickness and other symptoms of early pregnancy.

How Your Actions Affect Your Baby's Development

Using Over-the-Counter Medications and Preparations
Many people don't consider over-the-counter (OTC) preparations as medication and they take them at will, pregnant or not. Some researchers believe nonprescription, or over-the-counter, medication usage increases during pregnancy.

OTC medications and preparations may not be safe during pregnancy. Use them with as much caution as any other drug! Many OTC preparations are combinations of medications. For example, pain medication can contain aspirin, caffeine and phenacetin. Cough syrups or sleep medications can contain as much as 25% alcohol. This is no different than drinking wine or beer during pregnancy.

Another medication to be careful with is ibuprofen, a popular product available in prescription and nonprescription forms. Experience with this medication during pregnancy is limited; it hasn't been available that long. There are no known benefits of

A Visit with the Doctor

My patient Catherine called because she had a chronic knee problem and she used aspirin for pain and swelling. She asked if it was OK to use it during pregnancy.

I told her that full doses of aspirin are not advised because aspirin use can increase bleeding. This could cause problems for Catherine or her baby if she bled during pregnancy or delivery. Under medical supervision, small doses of aspirin may be used, but always discuss the situation with your healthcare provider.

taking ibuprofen during pregnancy, and there have been reports of possible harmful effects. Why take a chance? Ibuprofen products include Advil®, Motrin® and Rufen®.

Other popular over-the-counter products include naprosyn (Aleve®) and ketoprofen (Orudis®), both used to relieve pain or to reduce fever. Experience with these medications during pregnancy is limited. It is best to use them only under your doctor's supervision.

Tip for Week 7

Don't take any over-the-counter medications for longer than 48 hours without consulting your healthcare provider. If a problem doesn't resolve, your caregiver may have another treatment plan for you.

Talk to your doctor about taking any medication before you use it! Read package labels and package inserts about safety during pregnancy—nearly all medications contain this information. Some antacids contain sodium bicarbonate, which increases your intake of sodium (this can be important to avoid if you have water-retention problems) and can cause constipation and increased gas. Some antacids contain aluminum, which can cause constipation and affect the metabolism of other minerals (phosphate). Others contain magnesium; excessive use of these may cause magnesium poisoning.

Some over-the-counter medications and preparations can be used safely during pregnancy, if you use them wisely:

- acetaminophen (Tylenol®)
- some antacids (Amphojel, Gelusil, Maalox, Milk of Magnesia)
- throat lozenges (Sucrets®)
- some decongestants (Sudafed®)
- some cough medicines (Robitussin®)

If you think your symptoms or discomfort are more severe than they should be, call your healthcare provider. Follow his or her advice. In addition, take good care of yourself. Exercise, eat right and keep a positive mental attitude about your pregnancy.

Your Nutrition

Dairy products can be very important to you during pregnancy. They contain calcium, which is important to you and

your developing baby. Read food labels for information on the calcium content of many packaged foods. Some dairy foods you may choose, and their serving sizes, include the following:

- cottage cheese—¾ cup
- processed cheese (American)—2 ounces
- hard cheese (Parmesan or Romano)—1 ounce
- custard or pudding—1 cup
- milk (whole, 2%, 1%, skim)—8 ounces
- natural cheese (Cheddar)—1½ ounces
- yogurt (plain or flavored)—1 cup

If you must watch your calorie intake and want to keep it low, choose dairy products with a low-fat content. Some choices include skim milk, low-fat yogurt and low-fat cheese. Calcium content is unaffected in low-fat dairy products.

Do You Need Extra Minerals?
Nearly all diets that supply a sufficient number of calories for appropriate weight gain contain enough minerals (except iron) to prevent mineral deficiency. During pregnancy, your iron requirement increases. Very few women have sufficient iron stores to meet pregnancy demands. During a normal pregnancy, blood volume increases by about 50%. A large amount of iron is required to produce those additional blood cells.

Iron needs are most important in the latter half of pregnancy. Most women don't need to take iron supplements during the first trimester. If prescribed at this time, they can worsen symptoms of nausea and vomiting.

The iron content of prenatal vitamins can irritate your stomach. Iron supplements may also cause constipation. You may not be able to take iron supplements until after the first trimester.

Caution
Avoid unpasteurized milk and any foods made from unpasteurized milk. Also avoid soft cheeses, such as Camembert, Brie, feta and Roquefort. These products are a common source of *listeriosis,* a form of food poisoning. Undercooked poultry, red meat, seafood and hot dogs can contain listeriosis. Cook all meat and seafood thoroughly before eating.

Prenatal Vitamins

Prenatal vitamins are usually prescribed for a pregnant woman by her healthcare provider. Some women like to begin taking prenatal vitamins while they are trying to get pregnant. Supplements contain the daily amounts of vitamins and minerals recommended for you during pregnancy.

Your prenatal vitamin is different from a regular multivitamin because of its iron and folic-acid content. It is the most important supplement for you in pregnancy. Prenatal vitamins are best tolerated if you take them with meals or at night before bed.

Prenatal vitamins contain many essential ingredients for the development of your baby and your continued good health. That's why you should take them until your baby is born. A typical prenatal vitamin contains the following:

- **calcium** to build baby's teeth and bones, and to help strengthen your own
- **copper** to help prevent anemia and to help in bone formation
- **folic acid** to reduce the risk of neural-tube defects and to help in blood-cell production
- **iodine** to help control metabolism
- **iron** to prevent anemia and to help baby's blood development
- **vitamin A** for general health and body metabolism
- **vitamin B$_1$** for general health and body metabolism
- **vitamin B$_2$** for general health and body metabolism
- **vitamin B$_3$** for general health and body metabolism
- **vitamin B$_6$** for general health and body metabolism
- **vitamin B$_{12}$** to promote formation of blood
- **vitamin C** to aid in your body's absorption of iron
- **vitamin D** to strengthen baby's bones and teeth, and to help your body use phosphorus and calcium
- **vitamin E** for general health and body metabolism
- **zinc** to help balance fluids in your body and to aid nerve and muscle function

Some doctors prescribe calcium supplementation. Calcium is important for every pregnant woman. It helps build strong bones and teeth in the baby and helps keep the woman's bones healthy. During pregnancy, you need 1,200 to 1,500mg a day. That's about 3 to 4 glasses of skim milk a day.

Calcium supplementation may help control blood pressure and reduce hypertension and the risk of pre-eclampsia. Some substances interfere with the body's absorption of calcium. Do not consume salt, protein foods, tea, coffee or unleavened bread with calcium-containing foods.

Research has found that zinc may be helpful to a thin or underweight woman during pregnancy. We believe this mineral helps a thin woman increase her chances of giving birth to a bigger, healthier baby.

The value of fluoride and fluoride supplementation in a pregnant woman is unclear. Some researchers believe fluoride supplementation during pregnancy results in improved teeth in the child; not everyone agrees. Fluoride supplementation in a pregnant woman has not been proved to harm her baby. Some prenatal vitamins contain fluoride.

A Visit with the Doctor

Andrea was very upset at her second visit. Crying, she told me, "Todd doesn't find me attractive now. We haven't had sex since I got pregnant." Todd, who was with her, said that wasn't true; he thought she was more beautiful than ever. But he was afraid sex would hurt the baby.

I explained to them that intimacy during pregnancy is natural and OK. It wouldn't hurt the baby as long as Andrea's pregnancy was normal and uncomplicated.

You Should Also Know

Sexual Intimacy during Pregnancy

Many couples question whether it is wise or permissible to have sexual intercourse during pregnancy. Sexual relations are

Dad Tip

Buy a present for your partner and the baby.

acceptable for a healthy pregnant woman and her partner. However, when miscarriage or premature labor threaten, avoid intercourse.

Some doctors recommend abstinence from intercourse during the last 4 weeks of pregnancy, but not all physicians agree with this. Discuss it with your healthcare provider.

If you've just found out you're pregnant, you might want to begin by reading the previous chapters.

Week 8

How Big Is Your Baby?

By your 8th week of pregnancy, the crown-to-rump length of your baby is 0.56 to 0.8 inch (14 to 20mm). This is about the size of a pinto bean.

How Big Are You?

Your uterus is getting bigger, but it probably still isn't big enough for you to be showing, especially if this is your first pregnancy. You will notice a gradual change in your waistline and the fit of your clothes. Your healthcare provider will see that your uterus is enlarged if you have a pelvic exam.

How Your Baby Is Growing and Developing

Your baby is continuing to grow and to change rapidly during these early weeks. Compare the illustration on page 95 with the illustration for the 7th week of pregnancy. Can you see the incredible changes?

Eyelid folds are forming on the face. The tip of the nose is present. Ears are forming, internally and externally.

In the heart, the aortic and pulmonary valves are present and distinct. Tubes leading from the throat to the functioning part of the lungs are branched, like the branches of a tree. The body's trunk area is getting longer and straightening out.

Elbows are present, and the arms and legs extend forward. Arms have grown longer. They bend at the elbows and curve slightly over the heart. The digital rays, which become fingers, are notched. Toe rays are present on the feet.

Changes in You

Changes in Your Uterus
Before pregnancy, your uterus was about the size of your fist. After 6 weeks of growth, it is about the size of a grapefruit. As the uterus grows, you may feel cramping or even pain in your lower abdomen or your sides. Some women feel tightening or contractions of the uterus.

The uterus tightens or contracts throughout pregnancy. If you don't feel this, don't worry. However, when contractions are accompanied by bleeding from the vagina, consult your healthcare provider.

Sciatic-Nerve Pain
Many women experience an occasional excruciating pain in their buttocks and down the back or side of their legs as pregnancy progresses. This is called *sciatic-nerve pain.* The sciatic nerve runs behind the uterus in the pelvis to the legs. We believe pain is caused by pressure on the nerve from the growing, expanding uterus.

The best treatment for the pain is to lie on your opposite side. This helps relieve pressure on the nerve.

How Your Actions Affect Your Baby's Development

Miscarriage
Miscarriage occurs when a pregnancy ends before the embryo or fetus can survive on its own outside the uterus. Nearly every pregnant woman thinks about miscarriage during pregnancy, but it occurs in only about 15% of all pregnancies.

What Causes a Miscarriage?
We don't usually know and are often unable to find out what causes a miscarriage. The most common finding in early miscarriages is an abnormality in the development of the early embryo. Studies

indicate more than half of all early miscarriages have chromosomal abnormalities.

Many factors can affect the embryo and its environment, including radiation, chemicals (drugs or medications) and infections. Called *teratogens,* these adverse factors are discussed in depth in Week 4.

We believe various maternal factors are important in some

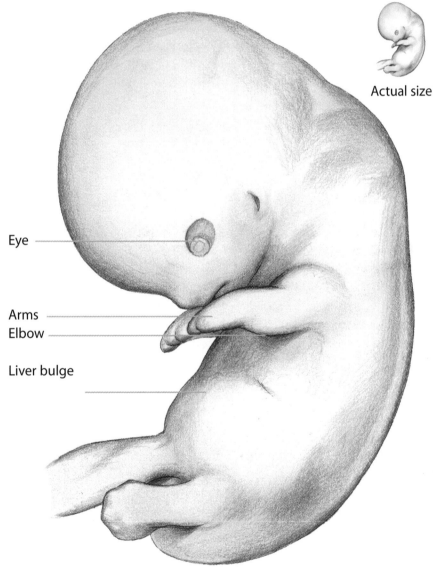

Actual size

Eye

Arms
Elbow

Liver bulge

Embryo at 8 weeks (fetal age—6 weeks).
Crown-to-rump length is about 0.8 inch (20mm).
Arms are longer and bend at the elbows.

A Visit with the Doctor

**Ruby, 8 weeks pregnant, was upset when
she came for her first prenatal visit. Her
last pregnancy had ended in miscarriage at
8 weeks, and she was scared she would
have a miscarriage with this
pregnancy. I assured her there were no
indications it would happen this time.
She left the office looking forward to
her next visit, when she could probably
hear the baby's heartbeat.**

miscarriages. Unusual infections, such as listeriosis, toxoplasmosis and syphilis, have been implicated in miscarriages.

We have no concrete evidence that deficiency of any particular nutrient or even a moderate deficiency of all nutrients causes a miscarriage. Women who smoke have a higher rate of miscarriage. Alcohol is also blamed for an increase in miscarriages.

The trauma of an accident or major surgery has been related to an increase in miscarriages, although this is difficult to verify. An incompetent cervix (see Week 24) is a cause of pregnancy loss after the first trimester. Many women have blamed emotional upset or trauma for a miscarriage, but this is hard to prove.

> **Nearly every pregnant woman thinks about miscarriage during pregnancy, but it occurs in only about 15% of all pregnancies.**

Below is a discussion of different types and causes of miscarriage. It is included to alert you about what to watch for if you have any symptoms of a miscarriage. If you have questions, discuss them with your healthcare provider.

Threatened Miscarriage

A threatened miscarriage may be presumed when there is a bloody discharge from the vagina during the first half of pregnancy. Bleeding may last for days or even weeks. There may or may not be any cramping or pain. Pain may feel like a menstrual cramp or a mild backache. Resting in bed is about all you can do, although being active does not cause miscarriage. No procedures or medication can keep a woman from miscarrying.

Threatened miscarriage is a common diagnosis because 20% of all women experience bleeding during early pregnancy but not all miscarry.

Inevitable Miscarriage

An inevitable miscarriage occurs with the rupture of membranes, dilatation of the cervix and passage of blood clots and even tissue. Miscarriage is almost certain under these circumstances. The uterus usually contracts, expelling the fetus or *products of conception* (so-called when no embryo or fetus is present).

Incomplete Miscarriage

With an incomplete miscarriage, the entire pregnancy may not be passed at once. Part of the pregnancy is passed while part of it remains in the uterus. Bleeding may be heavy and continues until the uterus is empty.

> **Tip for Week 8**
>
> **Wash your hands thoroughly throughout the day, especially after handling raw meat or using the bathroom. This simple activity can help prevent the spread of many bacteria and viruses that cause infection.**

Missed Miscarriage

A missed miscarriage can occur with prolonged retention of an embryo that died earlier. There may be no symptoms or bleeding. The time period from when the pregnancy failed to the time the miscarriage is discovered is usually weeks.

Habitual Miscarriage

This term usually refers to three or more consecutive miscarriages.

If You Have Problems

If you have problems, notify your doctor immediately! Bleeding usually appears first, followed by cramping. Ectopic pregnancy must be considered a possibility. A quantitative HCG may be useful in identifying a normal pregnancy, but a single test report usually won't help. Your caregiver needs to repeat the test over a period of days.

Ultrasound may help if you are more than 5 gestational weeks
into your pregnancy. You may continue to bleed, but seeing
your baby's heartbeat and a normal-appearing pregnancy may be
reassuring. If the first ultrasound is not reassuring, you may be asked
to wait a week or 10 days, then repeat the ultrasound.

The longer you bleed and cramp, the more likely you are having
a miscarriage. If you pass all of the pregnancy and bleeding stops
and cramping goes away, you may be done with it. However,
if everything is not expelled, it may be necessary to perform a
dilatation and curettage (D&C) to empty the uterus. It is preferable
to do this so you won't bleed for a long time, risking anemia and
infection.

Some women are given the hormone progesterone to help them
keep a pregnancy. The use of progesterone to prevent miscarriage is
controversial. Doctors do not agree on its use or its effectiveness.

Rh-Sensitivity and Miscarriage
If you're Rh-negative and you have a miscarriage, you will need to
receive RhoGAM. This applies *only* if you are Rh-negative. RhoGAM is
given to protect you from making antibodies to Rh-positive blood.
(This is discussed in Week 16.)

If You Have a Miscarriage
One miscarriage can be traumatic; two in a row can be very difficult
to deal with. Repeated miscarriages occur due to chance or "bad
luck" in most cases.

Most doctors don't recommend testing to find a reason for
miscarriage unless you have three or more. Chromosome analysis
can be done, and other tests investigate the possibility of infections,
diabetes and lupus.

Don't blame yourself or your partner for a miscarriage. It is
usually impossible to look back at everything you've done, eaten or
been exposed to and find the cause of a miscarriage.

Your Nutrition

You may not always get the nutrients you
need, in the amounts you need. Below is
a chart showing you where to get various
nutrients you should be eating every day. Your prenatal vitamin is

Sources of Food Nutrients

Nutrient (Daily Requirement)	Food Sources
Calcium (1,200mg)	dairy products, dark leafy vegetables, dried beans and peas, tofu
Folic acid (0.4mg)	liver, dried beans and peas, eggs, broccoli, whole-grain products, oranges and orange juice
Iron (30mg)	fish, liver, meat, poultry, egg yolks, nuts, dried beans and peas, dark leafy vegetables, dried fruit
Magnesium (320mg)	dried beans and peas, cocoa, seafoods, whole-grain products, nuts
Vitamin B$_6$ (2.2mg)	whole-grain products, liver, meat
Vitamin E (10mg)	milk, eggs, meat, fish, cereals, leafy vegetables, vegetable oils
Zinc (15mg)	seafood, meat, nuts, milk, dried beans and peas

not a substitute for food, so don't count on it to supply you with essential vitamins and minerals. Food is important, too!

You Should Also Know

Lab Tests Your Doctor May Order

At your first or second visit, routine lab tests are performed. You will have a pelvic exam, including a Pap smear. Other tests include a CBC (complete blood count), urinalysis and urine culture, a test for syphilis (VDRL or ART), and cervical cultures, as indicated. Many doctors test blood sugar (to look for diabetes). They also test for your immunity against rubella and your blood type and Rh-factor.

Tests are not performed at each visit; they are done at the beginning of pregnancy and as needed. Tests for hepatitis are now standard.

Toxoplasmosis

If you have a cat, you may be concerned about *toxoplasmosis*. The disease is spread by eating raw, infected meat or by contact with infected cat feces. It can cross the placenta to your baby. Usually an infection in the mother has no symptoms.

Infection during pregnancy can lead to miscarriage or an infected infant at birth. Antibiotics, such as pyrimethamine, sulfadiazine and erythromycin, can treat toxoplasmosis, but the best plan is prevention. Hygienic measures prevent transmission of the disease.

Avoid exposure to cat feces (get someone else to change the kitty litter). Wash hands thoroughly after petting your cat, and keep your cat off counters and tables. Wash your hands after contact with meat and soil, and cook meat thoroughly.

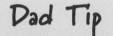

Dad Tip

If you have pets, take over their care during your partner's pregnancy. Change the litter box (she should *never* do this while pregnant). Walk the dog (the pull on the leash might hurt her back). Buy food and other pet supplies (again, save her back from the strain of lifting big food bags). Make and keep vet appointments.

If you've just found out you're pregnant, you might want to begin by reading the previous chapters.

Week 9

How Big Is Your Baby?

The crown-to-rump length of the embryo is 0.9 inch to 1.2 inches (22 to 30mm). This is close to the size of a medium green olive.

How Big Are You?

Each week your uterus grows larger with the baby growing inside it. You may begin to see your waistline growing thicker by this time. A pelvic exam will detect a uterus a little bigger than a grapefruit.

How Your Baby Is Growing and Developing

If you could look inside your uterus, you'd see many changes in your baby. The illustration on page 102 shows some of them.

Your baby's arms and legs are longer. Hands are flexed at the wrist and meet over the heart area. They continue to extend in front of the body. Fingers are longer, and the tips are slightly enlarged where touch pads are developing. The feet are approaching the midline of the body and may be long enough to meet in front of the torso.

The head is more erect, and the neck is more developed. The eyelids almost cover the eyes. Up to this time, the eyes have been uncovered. External ears are evident and well formed. Your baby now moves its body and limbs. This movement may be seen during an ultrasound exam.

The baby looks more recognizable as a human being, although it is still extremely small. It is probably impossible to distinguish a male from a female. External organs (external genitalia) of the male and female appear very similar and will not be distinguishable for another few weeks.

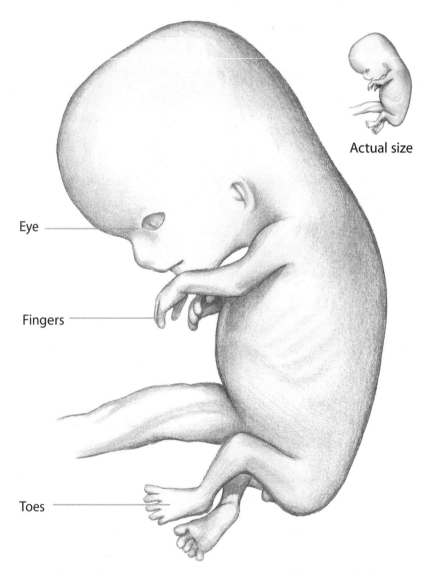

Actual size

Eye

Fingers

Toes

Embryo at 9 weeks of pregnancy
(fetal age—46 to 49 days).
Toes are formed, and feet are more recognizable.
Crown-to-rump length is about 1 inch (25mm).

Changes in You

Weight Change

Most women are interested in their weight during pregnancy; many watch their weight closely. As strange as it may seem, gaining weight is an important way to monitor the well-being of your developing baby. Even though your weight gain may be small, your body is changing.

How Is Pregnancy Weight Distributed?

7 pounds .... **Maternal stores (fat, protein and other nutrients)**
4 pounds .... **Increased fluid volume**
2 pounds .... **Breast enlargement**
2 pounds .... **Uterus**
7-1/2 pounds .... **Baby**
2 pounds .... **Amniotic fluid**
1-1/2 pounds .... **Placenta (connects mother and baby; brings nourishment and takes away waste)**

(Modified from A.C.O.G. Guide to Planning for Pregnancy, Birth and Beyond; 1990, American College of Obstetricians and Gynecologists)

Increased Blood Volume

Your blood system changes dramatically during pregnancy. Your blood volume increases greatly—to about 50% more than before you became pregnant. However, this amount varies from woman to woman.

Increased blood volume is important. It is designed to meet the demands of your growing uterus. This increase does not include the blood in the embryo, whose circulation is separate (fetal blood does not mix with your blood). It protects you and your baby from harmful effects when you lie down or stand up. It is also a safeguard during labor and delivery, when some blood is lost.

The increase in blood volume starts during the first trimester. The largest increase occurs during the second trimester. It continues to increase at a slower rate during the third trimester.

Blood is composed of fluid (plasma) and cells (red blood cells and white blood cells). Plasma and cells play an important role in your body's function.

Fluid and cells increase to different degrees. Usually there is an initial rise in plasma volume followed by an increase in red blood cells. The increase in red blood cells increases your body's demand for iron.

Red blood cells and plasma both increase during pregnancy; plasma increases more. This increase in plasma can cause anemia. If you're anemic, especially during pregnancy, you may feel tired, fatigue easily or experience a general feeling of ill health. (See Week 22 for a discussion of anemia.)

How Your Actions Affect Your Baby's Development

Saunas and Hot Tubs
Some women are concerned about using saunas, hot tubs and spas during pregnancy. They want to know if it is OK to relax in this way.

Your baby relies on you to maintain the correct body temperature. If your body temperature is elevated high enough and stays there for an extended period, it may damage the baby if it occurs at critical times in its development. Don't take a chance with a hot tub or sauna until more medical research confirms it is not harmful to your baby.

Electric Blankets
There has been controversy about using electric blankets to keep you warm during pregnancy. There is still much disagreement and discussion about their safety. Some experts question whether they can cause health problems.

Electric blankets produce a low-level electromagnetic field. The developing fetus may be more sensitive than an adult to these electromagnetic fields.

Because researchers are uncertain about acceptable levels of exposure for a pregnant woman and her baby, the safest alternative at this time is *not* to use an electric blanket during pregnancy. There are many other ways to keep warm, such as down comforters and wool blankets. One of these is a better choice.

Tip for Week 9

It's an old wives' tale that your hair won't curl if you have a permanent during pregnancy. Our only precaution is that if odors affect you, the fumes from a permanent or hair coloring could make you feel ill.

Microwave Ovens

Many women express concerns about the safety of microwave ovens. Are they exposed to radiation? Microwave ovens are helpful to busy people who prepare meals. However, we don't know if there is danger to you if you use a microwave oven during pregnancy. More research is needed.

Initial research indicates that tissues developing in the body, which would include the human fetus, may be particularly sensitive to the effects of microwaves. A microwave oven heats tissues from the inside. Follow the directions provided with your microwave oven and don't stand next to or directly in front of it while it is in use.

A Visit with the Doctor

Phoebe always had a tan. She told me she maintained her tan at a tanning booth with regular weekly visits. She wanted to know if she could continue these visits during her pregnancy. I advised her that we don't yet know the effects on the growing fetus of a pregnant woman lying in a tanning booth. It has not been studied by medical researchers. "Until medical studies indicate it's safe to get in a tanning booth," I told Phoebe, "it's best to avoid using them while you're pregnant."

Your Nutrition

Fruits and vegetables are important during pregnancy. Because different kinds of produce are available in different seasons, you can add variety to your diet  quite easily with them. They are excellent sources of vitamins, minerals and fiber. Eating a variety supplies you with iron, folic acid, calcium and vitamin C.

Each day, eat one or two servings of fruit rich in vitamin C and at least one dark green or deep yellow vegetable for extra iron, fiber and folic acid. Fruits and vegetables you may choose, and their serving sizes, include the following:

- grapes—¾ cup
- banana, orange, apple—
    1 medium piece
- dried fruit—¼ cup
- fruit juice—½ cup
- canned or cooked fruit—½ cup
- broccoli, carrots or other
    vegetable—½ cup
- potato—1 medium
- leafy green vegetables—1 cup
- vegetable juice—¾ cup

Alfalfa Sprouts

Be careful about adding alfalfa sprouts to foods you eat. Recent research has found that these sprouts can cause infections in people with a weakened immune system.

You Should Also Know

Having a Baby Costs Money!

Every couple wants to know what it will cost to have a baby. There are really two answers to that question—it costs a lot, and cost varies from one part of the country to another.

To determine how much it costs to have a baby in your area, you need to consider several different factors. Insurance makes a big difference. If you don't have it, you will pay for everything. If you do have insurance, you need to check out some things. Ask your employer the following questions.

- What type of coverage do I have?
- Are there maternity benefits? What are they?
- Do maternity benefits cover Cesarean deliveries?
- What kind of coverage is there for a high-risk pregnancy?
- Do I have to pay a deductible? If so, how much is it?
- How do I submit claims?
- Is there a cap (limit) on total coverage?
- What percentage of my costs are covered?
- Is the cost of taking childbirth-education classes covered?

- Does my coverage restrict the kind of hospital accommodations I may choose, such as a birthing center or a birthing room?
- What procedures must I follow before entering the hospital?
- Does my policy cover a nurse-midwife?
- Does coverage include medications?
- What tests during pregnancy are covered?
- What tests during labor and delivery are covered?
- What types of anesthesia are covered during labor and delivery?
- How long can I stay in the hospital?
- Does payment go directly to my healthcare provider or to me?
- What conditions or services are not covered?
- What kind of coverage is there for the baby after it is born?
- How long can the baby stay in the hospital?
- Is there an additional cost to add the baby to the policy?
- How do I add the baby to the policy?
- Can we collect a percentage of a fee from my husband's policy and the rest from mine?

Your insurance dictates a lot of the costs and decisions for you. Having a baby generates different costs. One is the hospital. Much of the covered amount for the hospital is determined by the length of stay and the services you use. In some cases, having an epidural or Cesarean delivery adds to this bill. Your doctor's bill is separate

A Visit with the Doctor

When my first daughter was born in 1974, a normal delivery and 2-day hospital stay for my wife (no C-section, anesthesia or complications) cost a total of $600 for hospital, doctor, nursery and pediatrician. When my youngest daughter was born in 1985, a similar stay (again no anesthesia, C-section or complications) cost about $3,500—an increase of almost 600% in 11 years!
Across the United States, prices for a delivery in 2000 range from $6,000 to $14,000, depending on complications and the type of delivery.

from this, except under some plans. A pediatrician usually examines the baby, does a physical and sees the baby each day in the hospital. This is another cost.

It would be nice to think about costs before pregnancy and be sure to have insurance to help out. However, many pregnancies are surprises.

What can you do? First, find the answers to your questions. Talk to your insurance carrier. Then talk to someone in your doctor's office who handles insurance claims. This person may have answers or know of resources you haven't thought about. Don't be embarrassed to ask questions. You will be happier if you get these issues resolved early. Pregnancy is not the time to cut corners to save money.

Call around so you can compare hospitals and prices. Sometimes it's worth spending a little more money to get more. When you call, ask for specifics about what is included in the prices you are quoted. You may get a price that seems lower and better than others but really doesn't cover everything you will want and need.

Today, some hospitals and medical centers offer "pregnancy packages." A package can cover many services for one fee. Ask about it in your area.

You want to be prepared well in advance. The last thing you need at this time is an unpleasant surprise about what is covered or how much you will have to pay for medical services.

Dad Tip

Ask your partner which visits to the doctor she'd like you to attend. Some couples attend every visit together, when possible. Ask her to let you know the date and time of each appointment.

Costs of Having a Baby in Canada

The Canadian healthcare system is different from the healthcare system in the United States. Canadians pay a healthcare premium on a monthly basis. Cost varies depending on the province you live in. The doctor who delivers your baby is paid by the government. He or she submits the bill to the government, not you.

If you've just found out you're pregnant, you might want to begin by reading the previous chapters.

Week 10

How Big Is Your Baby?

By the 10th week of pregnancy, the crown-to-rump length of your growing baby is about 1.25 to 1.68 inches (31 to 42mm). At this time, we can start measuring how much the baby weighs. Before this week, weight was too small to measure weekly differences. Now that the baby is starting to put on a little weight, weight is included in this section. The baby weighs close to 0.18 ounce (5g) and is the size of a small plum.

How Big Are You?

Changes are gradual, and you still may not show much. You may be thinking about and looking at maternity clothes, but you probably don't need them just yet.

Molar Pregnancy

A condition that can make you grow too big too fast is a *molar pregnancy*, sometimes called *gestational trophoblastic neoplasia* (GTN) or *hydatidiform mole*. The occurrence of GTN is easily monitored by checking HCG levels (see Week 5). Molar pregnancy can be treated with medications or surgery.

When a molar pregnancy occurs, an embryo does not usually develop. Other tissue grows, which is abnormal placental tissue. The most common symptom is bleeding during the first trimester. Another symptom is the discrepancy between the size of the

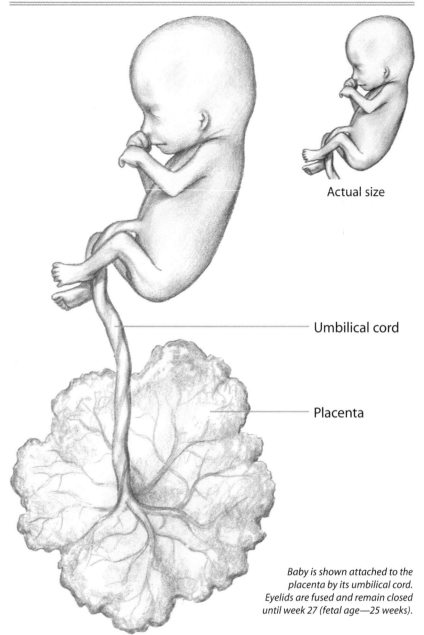

Actual size

Umbilical cord

Placenta

Baby is shown attached to the placenta by its umbilical cord. Eyelids are fused and remain closed until week 27 (fetal age—25 weeks).

mother-to-be and how far along she is supposed to be in pregnancy. Half the time, a woman is too large. Twenty-five percent of the time, she is too small. Excessive nausea and vomiting are other symptoms. Cysts may occur on the ovaries.

The most effective way to diagnose a molar pregnancy is by ultrasound. The ultrasound picture has a "snowflake" appearance. A molar pregnancy is usually found when ultrasound is done early in pregnancy to determine the cause of bleeding or rapid growth of the uterus.

When a molar pregnancy is diagnosed, a dilatation and curettage (D&C) is usually done as soon as possible. After a molar pregnancy occurs, effective birth control is important to be sure the molar pregnancy is completely gone. Most doctors recommend using reliable birth control for 1 year before attempting pregnancy again.

How Your Baby Is Growing and Developing

The end of week 10 is the end of the embryonic period. At this time, the fetal period begins. It is characterized by rapid growth of the fetus when the three germ layers are established. (See Week 4 for further information.) During the embryonic period, the embryo was most susceptible to things that could

> A critical part of your baby's development is safely behind you.

interfere with its development. Most congenital malformations occur before the end of week 10. It is encouraging to know that a critical part of your baby's development is safely behind you.

Few malformations occur during the fetal period. However, drugs and other harmful exposures, such as severe stress or radiation (X-ray), can destroy fetal cells at any time during pregnancy. Continue to avoid them.

By the end of week 10, development of organ systems and the body are well under way. Your baby is beginning to look more human.

Changes in You

Emotional Changes
When your pregnancy is confirmed by an exam or a pregnancy test, you may be affected in many ways. Pregnancy can change many of your expectations. Some women see pregnancy as a sign of womanhood. Some consider it a blessing. Still others feel it is a problem to be dealt with.

You will experience many changes in your body. You may wonder if you are still attractive. Will your partner still find you desirable? (Many men believe pregnant women are beautiful.) Will your partner help you? Clothing may become an issue. Can you look attractive? Can you learn to adapt?

If you aren't immediately excited about pregnancy, don't feel alone. You may question your condition—that's common. Some of this reaction is because you're not sure of what lies ahead.

When and how you begin to regard the fetus as a person is different for everyone. Some women say it is when their pregnancy test is positive. Others say it occurs when they hear the fetal heartbeat, usually at around 12 weeks. For still others, it happens when they first feel their baby move, at between 16 and 20 weeks.

You may find you are emotional about many things. You may feel moody, cry at the slightest thing or drift off in daydreams. Emotional swings are normal and continue to some degree throughout your pregnancy.

How can you help yourself deal with emotional changes? One of the most important things you can do is get good prenatal care. Follow your healthcare provider's recommendations. Keep all your prenatal appointments. Establish good communication with your caregiver and his or her office staff. Ask questions. If something bothers you or worries you, discuss it with someone reliable.

How Your Actions Affect Your Baby's Development

Vaccinations and Immunizations

Many vaccines are available that help prevent illness. A vaccine is given to provide you with protection against infection. A vaccine is usually given by injection or taken orally.

Most women of childbearing age in the United States and Canada should be immune to measles, mumps, rubella, tetanus and diphtheria. Most people born before 1957 were exposed to and infected naturally with measles, mumps and rubella and can be considered immune. They have antibodies and therefore are protected.

A Visit with the Doctor

Marcia was very upset when she called my office. She had cut her leg on a rusty piece of pipe and thought she might need a tetanus shot. We checked her records and assured her she was up to date on her vaccinations. You are considered immune to tetanus, diphtheria and whooping cough if you have received at least three doses of the DPT vaccine and if the last dose was given at least a year after the previous dose. A booster is required every 10 years. Marcia had had a booster shot 2 years before. If you aren't sure when or if you have been vaccinated, check with your doctor.

For women born after 1957, the situation may not be quite so clear. A blood test for measles is necessary to determine immunity. The diagnosis of rubella is difficult without a blood test because many other illnesses may have similar symptoms. Physician-diagnosed mumps or mumps vaccination is necessary evidence of immunity.

Vaccination for measles, mumps and rubella (MMR) should be administered only when a woman is practicing birth control. She must continue to use contraception for at least 3 months after receiving this immunization. Other vaccinations are also important, such as the tetanus (DPT; diphtheria, pertussis [whooping cough], tetanus) vaccine.

Risk of Exposure

It's important to consider your risk of exposure to various diseases when you are deciding whether to have a particular vaccination. Try to decrease your chance of exposure to disease and illness. Avoid visiting areas known to have prevalent diseases. Avoid people (usually children) with known illnesses.

It's impossible to avoid all exposure to disease. If you have been exposed, or if exposure is unavoidable, the risk of the disease must be balanced against the potential harmful effects of vaccination.

After that, the vaccine must be evaluated in terms of its effectiveness and its potential for complicating pregnancy. There is little information available on harmful effects on the developing fetus from vaccines. In general, killed vaccines are safe.

Live-measles vaccine should *never* be given to a pregnant woman. The only immunizing agent recommended for use during pregnancy is the DPT vaccine. MMR vaccine should be given before pregnancy or after delivery. A pregnant woman should receive primary vaccination against polio only if her risk of exposure to the disease is high; only inactivated polio vaccine should be used.

Effects of Infections on Your Baby

Some infections and illnesses a woman contracts can also affect her baby's development during this growth period. Below is a list of some infections and diseases, and the effects they may have on a developing baby.

Infections	Effects on Fetus
Cytomegalovirus (CMV)	microcephaly, brain damage, hearing loss
Rubella (German measles)	cataracts, deafness, heart lesions, can involve all organs
Syphilis	fetal death, skin defects
Toxoplasmosis	possible effects on all organs
Varicella	possible effects on all organs

Rubella during Pregnancy

It's a good idea to be checked for immunity to rubella before you get pregnant. Rubella (German measles) during pregnancy can be responsible for miscarriage or fetal malformation. Because there is no known treatment for rubella, the best approach is prevention.

If you're not immune, you can receive a vaccination while you take reliable birth control. Do not have a vaccination shortly before or during pregnancy because of the possibility of exposing the baby to the rubella virus.

Your Nutrition

Protein supplies you with amino acids, which are critical for the growth and repair of the embryo/fetus, placenta, uterus and breasts. Pregnancy increases your protein needs. Try to eat 50g of protein each day during the first trimester and 60g a day during the second and third trimesters. However, protein should only make up about 15% of your total calorie intake.

Many protein sources are high in fat. If you need to watch your calories, choose low-fat sources of poultry, fish, red meat,

eggs, nuts, seeds, and dried beans and peas. Some protein foods you may choose, and their serving sizes, include the following:

- chickpeas (garbanzo beans)—1 cup
- cheese, mozzarella—1 ounce
- chicken, roasted, skinless—½ breast
- eggs—1
- hamburger, broiled, lean—3½ ounces
- milk—8 ounces
- peanut butter—2 tablespoons
- tuna, canned in water—3 ounces
- yogurt—8 ounces

Brain Builders

Choline and docosahexaenoic acid (DHA) can help build baby's brain cells during fetal development and after birth, if baby breastfeeds. Choline is found in milk, eggs, peanuts, whole-wheat bread and beef. DHA is found in fish, egg yolks, poultry, meat, canola oil, walnuts and wheat germ. If you eat these foods during pregnancy and while you're breastfeeding, you can help your baby obtain these important supplements.

Dieting during Pregnancy?

Don't diet to lose weight during pregnancy! You should be *gaining* weight now; it can be harmful to your baby if you don't. A woman of normal weight can expect to gain between 25 and 35 pounds while pregnant. Your weight gain gives your doctor an indication of your and your baby's well-being.

Pregnancy is not a time to experiment with different diets or cut down on calories. However, this doesn't mean you have the go-ahead to eat anything you want, any time you want. Exercise and a proper nutrition plan, without junk food, will help you manage your weight. Be smart about food choices. It's true you're eating for two—however, you must eat wisely for both of you!

You Should Also Know

Chorionic Villus Sampling

Chorionic villus sampling (CVS) is a test used to detect genetic abnormalities. Sampling is done early in pregnancy, usually between the 9th and 11th week.

CVS is done for many reasons. The test helps identify problems related to genetic defects, such as Down syndrome. This test offers an advantage over amniocentesis because it is done much earlier in pregnancy; results are available in about 1 week. If the pregnancy will be terminated, it can be done earlier and may carry fewer risks to the woman.

Chorionic villus sampling involves placing an instrument through the cervix or abdomen to remove fetal tissue from the placenta. There is a small risk of miscarriage after this procedure, so the test should be performed only by someone experienced in the technique.

If your doctor recommends you have CVS, ask about its risks. The risk of miscarriage is small—between 1 and 2%.

Fetoscopy

Fetoscopy provides a view of the baby and placenta inside your uterus. In some cases, abnormalities and problems can be detected and corrected.

The goal of fetoscopy is to correct a defect before the problem worsens, which could prevent a fetus from developing normally. A doctor can see the problem more clearly with fetoscopy than with ultrasound.

> **Dad Tip**
>
> Are you concerned about sex during pregnancy? You both may have questions, so talk about them together and with your partner's doctor. Occasionally during a pregnancy you'll need to avoid intercourse. However, pregnancy is an opportunity for increased closeness and intimacy for you as a couple. Sex can be a positive part of this experience.

The test is done by placing a scope, like the one used in laparoscopy or arthroscopy, through the abdomen. The procedure is similar to amniocentesis, but the fetoscope is larger than the needle used for amniocentesis.

If your doctor suggests fetoscopy to you, discuss possible risks, advantages and disadvantages of the procedure with him or her. The test should be done only by someone experienced in the technique. Risk of miscarriage is 3 to 4% with this procedure. It is not available everywhere.

Notes

Week 11

How Big Is Your Baby?

By this week, the crown-to-rump length of your baby is 1.75 to 2.4 inches (44 to 60mm). Fetal weight is about 0.3 ounce (8g). Your baby is about the size of a large lime.

How Big Are You?

While big changes are occurring in your baby, changes are probably happening more slowly in you. You are almost at the end of the first trimester; your uterus has been growing along with the fetus inside it. It is almost big enough to fill your pelvis and may be felt in your lower abdomen, above the middle of your pubic bone.

You won't be able to feel your baby moving yet. If you think you feel your baby move at this time, you either have gas or are further along in your pregnancy than you thought.

How Your Baby Is Growing and Developing

Fetal growth is rapid now. The crown-to-rump length of your baby doubles in the next 3 weeks. As you can see in the illustration on page 120, the head is almost half the baby's entire length. As the head extends (uncurls or tips backward toward the spine), the chin rises from the chest, and the neck develops and lengthens. Fingernails appear.

External genitalia are beginning to show distinguishing features. Development of the fetus into a male or female is complete in another 3 weeks. If a miscarriage occurs after this point, it may be possible to tell if it was male or female.

All embryos begin life looking the same. Whether the embryo develops into a male or female is determined by the genetic information contained in the embryo.

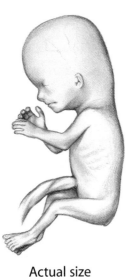

Actual size

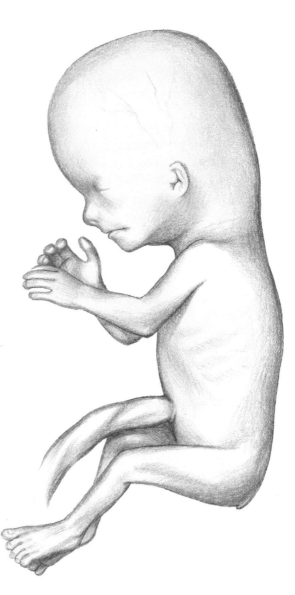

By week 11 of gestation (fetal age—9 weeks), fingernails are beginning to appear.

Changes in You

Some women notice changes in their hair, fingernails or toenails during pregnancy. This doesn't happen to everyone, but if it happens to you, don't worry about it. Some fortunate women notice an increase in hair and nail growth during pregnancy. Others find they lose some hair during this time.

Some doctors believe these changes occur during pregnancy because of increased circulation throughout your body. Others credit the hormonal changes occurring in you. Still others explain these differences with a change in "phase" of the growth cycle of the hair or nails. In any event, these differences are rarely permanent. There is little or nothing you can do about them.

How Your Actions Affect Your Baby's Development

Traveling during Pregnancy

Pregnant women frequently ask whether travel during pregnancy can hurt their baby. If your pregnancy is uncomplicated and you are not at high risk, travel is usually acceptable. Ask your healthcare provider about any travel you are considering *before* making firm plans or buying tickets.

Whether you travel by car, bus, train or airplane, it's wise to get up and walk at least every 2 hours. Regular visits to the bathroom may take care of this requirement.

The biggest risk of traveling during pregnancy is development of a complication while you are away from those who know your medical and pregnancy history. If you do decide to take a trip, be sensible in your planning. Don't overdo it. Take it easy!

You may want to keep these things in mind if you're considering flying during pregnancy.

• Avoid flights that are high altitude (nonstop overseas or cross-country flights) because the oxygen levels are lower. This increases your heartbeat, as well as your baby's; your baby also receives less oxygen.
• If you have problems with swelling, wear loose-fitting shoes and clothes. (This is good advice for every traveler.) Avoid pantyhose, tight clothes, knee-high socks or stockings, and tight waistlines.

- You can order special meals, such as low-sodium or vegetarian, if you want to avoid some foods that might cause you problems.
- Drink lots of water to keep you hydrated.
- Get up and move around when you can during the flight. Try to walk at least 10 minutes every hour. Sometimes just standing up helps your circulation.
- Try to get an aisle seat, close to the bathroom. If you have to go to the bathroom a lot, it's easier if you don't have to crawl over someone to get out.
- Be careful of any X-ray devices in the airport.

Auto Safety during Pregnancy

Many women are concerned about driving and using seat belts and shoulder harnesses during pregnancy. Wearing safety restraints dramatically decreases the incidence of injury in an accident. More than 50,000 deaths and 2 million injuries are directly related to auto accidents every year. Wearing a seat belt and shoulder harness can decrease these losses. There is no reason not to drive while you're pregnant, if your pregnancy is normal and you feel OK.

The Proper Way to Wear a Lap Belt and Shoulder Harness

Use a seat belt and shoulder harness throughout pregnancy.

There is a proper way for you to wear a seat belt during pregnancy. Place the lap-belt portion under your abdomen and across your upper thighs. It should be as snug as is comfortably possible. The shoulder belt should also be snug but comfortable. Adjust your position so the belt crosses your shoulder without cutting into your neck. Position the shoulder belt between your breasts. Do *not* slip this belt off your shoulder. If it's a long trip, adjust the belt as needed for comfort.

Some women believe using a safety restraint might be harmful to their pregnancy. Here are some common excuses (and our responses) for not using seat belts and shoulder harnesses in pregnancy.

"Using a safety belt will hurt my baby." There is no evidence that seat-belt use will increase the chance of fetal or uterine injury. Your chance of survival with a seat belt is better than without one. Your survival is important to your unborn baby.

"I don't want to be trapped in my car if there is a fire." Few automobile accidents result in fires. Even if a fire did occur, you could probably undo the restraint and escape if you were conscious. Ejection from a car accounts for about 25% of all deaths in automobile accidents. Seat-belt use prevents this.

"I'm a good driver." Defensive driving helps, but it doesn't prevent an accident.

"I don't need to use a safety belt; I'm just going a short distance." Most injuries occur within 25 miles of home.

A few studies have been done on pregnant women who used seat belts. In one California study, only 14% of all pregnant women used seat belts compared to 30% of nonpregnant women. We know the lap/shoulder seat-belt system is safe to wear during pregnancy, so buckle up for you *and* your baby.

Your Nutrition

Carbohydrate foods provide the primary source of energy for your developing baby. These foods also ensure that your body uses protein efficiently. Foods from this group are almost interchangeable, so it should be easy to get all the servings you need. Some carbohydrate foods you may choose, and their serving sizes, include the following:

- tortilla—1 large
- pasta, cereal or rice, cooked—½ cup
- cereal, ready-to-eat—1 ounce
- bagel—½
- bread—1 slice
- roll—1 medium

You Should Also Know

Ultrasound in Pregnancy

By this point, you may have discussed ultrasound with your doctor. Or you may already have had an ultrasound test. Ultrasound (also called *sonography* or *sonogram*) is one of our most valuable methods for evaluating a pregnancy. Although doctors, hospitals and insurance companies (yes, they get involved in this, too) don't agree as to when ultrasound should be done or if every pregnant woman should have an ultrasound test during pregnancy, it definitely has its place. The test has proved useful in improving the outcome in pregnancy. It is a noninvasive test, and there are no known risks associated with it.

Ultrasound involves the use of high-frequency sound waves made by applying an alternating current to a transducer. A lubricant is placed on the skin to improve contact with the transducer. The transducer passes over the abdomen above the uterus. Sound waves are projected from the transducer through the abdomen, into the pelvis. Sound waves bounce off tissues they are directed toward and back to the transducer. The reflection of sound waves can be compared to radar used by airplanes or ships.

Different tissues of the body reflect ultrasound signals differently, and we can distinguish among them. Motion can be distinguished, so we can detect motion of the baby or its parts such as the heart. With ultrasound, a fetal heart can be seen beating as early as 5 or 6 weeks into the pregnancy.

Ultrasound can detect fetal motion. Your baby's body and limbs can be seen moving as early as 4 weeks of embryonic growth (6th week of pregnancy).

You may be asked to drink a lot of water before an ultrasound examination. If you have had an ultrasound exam during a previous pregnancy, one of the main things you may remember is how uncomfortable you were with your bladder full to overflowing!

> **Tip for Week 11**
>
> You may be able to get a "picture" of your baby before birth from an ultrasound test. Some facilities can even make a videotape for you. Ask about it before the test, if you're scheduled to have one. You may be advised to bring a clean videotape.

Ultrasound

Your doctor can use ultrasound in many ways in relation to your pregnancy:

- helping in the early identification of pregnancy
- showing the size and growth rate of the embryo or fetus
- identifying the presence of two or more fetuses
- measuring the fetal head, abdomen or femur to determine the stage of pregnancy
- identifying some fetuses with Down syndrome
- identifying fetal abnormalities, such as hydrocephalus and microcephaly
- identifying abnormalities of internal organs, such as the kidneys or bladder
- measuring the amount of amniotic fluid to help determine fetal well-being
- identifying the location, size and maturity of the placenta
- identifying placental abnormalities
- identifying uterine abnormalities or tumors
- determining the position of an IUD
- differentiating between miscarriage, ectopic pregnancy and normal pregnancy
- in connection with various tests, such as amniocentesis, percutaneous blood-cord sampling (PUBS) and chorionic villus sampling (CVS), to select a safe place to do each test

Your bladder is in front of your uterus. When your bladder is empty, your uterus is harder to see because it is farther down inside the pelvic bones. Bones disrupt ultrasound signals and make the picture harder to interpret. With your bladder full, your uterus rises out of the pelvis and can be seen more easily. The bladder acts as a window to the uterus and the fetus inside.

There's a 3-dimensional ultrasound available in some areas that provides detailed, clear pictures of the fetus in the womb. They're so clear the image almost looks like a photograph. For the pregnant woman, the test is almost the same. The difference is that computer software translates the picture into a 3-D image. This ultrasound may be used when there is suspicion of fetal abnormalities and the doctor wants to take a closer look.

The ultrasound vaginal probe, also called the *transvaginal ultrasound,* can be used in early pregnancy for a better view of the baby and placenta. A probe is placed inside the vagina, and the pregnancy is viewed from this angle. You don't have to have your bladder full for this one!

Some couples ask for ultrasound to determine whether they are carrying a boy or girl. If the baby is in a good position and it is old enough for the genitals to have developed and they can be seen clearly, determination may be possible. However, many doctors feel this reason alone is not a good reason to do an ultrasound exam. Discuss it with your healthcare provider. Understand ultrasound is a test, and tests can occasionally be wrong.

Dad Tip

Remember that despite morning sickness, headaches and a changing waistline, pregnancy is a miracle! Pregnancy and childbirth happen only a limited number of times in your life. You'll look back fondly at the challenge of becoming parents and probably even say, "That wasn't so bad." We know that because people get pregnant again and have more kids!

Week 12

How Big Is Your Baby?

Your baby weighs between 0.3 and 0.5 ounce (8 to 14g), and crown-to-rump length is almost 2.5 inches (61mm). As you can see on page 128, your baby's size has almost doubled in the past 3 weeks! Length of the baby is a better measure at this time than fetal weight.

How Big Are You?

By the end of 12 weeks, your uterus is too large to remain completely in your pelvis. You may feel it above your pubic bone (pubic symphysis). The uterus has a remarkable ability to grow while you're pregnant. During pregnancy, it grows upward to fill the pelvis and abdomen, and returns to its usual size within a few weeks after delivery.

Before pregnancy, your uterus is almost solid. It holds about 0.3 ounce (10ml) or less. The uterus changes during pregnancy into a comparatively thin-walled, muscular container big enough to hold the fetus, placenta and amniotic fluid. The uterus increases its capacity 500 to 1,000 times during pregnancy! The weight of the uterus also changes. When your baby is born, your uterus weighs almost 40 ounces (1,100g) compared to 2.5 ounces (70g) before pregnancy.

The uterine wall grows during the first few months of pregnancy due to hormonal stimulation by estrogen and progesterone. Later in your pregnancy, the growth of the baby and the placenta stretch and thin the uterine wall.

How Your Baby Is Growing and Developing

Few, if any, structures in the baby are formed after this week in
pregnancy. However, the structures already formed continue to grow
and to develop. At your 12-week visit (or close to that time), you'll
probably be able to hear your baby's heartbeat! It can be heard with
doppler, a special listening machine (not a stethoscope). It magnifies
the sound of your baby's heartbeat so you can hear it.

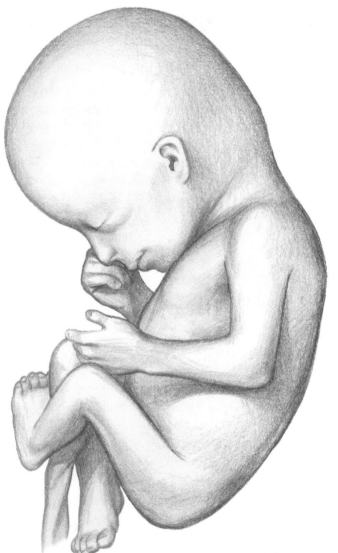

Your baby is growing rapidly.
It has doubled in length in the last 3 weeks.

The skeletal system now has centers of bone formation (ossification) in most bones. Fingers and toes have separated, and nails are growing. Scattered rudiments of hair appear on the body. External genitalia are beginning to show distinct signs of male or female sex characteristics.

The digestive system (small intestine) is capable of producing contractions that push food through the bowels. It is also able to absorb glucose (sugar).

At the base of your baby's brain, the pituitary gland is beginning to make many hormones. Hormones are chemicals that are made in one part of the body, but their action is exerted on another part of the body.

Other things are also happening. The fetal nervous system has developed further. Your baby is moving inside your uterus, but you probably won't feel it for a while yet. Stimulating the fetus in certain spots may cause it to squint, open its mouth and move its fingers or toes.

The amount of amniotic fluid is increasing. Total volume is now about 1.5 ounces (50ml). At this time, the fluid is similar to maternal plasma (the noncellular portion of your blood), except it contains much less protein.

Changes in You

You are probably starting to feel better than you have for most of your pregnancy. At this point, morning sickness often begins to improve. You aren't extremely big and are probably still quite comfortable.

If it's your first pregnancy, you may still be wearing regular clothes. If you've had other pregnancies, you may start to show earlier and to feel more comfortable in looser clothing, such as maternity clothes.

You may be getting bigger in places besides your tummy. Your breasts are probably getting larger. They may have been sore for some time. You may also notice weight gain in your hips, legs and at your sides.

Your Skin

Skin Changes

Your skin may change during pregnancy. In many women, skin along the midline of the abdomen becomes markedly darker or pigmented with a brown-black color. It forms a vertical line called the *linea nigra*.

Occasionally irregular brown patches of varying size appear on the face and neck called *chloasma* or *mask of pregnancy*. These disappear or get lighter after delivery. Oral contraceptives may cause similar pigmentation changes.

Vascular spiders (called *telangiectasias* or *angiomas*) are small red elevations on the skin, with branches extending outward. The condition develops in about 65% of white women and 10% of black women during pregnancy.

A similar condition is redness of the palms, called *palmar erythema*. It is seen in 65% of white women and 35% of black women.

Vascular spiders and palmar erythema often occur together. Symptoms are temporary and disappear shortly after delivery. The occurrence of either condition is probably caused by high levels of estrogen during pregnancy.

Stretch Marks

Stretch marks, called *striae distensae*, are seen often, and in varying degrees, during pregnancy. They may appear early or later in your pregnancy, usually on the abdomen, breasts, and hips or

buttocks. After pregnancy, they may fade to the same color as the rest of your skin, but they won't go away.

Many women want to know what they can do for the stretch marks they develop during pregnancy. Some new treatments being used today seem to help a lot. The use of Retin-A® or Renova®, in combination with glycolic acid, has been shown to be fairly effective. Prescriptions are needed for Retin-A and Renova; you can get glycolic acid from your dermatologist. Cellex-C®, with glycolic acid, also improves the appearance of stretch marks. The most effective treatment is laser treatment, but it's very costly. This is often done in combination with the medication methods described above. All of these treatments are for *after* pregnancy.

If you use steroid creams, such as hydrocortisone or topicort, to treat stretch marks during pregnancy, you absorb some of the steroid into your system. The substance can then pass to your developing baby. *Don't use steroid creams during pregnancy without first checking with your healthcare provider!* (See the opposite page for more information.)

Skin Tags and Moles

Pregnancy can make skin tags and moles change and grow. Skin tags are small tags of skin that may appear for the first time or may grow larger during pregnancy. Moles may appear for the first time during pregnancy, or existing moles may grow larger and darken. If a mole changes, it must be checked. If you notice any change, show it to your healthcare provider!

Accutane®

Some women notice an improvement in their acne during pregnancy. But this doesn't happen for everyone.

Accutane (isotretinoin) is commonly prescribed for the treatment of acne. *Do not take Accutane during pregnancy!* Taken during the first trimester, Accutane is responsible for a higher frequency of miscarriage and malformation of the fetus.

If you even think you might be pregnant, don't take Accutane. Use reliable birth control to avoid pregnancy if you do use it.

Retin-A

Retin-A (tretinoin), not to be confused with Accutane (isotretinoin), is a cream or lotion used to treat acne and to help get rid of fine wrinkles on the face. *If you are pregnant, stop using Retin-A.* We don't have enough data to know if it's safe to use during pregnancy. We do know any type of medication you use—whether taken internally, inhaled, injected or used topically (spread on the skin)—gets into your bloodstream. Any substance in your bloodstream can be passed to your baby.

Itching

Itching *(pruritus gravidarum)* is a common symptom during pregnancy. There are no bumps or lesions on the skin; it just itches. Nearly 20% of all pregnant women suffer from itching, usually in the last weeks of pregnancy, but it can occur at any time. It may occur with each pregnancy and may also appear when you use oral contraceptives. The condition doesn't present any risk to you or your baby.

Treatment for the itching consists of antihistamines or cooling lotions containing menthol or camphor. Often no treatment is needed.

Some medications a mother-to-be uses become concentrated in the baby. Your body can handle it, but your baby's body may not be able to. If some substances build up in the baby, they can have significant effects on its development. In the future, we may know more about its effects on a growing baby. At this time, it's best to avoid using Retin-A.

Steroid Creams and Ointments

Skin conditions may arise during pregnancy that require treatment with creams or ointments. This treatment could include steroid preparations. Before you use anything of this type, ask your healthcare provider for information.

How Your Actions Affect Your Baby's Development

Physical Injury during Pregnancy

Trauma (physical injury) occurs in about 6 to 7% of all pregnancies. Accidents involving motor vehicles account for 66% of these cases; falls and assaults account for the remaining 34%. More than 90% of these are minor injuries.

If you experience trauma during pregnancy, you may be taken care of by emergency-medicine personnel, trauma surgeons, general surgeons and your obstetrician. Most experts recommend observing a pregnant woman for a few hours after an accident. This provides adequate time to monitor the baby. Longer monitoring may be necessary in a more serious accident.

Your Nutrition

Some women misunderstand the concept of increasing their caloric intake during pregnancy. They think they can eat all they want. Don't fall into this trap! It's unhealthy for you and your baby if you gain too much weight during pregnancy. It makes carrying your baby more uncomfortable, and delivery may be more difficult. It's hard to shed the extra pounds after pregnancy. After their baby is born, most women are eager to return to "normal" clothes and to look the way they did before pregnancy. Having to deal with extra weight can interfere with reaching this goal.

> **Tip for Week 12**
>
> If you have diarrhea that doesn't go away in 24 hours, or if it keeps returning, call your doctor. Don't self-medicate for longer than 24 hours.

Junk Food

Is junk food your kind of food? Do you eat it several times a day? Pregnancy is the time to break that habit! Now that you're pregnant, your dietary habits affect someone besides just yourself—your growing baby. If you're used to skipping breakfast, getting something from a machine for lunch, then eating dinner at a fast-food restaurant, it doesn't help your pregnancy.

What and when you eat become more important when you realize how your actions affect your baby. Proper nutrition takes some planning on your part, but you can do it. If you work, take healthful foods with you for lunches and snacks. Stay away from fast food and junk food. (See page 351 for a list of snack ideas.)

Late-Night Snacks
Late-night nutritious snacks are beneficial for some women. However, for many women, snacking at night is unnecessary. If you're used to ice cream or other goodies before bed, you may pay for it during pregnancy with excessive weight gain. Food in your stomach late at night may also cause you more distress if you suffer from heartburn or nausea and vomiting.

> **Instead of selecting a food with little nutritional value, like potato chips or cookies, choose a piece of fruit, some cheese or a slice of whole-wheat bread with a little peanut butter.**

Fats and Sweets
You may need to be cautious with fats and sweets, unless you're underweight and need to gain some weight. Many of these foods are high in calories and low in nutritional value. Eat them sparingly. Instead of selecting a food with little nutritional value, like potato chips or cookies, choose a piece of fruit, some cheese or a slice of whole-wheat bread with a little peanut butter. You'll satisfy your hunger and your nutritional needs at the same time! Some fats and sweets you may choose, and their serving sizes, include the following:

- sugar or honey—1 tablespoon
- oil—1 tablespoon
- margarine or butter—1 pat
- jam or jelly—1 tablespoon
- salad dressing—1 tablespoon

You Should Also Know

Fifth Disease
Fifth disease, also called *parvo virus B19*, was the fifth disease to be described with a certain kind of rash. It is a mild, moderately contagious airborne infection. Fifth disease spreads easily through

Dad Tip

At this doctor's visit, it may be possible to hear the baby's heartbeat. If you can't be there, send a tape recorder or Dictaphone™ with your partner so she can record the heartbeat for you to listen to later.

groups, such as classrooms or day-care centers.

The rash looks like reddened skin caused by a slap. The reddening fades and recurs, and lasts from 2 to 34 days. There is no treatment.

This virus is important during pregnancy because it interferes with the production of red blood cells in the woman and the fetus. If you believe you have been exposed to fifth disease during pregnancy, contact your healthcare provider. A blood test can determine whether you have had the virus. If you haven't, your healthcare provider can monitor you to detect fetal problems. Some fetal problems can be dealt with before the baby is born.

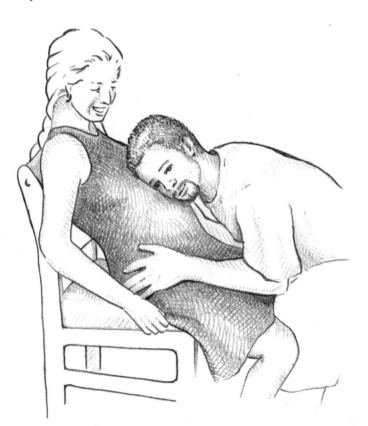

Week 13

How Big Is Your Baby?

Your baby is growing rapidly! Its crown-to-rump length is 2.6 to 3.1 inches (65 to 78mm), and it weighs between 0.5 and 0.7 ounce (13 to 20g). It is about the size of a peach.

How Big Are You?

Your uterus has grown quite a bit. You can probably feel its upper edge above the pubic bone in the lowest part of your abdomen, about 4 inches (10cm) below your bellybutton. At 12 to 13 weeks, your uterus fills your pelvis and starts growing upward into your abdomen. It feels like a soft, smooth ball.

You have probably gained some weight by now. If morning sickness has been a problem and you've had a hard time eating, you may not have gained much weight. As you feel better and as your baby rapidly starts to gain weight, you'll gain weight.

How Your Baby Is Growing and Developing

Fetal growth is particularly striking from now through about 24 weeks of pregnancy. The baby has doubled in length since the 7th week. Changes in fetal weight have also been tremendous during the last 8 to 10 weeks of your pregnancy.

One interesting change is the relative slowdown in the growth of your baby's head compared to the rest of its body. In week 13, the head is about half the crown-to-rump length. By week 21, the head is about one-third of the baby's body. At birth, your baby's head is only one-fourth the size of its body. Fetal body growth accelerates as fetal head growth slows.

Your baby's face is beginning to look more humanlike. Eyes, which started out on the side of the head, move closer together on the face. The ears come to lie in their normal position on the sides of the head. External genitalia have developed enough so that a male can be distinguished from a female if examined outside the womb.

Intestines initially develop within a large swelling in the umbilical cord outside the fetal body. About this time, they withdraw into the fetal abdominal cavity. If this doesn't occur and the intestines remain outside the fetal abdomen at birth, a condition called an *omphalocele* occurs. It is rare (occurs in 1 of 10,000 births). The condition can usually be repaired with surgery, and babies do well afterward.

Changes in You

You are losing your waist! Clothing fits snugly. It's time to start wearing loose-fitting clothing.

Your Breasts

Changes in Your Breasts

You have probably noticed your breasts are changing. (See the illustration below.) The mammary gland (another name for the breast) got its name from the Latin term for breast—*mamma*.

Your breast is made up of glands, connective tissue to provide support and fatty tissue to provide protection. Milk-producing sacs connect with the ducts leading to the nipple.

Before pregnancy, the average breast weighs about 7 ounces (200g). During pregnancy, breasts increase in size and weight. Near the end of pregnancy, each breast may weigh 14 to 28 ounces (400 to 800g). During nursing, each breast may weigh 28 ounces (800g) or more!

Size and shape of women's breasts vary greatly. Breast tissue usually projects under the arm. Glands that make up the breast open into ducts in the nipple. Each nipple contains nerve endings, muscle fibers, sebaceous glands, sweat glands and about 20 milk ducts.

The nipple is surrounded by the areola, a circular, pigmented area. Before pregnancy, the areola is usually pink. It turns brown or red-brown and enlarges during pregnancy and lactation. A darkened areola may act as a visual signal for the breastfeeding infant.

Breasts undergo many changes during pregnancy. In the early weeks, a common symptom of pregnancy is tingling or soreness of the breasts. After about 8 weeks of pregnancy, your breasts may grow larger and become nodular or lumpy as glands and ducts inside the breasts grow and develop. As your breasts change during pregnancy, you may notice veins appear just beneath the skin.

During the second trimester, a thin yellow fluid called *colostrum* begins to form. It can sometimes be expressed from the nipple by gentle massage. If your breasts

Ribs

Breast Ducts

Nipple

Development of the maternal breast by end of the first trimester (13 weeks pregnancy).

have grown, you may notice stretch marks on your breasts similar to those on your abdomen.

Mammary glands begin to develop in the 6-week-old embryo. By the time of birth, milk ducts are present. After birth, a newborn's breasts may be swollen and may even secrete a small amount of milk. This can occur in both male and female infants and is caused by the secretion of estrogen.

Discovering a Breast Lump

Discovering a breast lump is important, during pregnancy or any other time. It's important for you to learn at an early age how to do a breast exam on yourself and to perform this on a regular basis (usually after every menstrual period). Nine out of 10 breast lumps are found by women examining themselves.

Your caregiver will probably perform breast exams at regular intervals, usually when you have your annual Pap smear. If you have an exam every year and are lump-free, it helps assure you no lumps are present before beginning pregnancy.

Finding a breast lump may be delayed during pregnancy because of changes in your breasts. It may be more difficult to feel a lump. Enlargement of the breasts during pregnancy and nursing tends to hide lumps or masses in the tissue of the breast.

Examine your breasts during pregnancy as you do when you are not pregnant. Do it every 4 or 5 weeks—the first day of every month is a good time to do it.

Tests for Breast Lumps

The routine test for breast lumps is examination by yourself or your healthcare provider. Other tests include X-ray examination, called a *mammogram,* and ultrasound examination of the breast.

If a lump is found, it may be necessary to have an ultrasound exam performed on the breast, or a mammogram. Because a mammogram utilizes X-rays, your pregnancy must be protected during the procedure, usually by shielding your abdomen with a lead apron.

It has not been shown that pregnancy accelerates the course or growth of a breast lump. But we do know it is difficult to find a breast lump because of breast changes.

Treatment during Pregnancy

Often a lump in the breast can be drained or aspirated. Fluid removed from the cyst is sent to the lab for evaluation to ensure there are no abnormal cells in the fluid. If a lump or cyst cannot be drained by a needle, a biopsy of the cyst or lump may be necessary. If fluid is clear, it's a good sign. Bloody fluid is of more concern and must be studied under a microscope in the laboratory.

If examination of a lump indicates breast cancer, treatment may begin during pregnancy. Treatment complications during pregnancy include risks for the fetus related to chemotherapy, radiation or medication, such as anesthesia or pain medicine for a biopsy. If a lump is cancerous, the need for radiation therapy and chemotherapy must be considered, along with the needs of the pregnancy.

How Your Actions Affect Your Baby's Development

Working during Pregnancy

Today, many women work outside the home, and many continue to work during pregnancy. It is common for employers and patients to ask doctors about work and pregnancy.

> *"Is it safe to work while I'm pregnant?"*
> *"Can I work my entire pregnancy?"*
> *"Am I in danger of harming my baby if I work?"*

More than half of all women work or are seeking work. In the United States, more than 1 million babies are born to women who have been employed at some time during pregnancy. These women have understandable concerns about safety and occupational health.

Legislation that May Affect You

The U.S. Pregnancy Discrimination Act prohibits job discrimination on the basis of pregnancy or childbirth. It states that pregnancy and related conditions should be treated the same as any other disability or medical condition. A doctor may be asked to certify that a pregnant woman can work without endangering herself or her pregnancy. Pregnancy-related disability comes from any of the following:

- the pregnancy itself
- complications of pregnancy, such as pre-eclampsia, premature labor or other medical problems
- job exposure to chemicals, inhalants, gases, solvents or radiation

The Family and Medical Leave Act was passed in 1993. If you or your partner have spent at least 1 year working for a company, the

State or Provincial Laws and Parental Leave

State laws about parental leave differ, so check with your state labor office or consult the personnel director in your company's human resources department. A summary of state laws on family leave is also available:

The Women's Bureau Publications
U.S. Department of Labor, Box EX
200 Constitution Avenue, NW
Washington, DC 20210

In Canada, contact the Human Resources office for information:

Human Resources
Tele-Center of Canada
(416) 730-1211 • (800) 227-9914

law allows each of you to take up to 12 weeks of unpaid leave in any 12-month period for the birth of your baby. Leave may be taken intermittently or all at once. If you qualify for leave under the Family Medical Leave Act, you can take up to 12 unpaid weeks off in a year to take care of family or personal problems. However, any time you take off *before* the birth of your baby is counted toward the 12 weeks you are entitled to in any given year. For information on the Family Medical Leave Act, call their hotline at 800-522-0925.

Under the law, you must be restored to an equivalent position with equal benefits when you return. However, the act applies only to companies that employ 50 or more people within a 75-mile radius. States may allow an employer to deny job restoration to those in the top 10% compensation bracket.

At this time, about half the states have passed state legislation that deals with parental leave. Some states provide disability insurance if you have to leave work because of pregnancy or birth.

In Canada, unpaid parental leave is available. The length of time you may take off from work varies from province to province.

Risks if You Work during Pregnancy
It may be difficult to know the exact risk of a particular job. In most cases, we don't have enough information to know all the specific substances that can harm a developing baby.

The goal is to minimize the risk to the mother and baby while still enabling the woman to work. A normal woman with a normal job should be able to work throughout her pregnancy. However, she may need to modify her job somewhat. For example, she may need to spend less time standing. Studies show that women who stand in the same position for prolonged periods are more likely to give birth to premature babies and babies with low birthweight.

Work with your healthcare provider and your employer. If problems arise, such as premature labor or bleeding, listen to your caregiver. If bed rest at home is suggested, follow your caregiver's advice. As your pregnancy progresses, you may have to work fewer hours or do lighter work. Be flexible. It doesn't help you or your baby if you wear yourself out and make complications of pregnancy worse.

Your Nutrition

Caffeine is a central-nervous-system stimulant found in many beverages and foods, including coffee, tea, cola drinks and chocolate. Research shows that you may be more sensitive to caffeine during pregnancy. The stimulant is also found in some medications, such as diet aids and headache medications. For over 20 years, the Food and Drug Administration (FDA) has recommended that pregnant women avoid caffeine. To date, no benefits to you or your unborn baby have been found with its use.

As little as 4 cups of coffee (400 mg of caffeine) a day have been associated with a decreased birthweight and a smaller head size in newborns. Some researchers also believe there is an association between caffeine use and miscarriage, stillbirth and premature labor.

Cut down on caffeine or cut caffeine from your diet. It crosses the placenta to the baby. It can affect your calcium metabolism and your baby's, too. If you're jittery, your baby may suffer from the same effects. Increased caffeine consumption may increase the chances of breathing problems

Tip for Week 13

When cutting down on caffeine during pregnancy, read labels. More than 200 foods, beverages and over-the-counter medications contain caffeine!

in a newborn. Caffeine passes to breast milk, which can cause irritability and sleeplessness in a breastfed baby. An infant metabolizes caffeine slower than an adult, and caffeine can collect in the infant.

A New Caffeine Warning

High levels of caffeine in a pregnant woman—400mg a day, equal to four cups of tea, soda or coffee—may affect a baby's developing respiratory system. One study showed this exposure before birth might be linked to sudden infant death syndrome (SIDS).

Effects of caffeine on you during pregnancy may include irritability, headaches, stomach upset, sleeplessness and jitters. Smoking may compound the stimulant effect of caffeine.

Limit the amount of caffeine you consume. Read labels on over-the-counter medications for caffeine. Most professionals agree that up to two cups *(not mugs)* of regular coffee or its equivalent each day is probably OK. That's less than 200mg a day. However, it may be a good idea to eliminate as much as you can from your diet. It's healthier for your baby, and you'll probably feel better, too. The list below details the amounts of caffeine in various sources:

- coffee, 5 ounces—from 60 to 140mg
- tea, 5 ounces—from 30 to 65mg
- baking chocolate, 1 ounce—25mg
- chocolate candy, 1 ounce—6mg
- soft drinks, 12 ounces—from 35 to 55mg
- pain relief tablets, standard dose—40mg
- allergy and cold remedies, standard dose—25mg

You Should Also Know

Lyme Disease

Lyme disease refers to an infection transmitted to humans by ticks. There are several stages of the illness. In about 80% of those bitten, there is a skin lesion with a distinctive look, called a *bull's eye*. There may be flulike symptoms. After 4 to 6 weeks, symptoms may become more serious.

At the beginning of the illness, blood tests may not diagnose Lyme disease. A blood test done later in the illness can establish the diagnosis.

We know Lyme disease can cross the placenta. At this time, we don't know if it is dangerous to the baby. Researchers are studying it.

Treatment for Lyme disease requires long-term antibiotic therapy and sometimes intravenous antibiotic therapy. Many medications used to treat Lyme disease are safe to use during pregnancy.

Avoid exposure to Lyme disease, if possible. Stay out of areas known to have ticks, especially heavily wooded areas. If you can't avoid these areas, wear long-sleeved shirts, long pants, a hat or scarf, socks and boots or closed shoes. Be sure to check your hair when you come in; ticks often attach themselves there. Also, check your clothing to make sure no ticks remain in folds, cuffs or pockets.

Dad Tip

Ask the doctor if there is some exercise you can do together on a regular basis during pregnancy, such as walking, swimming, or playing golf or tennis.

Second Trimester Journal

Topics to discuss at my next doctor's appointment:

_____

_____

_____

_____

My goals for my second trimester (changing a habit or adjusting my exercise routine):

_____

_____

_____

Issues to discuss with my partner (childcare, discipline, breast or bottle): _____

_____

My concerns about pregnancy, labor, the baby, being a parent:

_____

_____

_____

_____

Other journal ideas:

- Write a letter to your child.
- Record your dreams.
- Write about what your future will be like after your baby is born.
- Write about the present: your body, where you live, the people helping you out—use all your senses.

_____

_____

_____

_____

_____

_____

_____

_____

_____

_____

_____

_____

_____

_____

Notes

Week 14

How Big Is Your Baby?

The crown-to-rump length is 3.2 to 4.1 inches (80 to 93mm). Your baby is about the size of your fist and weighs almost 1 ounce (25g).

How Big Are You?

Maternity clothes may be a "must" by now. Some women try to get by for a while by not buttoning or zipping their pants all the way or by using rubber bands or safety pins to increase their waistbands. Others wear their partner's clothing, but that usually works for only a short time. You're going to get even bigger. You'll enjoy your pregnancy more and feel more comfortable with clothing that fits comfortably and provides you room to grow.

How your body responds to this growth is influenced by any previous pregnancies and the changes your body experienced then. Your skin and muscles stretched to accommodate your uterus, placenta and baby, and that changed them permanently. Skin and muscles may give way faster to accommodate your growing uterus and baby. This means you show sooner and feel bigger.

How Your Baby Is Growing and Developing

As you can see in the illustration on page 148, by this week your baby's ears have moved from the neck to the sides of the head. Eyes have been moving gradually to the front of the face from the side of

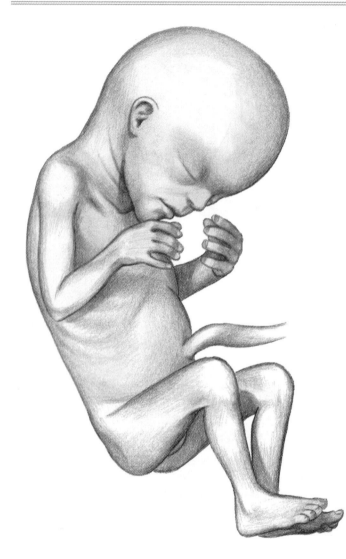

Your baby continues to change. Ears and eyes move to a more normal position by this week.

the head. The neck continues to get longer, and the chin no longer rests on the chest.

Sexual development continues. It is becoming easier to determine male from female by looking at external genitalia, which are more developed.

Changes in You

Do You Have Hemorrhoids?

Hemorrhoids, dilated blood vessels around or inside the anus, are a common problem during or following pregnancy. They are caused during pregnancy by the increased blood flow in the area around the uterus and the pelvis because of the weight of the uterus, causing congestion or blockage of circulation. Hemorrhoids may worsen toward the end of pregnancy. They may also get worse with each succeeding pregnancy.

Hemorrhoid treatment includes avoiding constipation by eating adequate amounts of fiber and drinking lots of fluid. You may avoid hemorrhoids by using stool softeners. Other measures include sitz baths or suppository medications. You can buy these without a prescription. Rarely, hemorrhoids are treated during pregnancy with surgery.

After pregnancy, hemorrhoids usually improve, but they may not go away completely. You can use the treatment methods mentioned above when pregnancy is over.

If hemorrhoids cause you a great deal of discomfort, discuss it with your healthcare provider. He or she will know what treatment method is best for you.

Relieving the Discomfort of Hemorrhoids

If hemorrhoids are a problem, try any of the following suggestions for relief.

- Rest at least 1 hour every day with your feet and hips elevated.
- Lie with your legs elevated and knees slightly bent (Sims position) when you sleep at night.
- Eat adequate amounts of fiber and drink lots of fluid.
- Take warm (not hot) baths for relief.
- Suppository medications, available without a prescription, may help.
- Apply ice packs, or cotton balls soaked in witch hazel, to the affected area.
- Don't sit for long periods.

How Your Actions Affect Your Baby's Development

X-Rays, CT Scans and MRIs during Pregnancy
Some women are concerned about tests that use radiation during pregnancy. Can they hurt the baby? Can you have them at any time in pregnancy?

No known amount of radiation is safe for a developing baby. Dangers to your baby include an increased risk of mutations and an increased risk of cancer later in life. Some doctors believe the only safe amount of X-ray during pregnancy is none.

Researchers are becoming more aware of the potential dangers of radiation to a developing fetus. At present, they believe the fetus is at greatest risk between 8 and 15 weeks' gestation (between the fetal age of 6 weeks and 13 weeks).

Problems, such as pneumonia or appendicitis, can and do occur in pregnant women and may require an X-ray for proper diagnosis and treatment. Discuss the need for X-rays with your healthcare provider. It is your responsibility to let your caregiver and others involved in your health care know you are pregnant or may be pregnant before you undergo any medical test. It's easier to deal with the questions of safety and risk *before* a test is performed.

If you have an X-ray or series of X-rays, then discover you are pregnant, talk to your healthcare provider about the possible risk to your baby. He or she will be able to advise you.

> ### Tip for Week 14
>
> **If you must have dental work or diagnostic tests, tell your dentist or your physician you are pregnant so they can take extra care with you. It may be helpful for your dentist and doctor to talk before any decisions are made.**

Computerized tomographic scans, also called *CT scans*, are a form of specialized X-ray. This technique combines X-ray with computer analysis. Many researchers believe the amount of radiation received by a fetus from a CT scan is much lower than that received from a regular X-ray. However, these tests should be undertaken with caution until we know more about the effects even this small amount of radiation has on a developing fetus.

Magnetic resonance imaging, also called *MRI*, is another diagnostic tool widely used today. At this time, no harmful effects in pregnancy have been reported from the use of MRI. However, it is probably best to avoid MRI during the first trimester of pregnancy.

Dental Care

Don't avoid your dentist or ignore your teeth while you're pregnant. See your dentist at least once during pregnancy. Tell your dentist you're pregnant. If you need dental work, postpone it until after the first 12 weeks, if possible. You may not be able to wait if you have an infection. An untreated infection could be harmful to you and your baby.

Antibiotics or pain medications may be necessary. If you need medication, consult with your physician before taking anything. Be careful with regard to anesthesia for dental work during pregnancy. Avoid general anesthesia. If general anesthesia is necessary, make sure an experienced anesthesiologist who knows you are pregnant administers it.

Dental Emergencies

Dental emergencies do occur. Emergencies you might face include root canal, tooth extraction, a large cavity, an abscessed tooth or problems resulting from an accident or injury. Any of these emergencies can occur during pregnancy. A serious dental problem must be treated. Problems that could result from not treating it are more serious than the risks you might be exposed to with treatment.

Dental X-rays are sometimes necessary and can be done during pregnancy. Your abdomen must be shielded with a lead apron before X-rays are taken. If possible, wait until after the end of the first

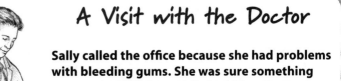

A Visit with the Doctor

Sally called the office because she had problems with bleeding gums. She was sure something was wrong with her teeth. I told her that a pregnant woman's gums can change during pregnancy. Gums may be affected by the hormones of pregnancy and become sensitive and bleed more easily. I advised Sally to floss and to brush regularly, and that using mouthwash and gargles was also OK.

trimester to have any dental work done.

Avoid gas or general anesthesia for a dental procedure during pregnancy. Local anesthetics are OK, and so are many antibiotics and pain medications. Be sure to consult your healthcare provider before taking any medications.

Your Nutrition

Being overweight when pregnancy begins may present special problems for you. Your doctor may advise you to gain a smaller amount of weight than the average 25 to 35 pounds recommended for a normal-weight woman. You will probably have to choose lower-calorie, lower-fat foods to eat. A visit with a nutritionist may be necessary to help you develop a healthful food plan. You will be advised not to diet during pregnancy.

Extra weight may cause more problems, including gestational diabetes or high blood pressure. Backaches, varicose veins and fatigue may also be more troublesome. If you gain too much weight during your pregnancy—beyond the amount of weight your physician recommends—you may have a greater chance of needing a Cesarean delivery.

If you're overweight, your healthcare provider may want to see you more often during your pregnancy. Ultrasound may be needed to help establish your due date because it's harder to determine the position and size of the fetus. Extra layers of abdominal fat may make manual examination difficult. Your caregiver may order tests for gestational diabetes. Other diagnostic tests may also be necessary as your due date nears.

You Should Also Know

Taking Others to Your Doctor Visits

Take your partner with you to an appointment with your healthcare provider. It's nice for your partner and caregiver to meet before labor begins. Maybe your mother or the other grandmother-to-be would like to go with you to hear their grandchild's heartbeat. Or you may want to take a tape recorder and record the heartbeat for others to hear. Things have changed since your mother carried you; many grandmothers-to-be enjoy this type of visit.

It's a good idea to wait until you have heard your baby's heartbeat before bringing other people. You don't always hear it the first time, and this can be frustrating and disappointing.

Bringing Children to an Office Visit

Some women bring their children with them to an office appointment. Most office personnel don't mind if you bring your children with you occasionally. They understand it may not always be possible to find someone to watch your children. However, if you are having problems or have a lot to discuss with your doctor, don't bring your child.

If a child is sick, has just gotten over chickenpox or is getting a cold, leave him or her at home. Don't expose everyone else in the waiting room.

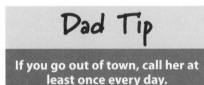

Dad Tip

If you go out of town, call her at least once every day.

Some women like to bring one child at a time to a visit if they have more than one child. That makes it special for you and for them. Crying or complaining children can create a difficult situation, however, so ask your doctor when it's good to bring family members with you before you come in with them.

Notes

Week 15

How Big Is Your Baby?

The fetal crown-to-rump length by this week of pregnancy is 4.1 to 4.5 inches (93 to 103mm). The fetus weighs about 1.75 ounces (50g). It's close to the size of a softball.

How Big Are You?

You can easily tell you're pregnant by the changes in your lower abdomen, which alter the way your clothes fit. You may be able to feel your uterus about 3 or 4 inches (7.6 to 10cm) below your bellybutton (also called the *umbilicus* or *navel*).

Your pregnancy may not be obvious to other people when you wear regular street clothes. But it may become obvious if you start wearing maternity clothes or put on a swimming suit.

It's still a little early to feel movement, although you should feel your baby move in the next few weeks!

How Your Baby Is Growing and Developing

Your baby's rapid growth continues. Its skin is thin. At this point in its development, you can see blood vessels through the skin. Fine hair called *lanugo hair* covers the baby's body.

By this time, your baby may be sucking its thumb. This has been seen with ultrasound examination. Eyes continue to move to the front of the face but are still widely separated.

Ears continue to develop externally. As you can see in the illustration on page 157, they now look more like normal ears. In fact, your baby looks more human with each passing day.

Bones that already formed are getting harder and retaining calcium (ossifying) rapidly. If an X-ray were performed at this time, the baby's skeleton would be visible.

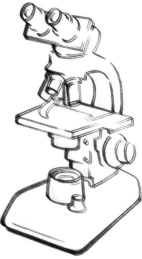

Alpha-fetoprotein Testing

As your baby grows inside you, it produces *alpha-fetoprotein*. This protein is found in increasing amounts in the amniotic fluid. Some alpha-fetoprotein crosses fetal membranes and enters your circulation. It is possible to measure the amount of alpha-fetoprotein by drawing your blood.

The level of this protein can be meaningful during pregnancy. An alpha-fetoprotein (AFP) test is usually done between 16 and 18 weeks of gestation. The timing of the test is important and must be correlated to the gestational age of your pregnancy and to your weight.

An elevated level of alpha-fetoprotein can indicate problems with the fetus, such as spina bifida (spinal-cord problem) or anencephaly (serious central-nervous-system defect). Some researchers have even found an association between a low level of alpha-fetoprotein and Down syndrome. In the past, amniocentesis was the only way to test for Down syndrome.

If the level of alpha-fetoprotein is abnormal, a careful ultrasound examination is done to look for spina bifida, anencephaly and Down syndrome. This ultrasound may help determine how far along in pregnancy you are.

This test is not done on all pregnant women, although it is required in some states. It is not used routinely in Canada. If the test isn't offered to you, ask about it. There is relatively little risk to you, and it tells your caregiver how your fetus is growing and developing.

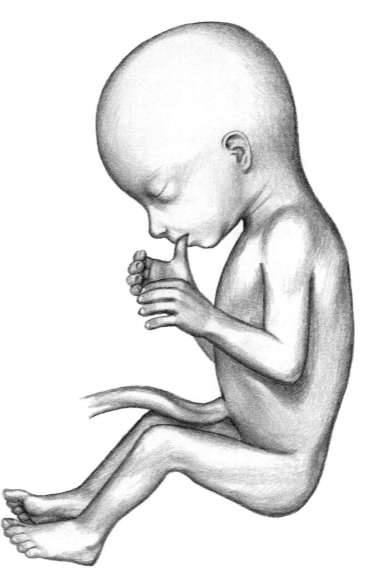

By week 15 of pregnancy (fetal age—13 weeks), your baby may suck its thumb. Eyes are at the front of the face but are still widely separated.

Changes in You

Pap Smears during Pregnancy

During your first visit to your healthcare provider, you probably had a Pap smear. A Pap smear is usually done at the beginning of pregnancy. By now, the result is back and you have discussed it with your caregiver, particularly if it was abnormal.

The Pap smear (short for Papanicolaou smear) is a screening test done at the time of a pelvic exam. It identifies cancerous or precancerous cells coming from the cervix, which is located at the top of the vagina. This test has contributed to a significant decrease in mortality from cervical cancer because of early detection and treatment.

> **Tip for Week 15**
>
> Start now to learn to sleep on your side. It will pay off later as you get bigger. Sometimes it helps to use a few extra pillows. Put one behind you so if you roll onto your back, you won't lie flat. Put another pillow between your legs or rest your "top" leg on a pillow. Some manufacturers make a "pregnancy pillow" that supports your entire body easily and effectively.

An Abnormal Pap Smear

If you have had an abnormal Pap smear or have been treated for an abnormal Pap test, continue to get checked as your caregiver suggests. Pap smears are screening tests. If a test is abnormal, your healthcare provider must verify the findings and decide on treatment. If you are not pregnant, most doctors will suggest a biopsy of the cervix.

Women who deliver vaginally may see a change in abnormal Pap smears. One study showed that 60% of a group of women who were diagnosed with high-grade squamous intra-epithelial lesions in the cervix before giving birth had normal Pap smears after their baby was born.

An abnormal Pap smear during pregnancy must be handled individually. When abnormal cells are "not too bad" (premalignant or not as serious), it may be possible to watch them during pregnancy with colposcopy or Pap smears; biopsies are not usually done at this time. The cervix bleeds easily during pregnancy because of changes in circulation. This situation must be handled carefully.

When Is a Biopsy Necessary?

A biopsy of the cervix is done in your doctor's office, without anesthesia, with *colposcopy*. Colposcopy is a procedure that uses an instrument similar to a pair of binoculars or a microscope to look at the cervix. This enables your doctor to see where abnormal areas are so biopsies can be taken. Most obstetricians/gynecologists are able to do this procedure without sending you to a specialist.

A biopsy provides a better idea of the nature and extent of the problem. If there is a possibility that abnormal cells could spread to other parts of the body, a *cone biopsy* may need to be done. A cone biopsy precisely determines the extent of more severe disease and removes abnormal tissue. This surgery is done with anesthesia but is not usually performed during pregnancy.

Treating Abnormal Cells

There are several ways to treat abnormal cells on the cervix, but most treatment methods cannot be performed during pregnancy. These treatments include surgically removing the abnormal spot (if it can be seen), electric cautery to remove or "burn" small abnormal spots, cryocautery to freeze small lesions, laser treatment to destroy abnormal areas on the cervix and cone biopsy for more-involved lesions.

How Your Actions Affect Your Baby's Development

Change Sleeping Positions Now

Some women have questions and concerns about their sleeping positions and sleep habits while they're pregnant. Some want to know if they can sleep on their stomachs. Others want to know if they should stop sleeping on their waterbed. (It is OK to continue sleeping in a waterbed.)

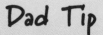

Dad Tip

When you need to be away or out of touch, ask friends and family to check on your partner or to be available to help out.

As you grow during pregnancy, finding comfortable sleeping positions will become more difficult. Don't lie on your back when you sleep. As your uterus gets larger, lying on your back can place the uterus on top of important blood vessels (the aorta and the inferior vena cava) that run down the back of your abdomen. This can decrease circulation to your baby and parts of your body. Some pregnant women also find it harder to breathe when lying on their backs.

Lying on your stomach puts extra pressure on your growing uterus. This is another reason to learn to sleep on your side. For some women, their favorite thing after delivery is to be able to sleep on their stomachs again!

Your Nutrition

About this time, you'll probably need to start adding an extra 300 calories to your meal plan to meet the needs of your growing fetus and your changing body. Below are some choices of extra food for one day to get those 300 calories. Be careful—300 calories is not a lot of food.

Choice 1—2 thin slices pork, ½ cup cabbage, 1 carrot

Choice 2—½ cup cooked brown rice, ¾ cup strawberries, 1 cup orange juice, 1 slice fresh pineapple

Choice 3—4½-ounce salmon steak, 1 cup asparagus, 2 cups Romaine lettuce

Choice 4—1 cup cooked pasta, 1 slice fresh tomato, 1 cup 1% milk, ½ cup cooked green beans, ¼ cantaloupe

Choice 5—1 container of yogurt, 1 medium apple, 1 cup lettuce

You Should Also Know

Getting a Good Night's Sleep

Getting a good night's sleep may be difficult for you now or later in pregnancy. Try some of the following suggestions to ensure a restful sleep.

- Go to bed and wake up at the same time each day.
- Don't drink too much fluid at night. Slow down after 6 P.M.
- Avoid caffeine after late afternoon.
- Get regular exercise.
- Sleep in a cool bedroom—70F (21.1C) is about the highest temperature for comfortable sleeping.
- If you experience heartburn at night, sleep propped up.

Week 16

How Big Is Your Baby?

The crown-to-rump length of your baby by this week is 4.3 to 4.6 inches (108 to 116mm). Weight is about 2.8 ounces (80g).

How Big Are You?

As your baby grows, your uterus and placenta are also growing. Six weeks ago, your uterus weighed about 5 ounces (140g). Today, it weighs about 8.75 ounces (250g). The amount of amniotic fluid around the baby is also increasing. There is now about 7.5 ounces (250ml) of fluid. You can easily feel your uterus about 3 inches (7.6cm) below your bellybutton.

How Your Baby Is Growing and Developing

Fine lanugo hair covers your baby's head. The umbilical cord is attached to the abdomen; this attachment has moved lower on the body of the fetus.

Fingernails are well formed. The illustration on page 162 shows that legs are longer than arms. Arms and legs are moving. You can see this movement during an ultrasound examination. You may also be able to feel your baby move at this point in your pregnancy.

Many women describe feelings of movement as a "gas bubble" or "fluttering." Often, it's something you have noticed for a few days

By this week, fine lanugo hair covers the baby's body and head.

or more, but you didn't realize what you were feeling. Then it occurs to you: You're feeling the baby moving inside you!

Changes in You

Triple-Screen Test

Tests are now available that go beyond alpha-fetoprotein testing in helping your healthcare provider determine if you might be carrying a child with Down syndrome. With the triple-screen test, your alpha-fetoprotein level is checked, along with the amounts of human chorionic gonadotropin (HCG: a pregnancy hormone) and unconjugated estriol (a form of estrogen produced by the placenta).

The levels of these three chemicals in your blood may indicate the presence of Down syndrome. For older mothers, the detection rate of the problem is higher than 60%, with a false-positive rate of nearly 25%.

If you have an abnormal result with a triple-screen test, an ultrasound and amniocentesis may be recommended. An elevated alpha-fetoprotein level can indicate an increased risk of a neural-tube defect (such as spina bifida). HCG and estriol are normal in this case.

Remember: These blood tests are used to find *possible* problems. They are screening tests. A diagnostic test will usually be done to confirm the diagnosis.

> ## Quickening
>
> If you haven't felt your baby move yet, don't worry. Fetal movement, also called *quickening,* is usually felt between 16 and 20 weeks of pregnancy. The time is different for every woman. It can also be different from one pregnancy to another. One baby may be more active than another and produce more movement. The size of the baby or the number of fetuses can also affect what you feel.

How Your Actions Affect Your Baby's Development

Amniocentesis

If it is necessary, the amniocentesis test is usually performed for prenatal evaluation around 16 to 18 weeks of pregnancy. By this point, your uterus is large enough and there is enough fluid surrounding the baby to make the test possible. Doing the procedure at this time allows the woman enough time to make a decision about terminating the pregnancy, if that is what she desires.

With amniocentesis, ultrasound is used to locate a pocket of fluid where the fetus and placenta are not in the way. The part of the abdomen above the uterus is cleaned. Skin is numbed, and a needle is placed through the abdominal wall into the uterus. Fluid is withdrawn

Tip for Week 16

Some of the foods you normally love to eat may make you sick to your stomach during pregnancy. You may need to substitute other nutritious foods you tolerate better.

from the amniotic cavity (area around the baby) with a syringe. About 1 ounce (30ml) of amniotic fluid is needed to perform various tests.

Fetal cells that float in the amniotic fluid can be grown in cultures. They are the cells used to identify fetal abnormalities. We know of more than 400 abnormalities a child can be born with—amniocentesis identifies about 40 (10%) of them, including the following:

- chromosomal problems, particularly Down syndrome
- fetal sex, if sex-specific problems such as hemophilia must be identified
- skeletal diseases, such as osteogenesis imperfecta
- fetal infections, such as herpes or rubella
- central-nervous-system diseases, such as anencephaly
- hematologic (blood) diseases, such as erythroblastosis fetalis
- inborn errors of metabolism (chemical problems or deficiencies of enzymes), such as cystinuria or maple-syrup–urine disease

Risks from amniocentesis include injury to the fetus, placenta or umbilical cord; infection; miscarriage or premature labor. The use of ultrasound to guide the needle helps avoid complications but doesn't eliminate all risk. There can be bleeding from the fetus to the mother, which can be a problem because fetal and maternal blood are separate and may be different types. This is a particular risk to an Rh-negative mother carrying an Rh-positive baby (see You Should Also Know, opposite). This type of bleeding can cause isoimmunization. An Rh-negative woman should receive RhoGAM at the time of amniocentesis to prevent isoimmunization.

Fetal loss from amniocentesis complications is estimated to be less than 3%. The procedure should be done only by someone who has experience doing it.

Your Nutrition

Good news—pregnant women should snack often, particularly during the second half of pregnancy! You should have three or four snacks a day, in addition to your regular meals. There are a couple of catches, though. First, snacks must be nutritious. Second, meals may need to be smaller so you can eat those snacks. One nutritional goal in pregnancy is to eat enough so important nutrients are always available for your body's use.

Usually you want a snack to be quick and easy. It may take some planning and effort on your part to make sure nutritious foods are available for snacking. Prepare things in advance. Cut up fresh vegetables for later use in salads and for munching with low-cal dip. Keep some hard-boiled eggs on

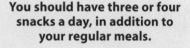

You should have three or four snacks a day, in addition to your regular meals.

hand. Peanut butter (reduced-calorie or regular), pretzels and plain popcorn are good choices. Low-fat cheese and cottage cheese provide calcium. Fruit juice can replace soda. If juice has more sugar than you need, cut it with water. Herbal teas can be healthful. (See the discussion of herbal teas on page 276.)

You Should Also Know

Rh-sensitivity

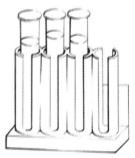

The lab tests you've already had determined your blood type and Rh-factor. You may know this information by now. Your blood type (such as O, A, B, AB) and the Rh-factor are important. In the past, an Rh-negative woman who carried an Rh-positive child faced a complicated pregnancy, which could result in a very sick baby.

Your blood is separate from your baby's blood. If you are Rh-positive, you don't have to worry about any of this. If you are Rh-negative, you need to know about it.

If you are Rh-negative and your baby is Rh-positive or if you have had a blood transfusion or received blood products of some kind, there's a risk you could become *Rh-sensitized* or *isoimmunized*. Isoimmunized means you make antibodies that circulate inside your system, which don't harm you but can attack the Rh-positive blood of your growing baby. (If your baby is Rh-negative, there is no problem.) Your antibodies can cross the placenta and attack your baby's blood. This can cause blood disease of the fetus or newborn. It can make your baby anemic while still inside the uterus, and it can be serious.

Fortunately, this reaction is preventable. The use of *Rh-immune globulin* (RhoGAM) has alleviated many problems. It is given at 28 weeks' gestation to prevent sensitization before delivery. Few women today are sensitized. If you are Rh-negative and pregnant, a RhoGAM injection should be part of your pregnancy. RhoGAM is a product that is extracted from human blood. If you have religious, ethical or personal reasons for not using blood or blood products, consult your physician or minister.

RhoGAM is also given to you within 72 hours after delivery, if your baby is Rh-positive. If your baby is Rh-negative, you don't need RhoGAM after delivery and you didn't need the shot during pregnancy. But it's better not to take that risk and to have the RhoGAM injection during pregnancy.

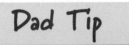

Dad Tip

Do you have concerns that you haven't shared with anyone? Are you concerned about your partner's health or the baby's? Do you wonder about your role in the labor and delivery? Are you worried about being a good father? Share your thoughts with your partner. You won't burden her. In fact, she'll probably be relieved to know she's not alone in feeling a little overwhelmed by this monumental life change.

If you have an ectopic pregnancy and are Rh-negative, you should receive RhoGAM. This applies to miscarriages and abortions as well. If amniocentesis is performed during pregnancy and you are Rh-negative, you should receive RhoGAM.

Week 17

How Big Is Your Baby?

The crown-to-rump length of your baby is 4.4 to 4.8 inches (110 to 120mm: 11 or 12cm). Fetal weight has doubled in 2 weeks and is about 3.5 ounces (100g). By this week, your baby is about the size of your hand spread open wide.

How Big Are You?

Your uterus is 1.5 to 2 inches (3.8 to 5cm) below your bellybutton. You are showing more now and have an obvious swelling in your lower abdomen. By this time, expanding or maternity clothing is a must for comfort's sake. When your partner gives you a hug, he may feel the difference in your lower abdomen.

The rest of your body is still changing. A total 5- to 10-pound (2.25- to 4.5-kg) gain by this point in your pregnancy is normal.

How Your Baby Is Growing and Developing

If you look at the illustration on page 170, then look at earlier chapters, you'll see the huge changes that are occurring. Fat begins to form during this week and the weeks that follow. Also called *adipose tissue*, fat is important to the body's heat production and metabolism.

At 17 weeks of development, water makes up about 3 ounces (89g) and fat 0.018 ounce (0.5g) of your baby's body. In a baby at term, fat makes up about 5.25 pounds (2.4kg) of the total average weight of 7.7 pounds (3.5kg).

You have felt your baby move, or you will soon. You may not feel it every day. As pregnancy progresses, movements become stronger and probably more frequent.

Changes in You

Feeling your baby move can reassure you that things are going well with your pregnancy. This is especially true if you've had problems.

As your pregnancy advances, the top of the uterus becomes almost spherical. It increases more rapidly in length (upward into your abdomen) than in width, so the uterus becomes more oval than round. The uterus fills the pelvis and starts to grow into the abdomen. Your intestines are pushed upward and to the sides. The uterus eventually reaches almost to your liver. The uterus doesn't

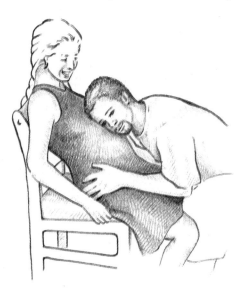

float around, but it is not firmly attached to one spot.

When you stand, your uterus touches your abdominal wall in the front. You may feel it most easily in this position. When you lie down, it can fall backward onto your spine and blood vessels (vena cava and aorta).

Round ligaments are attached to each side of the upper uterus and to the pelvic side wall. During pregnancy and the growth of the uterus, these ligaments are stretched and pulled. They become longer and thicker. Your movements can stretch and pull these ligaments, causing pain or discomfort called *round-ligament* pain. It doesn't signal a problem; it indicates your uterus is growing.

Pain may occur on one side only or both sides, or it may be worse on one side than another. This pain does not harm you or the baby.

If you experience pain, you may feel better if you lie down and rest. Talk to your healthcare provider about the pain if it is severe or if other symptoms arise. Warning signs of serious problems include bleeding from the vagina, loss of fluid from the vagina or severe pain.

How Your Actions Affect Your Baby's Development

Increased Vaginal Discharge
During pregnancy, it is normal to have an increase in vaginal discharge, or vaginal secretions, called *leukorrhea*. This discharge is usually white or yellow and fairly thick. It is not an infection. We believe it is caused by the increased blood flow to the skin and muscles around the vagina, which causes a violet or blue coloration of the vagina. This appearance, visible to your doctor early in pregnancy, is called *Chadwick's sign*.

You may have to wear sanitary pads if you have heavy discharge. Avoid wearing pantyhose and nylon underwear; choose underwear with a cotton crotch.

Vaginal infections can and do occur during pregnancy. The discharge that accompanies these infections is often foul-smelling, is yellow or green, and causes irritation or itching around or inside the vagina. If you suffer from any of these symptoms, call your healthcare provider. Many creams and antibiotics that treat vaginal infections are safe to use during pregnancy.

Douching during Pregnancy
Most doctors agree you should *not* douche during pregnancy. Bulb-syringe douches are definitely out!

Using a douche may cause you to bleed or may cause more serious problems, such as an *air embolus*. An air embolus results

> **Most doctors agree you should *not* douche during pregnancy.**

when air gets into your bloodstream from the pressure of the douche. It is rare, but it can cause serious problems for you.

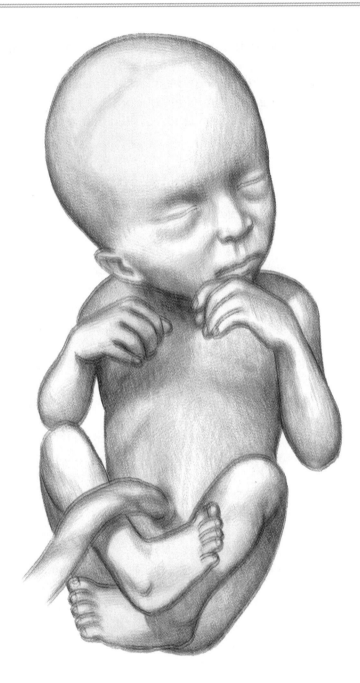

Your baby's fingernails are well formed.
The baby is beginning to accumulate a little fat.

Your Nutrition

Some women choose to eat a vegetarian diet because of personal or religious preferences. Some women are nauseated by meat during pregnancy. Is it safe to eat vegetarian while you're pregnant? It can be, if you pay close attention to the types of foods and the combinations of foods you eat.

If you eliminate meat from your diet, you need to eat enough calories to meet your energy needs. These need to be the right kind of calories, such as fresh fruits and vegetables. Avoid empty calories that have little or no nutritional value. You want to eat enough different sources of protein to provide energy for the fetus and for you.

It's important to get the vitamins and minerals you need. If you eat a wide variety of whole grains, dried beans and peas, dried fruit and wheat germ, you should be able to meet your body's demands for iron, zinc and other trace minerals. You must find other sources of calcium and vitamins B_2, B_{12} and D.

> ### Tip for Week 17
>
> If you experience leg cramps during pregnancy, don't stand for long periods. Rest on your side as often as possible. Careful stretching exercises may help. You may also use a heating pad on the cramped area, but don't use it for longer than 15 minutes at a time.

If you're not eating meat because it makes you ill during pregnancy, ask your physician for a referral to a nutritionist. You'll probably need help developing a good eating plan. If you're a vegetarian by choice, and have been for a while, you may know how to get many of the nutrients you need. However, if you have questions, be sure to discuss them with your healthcare provider.

You Should Also Know

Quad-screen Test
The quad-screen test can help your healthcare provider determine if you might be carrying a baby with Down syndrome. This blood test can also help rule out other problems in your pregnancy, such as neural-tube defects.

The quad-screen test is the same as the triple-screen, with the addition of a fourth measurement: your inhibin-A level. This fourth measurement raises the sensitivity of the standard triple-screen test by 20% in determining whether a fetus has Down syndrome.

The quad-screen test is able to identify 79% of those fetuses with Down syndrome. It has a false-positive result 5% of the time.

Dad Tip

Offer your partner tension-relieving, muscle-relaxing head, back or foot massages.

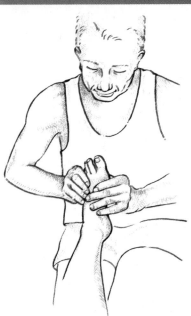

Week 18

How Big Is Your Baby?

The crown-to-rump length of your growing baby is 5 to
5.6 inches (12.5 to 14cm) by this week. Weight of the fetus is
about 5.25 ounces (150g).

How Big Are You?

You can feel your uterus just below your bellybutton. If you put your
fingers sideways and measure, it is about two finger-widths (1 inch)
below your bellybutton. Your uterus is the size of a cantaloupe or
a little larger.

Your total weight gain to this point should be 10 to 13 pounds
(4.5 to 5.8kg). However, this can vary widely. If you have gained more
weight than this, talk to your healthcare provider. You may need to
see a nutritionist. You still have more than half of your pregnancy
ahead of you, and you're going to gain more weight.

Gaining more than the
recommended weight can make
pregnancy and delivery harder on
you. Extra pounds are hard to lose
afterward.

> **Dieting during pregnancy is not a wise idea, but that doesn't mean you don't have to watch what you eat.**

Dieting during pregnancy is not a wise idea, but that doesn't
mean you don't have to watch what you eat. You should! Choose
food for the nutrition it provides you and your growing baby.

How Your Baby Is Growing and Developing

Your baby is continuing to grow and to develop, but now the rapid growth rate slows down a little. As you can see in the illustration on page 175, your baby has a human appearance now.

Development of the Heart and Circulatory System
At about the third week of fetal development, two tubes join to form the heart. The heart begins to contract by day 22 of development or about the beginning of the 5th week of gestation. A beating heart is visible as early as 5 to 6 weeks of pregnancy during an ultrasound examination.

> A beating heart is visible as early as 5 to 6 weeks of pregnancy during an ultrasound examination.

The heart tube divides into bulges. These bulges develop into heart chambers, called *ventricles* (left and right) and *atria* (left atrium and right atrium). These divisions occur between weeks 6 and 7. During week 7, tissue separating the left and right atria grows, and an opening between the atria called the *foramen ovale* appears. This opening lets blood pass from one atrium to the other, allowing it to bypass the lungs. At birth, the opening closes.

The ventricles, the lower chambers of the heart (lying below the atria), also develop a partition. The ventricle walls are muscular. The left ventricle pumps blood to the body and brain, and the right ventricle pumps blood to the lungs.

Heart valves develop at the same time as the chambers. These valves fill and empty the heart. Heart sounds and heart murmurs are caused by blood passing through these valves.

Your baby gets oxygen from you. Blood from your baby flows to the placenta through the umbilical cord. In the placenta, oxygen and nutrients are transported from your blood to the fetal blood. Although the circulation of your blood and that of your baby come close, there is no direct connection. These circulation systems are completely separate.

At birth, the baby has to go rapidly from depending entirely on you for oxygen to depending on its own heart and lungs. The foramen ovale closes. Blood goes to the right ventricle, the right atrium and the lungs for oxygenation for the first time. It is truly a miraculous conversion.

Your baby continues to grow. By this week, it is about 5 inches (12.5cm) from crown to rump. It looks much more human now.

At 18 weeks of gestation, ultrasound can detect some abnormalities of the heart. This can be helpful in identifying problems such as Down syndrome. A skilled ultrasonographer looks for specific heart defects. If an abnormality is suspected, further ultrasound exams may be ordered to follow a baby's development as pregnancy progresses.

Changes in You

Does Your Back Ache?

Nearly every pregnant woman experiences backache at some time in pregnancy. You may have felt it already or it may come later

as you get bigger. Some women have severe back pain following excessive exercise, walking, bending, lifting or standing. It is more common to have mild backache than severe problems. Some women need to take special care getting out of bed or getting up from sitting. In severe instances, some women find it difficult to walk.

A change in joint mobility may contribute to the change in your posture and may cause discomfort in the lower back. This is particularly true in the latter part of pregnancy.

The growth of the uterus moves your center of gravity forward, over your legs, which can affect the joints around the pelvis. All of your joints are looser. Hormonal increases are potential causes; however, pain may also be an indication of more serious problems, such as pyelonephritis or a kidney stone (see page 182). Check with your healthcare provider if back pain is a chronic problem for you.

What can you do to prevent or lessen your pain? Try some or all of the following tips as early in your pregnancy as possible, and they will pay off as your pregnancy progresses.

- Watch your diet and weight gain.
- Continue exercising within guidelines during pregnancy.
- Get in the habit of lying on your side when you sleep.

- Find time during the day to get off your feet and lie down for 30 minutes on your side.
- If you have other children, take a nap when they take theirs.
- It's OK to take acetaminophen (Tylenol) for back pain.
- Use heat on the area that is painful.
- If pain becomes constant or more severe, talk to your healthcare provider about it.

How Your Actions Affect Your Baby's Development

Exercise in the Second Trimester
Everyone has heard stories of women who continued with strenuous exercise or strenuous activities until the day of delivery without problems. Stories are told of Olympic athletes who were pregnant at the time they won medals in the Olympic games. This kind of training and physical stress isn't a good idea for most women.

As your uterus grows and your abdomen gets larger, your sense of balance may be affected. You may feel clumsy. This isn't the time for contact sports, such as basketball, or sports where you might fall easily, injure yourself or be struck in the abdomen.

Pregnant women can participate safely in many sports and other activities throughout their pregnancy. This is a different attitude from those held 20, 30 and 40 years ago. Bed rest and decreased activity were common then. Today, we believe exercise and activity can benefit you and your growing baby.

A Visit with the Doctor

Tina came to the office after a long day at the grocery store, where she was a clerk. She told me her back ached a lot, and she wanted to know what to do. I told her that backache can often be helped with heat, rest and analgesics, such as acetaminophen (Tylenol). Special maternity girdles are available that can provide some support. Keeping weight under control and exercising may also help. In a severe case, physical therapy or a consultation with an orthopedic surgeon may be necessary.

Discuss your particular activities with your healthcare provider. If your pregnancy is high risk or if you have had several miscarriages, it's particularly important to discuss exercise with your healthcare provider before starting an activity. Now is not the time to train for any sport or to increase activity. In fact, this may be a good time to decrease the amount or intensity of exercise you are doing. Listen to your body. It will tell you when it's time to slow down.

What about the activities you are already involved in or would like to begin? Below is a discussion of various activities and how they will affect you in your second and third trimester. (See Week 3 for information on exercise before pregnancy and in early pregnancy.)

Swimming

Swimming can be good for you when you're pregnant. The support and buoyancy of the water can be relaxing. If you swim, swim throughout pregnancy. If you can't swim and have been involved in water exercises (exercising in the shallow end of a swimming pool), you can continue this throughout your pregnancy as well. This is an exercise you can begin at any time during pregnancy, if you don't overdo it.

> **Pregnant women can participate safely in many sports and other activities throughout their pregnancy.**

Bicycling

Now is not the time to learn to ride a bike. If you're comfortable riding and have safe places to ride, you can enjoy this exercise with your partner or family.

Your balance will change as your body changes. This can make getting on and off a bicycle difficult. A fall from a bicycle could injure you or your baby.

A stationary bicycle is good for bad weather and for later in pregnancy. Many doctors suggest you ride a stationary bike to avoid the danger of a fall in the last 2 to 3 months of pregnancy.

Tip for Week 18

During exercise, your oxygen demands increase. Your body is heavier and your balance may change. You may also tire more easily. Keep these points in mind as you adjust your fitness program.

Walking

Walking is a desirable exercise during pregnancy. It can be a good time for you and your partner to talk. Even when the weather is bad, you can walk in places such as enclosed shopping malls to get a good workout. Two miles of walking at a good pace is adequate. As pregnancy progresses, you may need to decrease your speed and distance. Walking is an exercise you can begin at any time during pregnancy, if you don't overdo it.

Jogging

Many women continue to jog during pregnancy. Jogging may be permitted during pregnancy, but check with your healthcare provider first. If your pregnancy is high risk, jogging may not be a good idea.

Pregnancy is not the time to increase mileage or to train for a race. Wear comfortable clothing and shoes with good cushioning. Allow plenty of time to cool down.

During the course of your pregnancy, you'll probably need to slow down and decrease the number of miles you run. You may even change to walking. If you notice pain, contractions, bleeding or other symptoms during or after jogging, call your healthcare provider immediately.

Other Sports Activities

- Tennis and golf are safe to continue in the second and third trimesters but may provide little actual exercise.

- Horseback riding is not advisable during pregnancy *at any time.*
- Avoid water skiing while you're pregnant.
- Bowling is OK, although the amount of exercise you get varies. Be careful in late pregnancy; back strain could occur. Your balance changes, which could make bowling difficult for you.
- Talk to your healthcare provider about snow skiing before you hit the slopes. Again, in the latter part of pregnancy, your balance changes significantly. A fall could be harmful to you and your baby. Most physicians agree that skiing in the second half of pregnancy is not a good idea. Some doctors may allow skiing in early pregnancy, but only if there are no complications with this or a previous pregnancy.
- Riding snowmobiles or motorcycles is not advised. Some doctors may allow you to ride if it is not strenuous. However, most believe the risk is too great, especially if you have had problems during this or another pregnancy.

Your Nutrition

Iron is important to you while you're pregnant. You need about 30mg a day to meet the increased needs of pregnancy, due to the increase in your blood volume.
During your pregnancy, your baby draws on your iron stores to create its own stores for its first few months of life. This protects baby from iron deficiency if you breastfeed.

> An easy way to check your iron level is to examine the inside of your lower eyelid. If you're getting enough iron, it should be dark pink.

Most prenatal vitamins contain enough iron to meet your needs. If you must take iron supplements, take your iron pill with a glass of orange juice or grapefruit juice to increase its absorption. Avoid drinking milk, coffee or tea when you take an iron supplement or eat iron-rich foods. They prevent the body from absorbing the iron it needs.

If you feel tired, have trouble concentrating, suffer from headaches, dizziness or indigestion, or if you get sick easily, you may have an iron deficiency. An easy way to check is to examine the inside of your lower eyelid. If you're getting enough iron, it should be dark pink. Your nail beds should be pink, too.

Only 10 to 15% of the iron you consume is absorbed by the body. Your body stores it efficiently, but you need to eat iron-rich foods on a regular basis to maintain those stores. Foods that are rich in iron include chicken, red meat, organ meats (liver, heart, kidneys), egg yolks, dried fruit, spinach, kale and tofu. Combining a vitamin-C food and an iron-rich food ensures better iron absorption by the body. A spinach salad with orange or grapefruit sections is a good example.

Your prenatal vitamin contains about 60mg of iron. If you eat a well-balanced diet and take your prenatal vitamin every day, you may not need additional iron. Discuss it with your healthcare provider if you are concerned.

You Should Also Know

Bladder Infections
One of the most common problems of pregnancy is frequent urination. Urinary-tract infections (UTIs) may cause you to urinate even more frequently while you're pregnant. A UTI is the most common problem involving your bladder or kidneys during pregnancy. As the uterus grows larger, it sits directly on top of the bladder and on the ureters, the tubes leading from the kidneys to the bladder. This blocks the flow of urine. Other names for urinary-tract infections are *bladder infections* and *cystitis.*

Symptoms of a bladder infection include painful urination, particularly at the end of urination, the feeling of urgency to urinate and frequent urination. A severe urinary-tract infection may cause blood to appear in the urine.

Your healthcare provider may do a urinalysis and urine culture at your first prenatal visit. He or she may check your urine for infection at other times during pregnancy and when bothersome symptoms arise.

You can help avoid infection by not holding your urine. Empty your bladder as soon as you feel the need to. Don't wait to go to the bathroom; it could lead to a urinary-tract infection. Drink plenty of fluid; cranberry juice may help you avoid infections. For some women, it helps to empty the bladder after having intercourse.

See your healthcare provider if you think you have a bladder infection. It should be treated. Some antibiotics are safe to use during pregnancy for this problem. If left untreated, urinary-tract infections can get worse. They can even lead to *pyelonephritis*, a serious kidney infection (see below).

A urinary-tract infection during pregnancy might be a cause of premature labor or a low-birthweight infant. If you think you have an infection, talk to your healthcare provider. If you are diagnosed as having a UTI, take the full course of antibiotics prescribed for you.

Pyelonephritis
A more serious problem resulting from a bladder infection is pyelonephritis (kidney infection). This type of infection occurs in 1 to 2% of all pregnant women. The right kidney is most often affected.

Symptoms include frequent urination, a burning sensation during urination, the feeling you need to urinate and nothing will come out, high fever, chills and back pain. Pyelonephritis may require hospitalization and treatment with intravenous antibiotics.

If you have pyelonephritis or recurrent bladder infections during pregnancy, you may have to take antibiotics throughout pregnancy to prevent reinfection.

Kidney Stones
Another problem involving the kidneys and bladder is *kidney stones* (or *renal calculi*). They occur about once in every 1,500 pregnancies. Kidney stones cause severe pain in the back or lower abdomen. They may also be associated with blood in the urine.

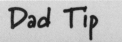

Dad Tip

Offer to run errands: Take her dry cleaning in and pick it up when it's done. Stop by the bank for her. Take her car to a car wash. Return her library books or rented videos.

A kidney stone during pregnancy can usually be treated with pain medication and by drinking lots of fluids. In this way, the stone may be passed without surgical removal or *lithotripsy* (an ultrasound procedure).

Week 19

How Big Is Your Baby?

Crown-to-rump length of the growing fetus is 5.2 to 6 inches (13 to 15cm) by this week. Your baby weighs about 7 ounces (200g). It's incredible to think your baby will increase its weight more than 15 times between now and delivery!

How Big Are You?

You can feel your uterus about 0.5 inch (1.3cm) below your umbilicus. The illustration on page 184 gives you a good idea of the relative size of you, your uterus and your developing baby. A side view really shows the change in you!

Your total weight gain at this point is between 8 and 14 pounds (3.6 and 6.3kg). Of this weight, only about 7 ounces (200g) is your baby! The placenta weighs about 6 ounces (170g); the amniotic fluid weighs another 11 ounces (320g). The uterus weighs 11 ounces (320g). Your breasts have each increased in weight by 6.3 ounces (180g).

How Your Baby Is Growing and Developing

Your Baby's Nervous System

The beginning of the baby's nervous system (brain and other structures, such as the spinal cord) is seen as early as week 4 as the neural plate begins to develop. By week 6 of gestation, the main divisions of the central nervous system are established.

These divisions consist of the forebrain, midbrain, hindbrain and spinal cord. In week 7, the forebrain divides into the two hemispheres that will become the two cerebral hemispheres of the brain.

Hydrocephalus

Organization and development of the brain continues from this early beginning. Cerebral spinal fluid (CSF), which circulates around the brain and the spinal cord, is made by the choroid plexus. Fluid must be able to flow without restriction. If openings are blocked and flow is restricted for any reason, it can cause *hydrocephalus* (water on the brain).

Hydrocephalus causes enlargement of the head. Occurring in about 1 in 2,000 babies, it is responsible for about 12% of all severe fetal malformations found at birth.

Hydrocephalus is often associated with spina bifida and occurs in about 33% of those cases. It can also be associated with *meningomyelocele* and *omphalocele* (hernias of the spine and navel). Between 15 and 45 ounces of fluid (500 to 1,500ml) can accumulate, but much more than that has been found. Brain tissue is compressed by all this fluid, which is a major concern.

Ultrasound is the best way to diagnose the problem. Hydrocephalus can usually be seen on ultrasound by 19 weeks

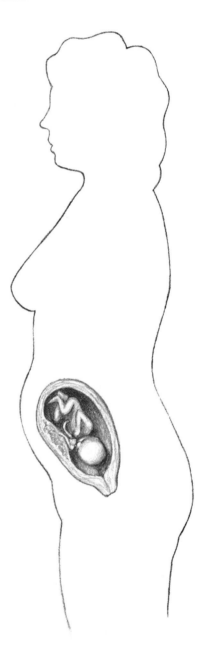

Comparative size of the uterus at 19 weeks of pregnancy (fetal age—17 weeks). The uterus can be felt just under the umbilicus (bellybutton).

of pregnancy. Occasionally it is found by routine exams and feeling your uterus.

In the past, nothing could be done about hydrocephalus until after delivery. Today, *intrauterine therapy*—treatment while the fetus is still in the uterus—can be performed in some cases.

There are two methods of treating hydrocephalus *in utero* (in the uterus). In one method, a needle passes through the mother's abdomen into the area of the baby's brain where fluid is collecting. Some fluid is removed to relieve pressure on the baby's brain. In another method, a small plastic tube is placed into the area where fluid collects in the baby's brain. This tube is left in place to drain fluid continuously.

Hydrocephalus is a high-risk problem. These procedures are highly specialized and should be performed only by someone experienced in the latest techniques. This requires consultation with a perinatologist specializing in high-risk pregnancies.

Changes in You

Feeling Dizzy

Feeling dizzy during pregnancy is a fairly common symptom, often caused by *hypotension* (low blood pressure). It usually doesn't appear until the second trimester but may occur earlier.

There are two common reasons for hypotension during pregnancy. It can be caused by the enlarging uterus putting pressure on your aorta and vena cava. This is called *supine hypotension* and occurs when you lie down. You can alleviate or prevent it by not sleeping or lying on your back.

> **Your blood pressure drops when you rise rapidly as blood leaves your brain because of gravity.**

The second cause of hypotension is rising rapidly from a sitting, kneeling or squatting position. This is called *postural hypotension*. Your blood pressure drops when you rise rapidly as blood leaves your brain because of gravity. This problem is cured by rising slowly from a sitting or lying position.

If you are anemic, you may feel dizzy, faint or tired, or you may fatigue easily. Your blood is checked routinely during pregnancy. Your caregiver will tell you if you have anemia. (See Week 22 for more information about anemia.)

Pregnancy also affects your blood-sugar level. High blood sugar (hyperglycemia) or low blood sugar (hypoglycemia) can make you feel dizzy or faint. Many doctors routinely test pregnant women for problems with blood sugar during pregnancy, particularly if they have a family history of diabetes or problems with dizziness. Most women can avoid or improve the problem by eating a balanced diet, not skipping meals and not going a long time without eating. Carry a piece of fruit or several crackers with you for a quick boost in blood sugar when you need it.

How Your Actions Affect Your Baby's Development

Warning Signs during Pregnancy

Many women are nervous because they don't think they would know if something important or serious happened during

pregnancy. Most women have few, if any, problems during pregnancy. If you are concerned, read the list below of the most important

> **Most women have few, if any, problems during pregnancy.**

symptoms to be aware of. Call your healthcare provider if you experience any of them:

- vaginal bleeding
- severe swelling of the face or fingers
- severe abdominal pain
- loss of fluid from the vagina, usually a gush of fluid, but sometimes a trickle or continuous wetness
- a big change in the baby's movement or a lack of movement
- high fever (more than 101.6F; 38.7C) or chills
- severe vomiting or an inability to keep food or liquid down
- blurring of vision
- painful urination
- a headache that won't go away or a severe headache
- an injury or accident, such as a fall or automobile accident, that causes you concern about the well-being of your baby

One way to get to know your healthcare provider is to ask his or her opinion about your concerns. When you talk to your caregiver, don't be embarrassed to ask questions about anything.

Your caregiver would rather know about problems while they are easier to deal with.

If problems warrant it, you may be referred to a perinatologist, an obstetrician who has spent an additional 2 years or more in specialized training. These specialists have experience caring for women with high-risk pregnancies.

You may not have a high-risk pregnancy at the beginning. However, if problems develop with you (such as premature labor) or your baby (such as spina bifida), you may be referred to a perinatologist for consultation and possibly care during your pregnancy. You may be able to return to your regular healthcare provider for your delivery.

If you are seeing a perinatologist, you may have to deliver your baby at a hospital other than the one you had chosen. This is usually because the hospital has specialized facilities or can administer specialized tests to you or your baby.

Your Nutrition

Calcium is important to you and your developing fetus. You need it to keep your bones healthy. Baby needs it to develop strong bones and teeth. During pregnancy, you need about 1,200mg of calcium a day. Your body stores calcium in the latter part of pregnancy to draw on if you breastfeed.

Dairy products are good sources of calcium. They also contain vitamin D, which aids in calcium absorption. Milk, cheese, yogurt and ice cream are calcium sources we commonly think of. Other foods that contain calcium include broccoli, bok choy, collards, spinach, salmon, sardines, garbanzo beans (chickpeas), sesame seeds, almonds, cooked dried beans, tofu and trout. Some foods are now calcium fortified, such as orange juice and some breads.

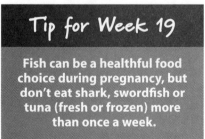

Tip for Week 19

Fish can be a healthful food choice during pregnancy, but don't eat shark, swordfish or tuna (fresh or frozen) more than once a week.

You can increase the calcium in your diet in other ways, too. Add powdered nonfat milk to recipes, such as soup, mashed potatoes and meat loaf. Make fruit shakes with fresh fruit and milk; add a scoop of ice milk or ice cream. Cook rice and oatmeal in skim or low-fat milk.

Some foods interfere with the body's calcium absorption. Salt, tea, coffee, protein and unleavened bread decrease the amount of calcium absorbed.

If you need to be careful with your calories, choose calcium sources wisely. There are many nonfat and low-fat products available. If your healthcare provider decides you need calcium supplementation, calcium carbonate combined with magnesium (to aid calcium absorption) is a good choice. Avoid any supplement derived from animal bones, oyster shells or dolomite because it may contain lead.

You Should Also Know

Allergies during Pregnancy

Allergies sometimes get a little worse during pregnancy. To help deal with the problem, drink plenty of fluids. If you have allergy medication, don't assume it's safe to take. Ask your healthcare provider about your medicine, whether prescription or nonprescription. This advice also applies to nasal sprays. Some types of allergy medication may not be advised. Many allergy medicines are combinations of several medicines, including aspirin, which you should not take during pregnancy.

Some women notice their allergies get better during pregnancy, and symptoms improve. Certain things they had trouble with before pregnancy are no longer a problem. (See also Nasal Problems, page 227.)

Dad Tip

When you can, take some time off from work or other obligations to spend time with your partner. Together, focus on planning your pregnancy and preparing for the birth of your baby.

Week 20

How Big Is Your Baby?

At this point in development, the crown-to-rump length is 5.6 to 6.4 inches (14 to 16cm). Your baby weighs about 9 ounces (260g).

How Big Are You?

Congratulations—20 weeks marks the midpoint, and you're halfway through your pregnancy! Remember, the entire pregnancy is 40 weeks from the beginning of your last period if you go full term.

Your uterus is probably about even with your bellybutton. Your healthcare provider has been watching your growth and the enlargement of your uterus. Growth to this point may have been irregular but usually becomes more regular after the 20th week.

Measuring the Growth of Your Uterus

Your uterus is measured often to keep track of your baby's growth. Your healthcare provider may use a measuring tape or his or her fingers and measure by finger breadth.

Your caregiver needs a point of reference against which to measure your growth. Some doctors measure from your bellybutton. Many measure from the pubic symphysis. The pubic symphysis is the place where the pubic bones meet in the middle-lower part of your abdomen. This bony area is just above your urethra (where urine comes out), 6 to 10 inches (15.2 to 25.4cm) below the bellybutton, depending on how tall you are. It may be felt 1 or 2 inches (2.5 to 5cm) below your pubic hairline.

Measurements are made from the pubic symphysis to the top of the uterus. After 20 weeks of pregnancy, you should grow about 0.4 inch (1cm) each week. If you are 8 inches (20cm) at 20 weeks, at your next visit (4 weeks later), you should measure about 9.6 inches (24cm).

If you measure 11.2 inches (28cm) at this point in pregnancy, you may require further evaluation with ultrasound to determine if you are carrying twins or to see if your due date is correct. If you measure 6 inches (15 to 16cm) at this point, it may be a reason to do further evaluation by ultrasound. Your due date could be wrong, or there may be a concern about intrauterine-growth retardation or some other problem.

> **Measurements differ among women and are often different for a woman from one pregnancy to another.**

Not every doctor measures the same way, and not every woman is the same size. Babies vary in size. If pregnant friends ask, "How much did you measure?" don't worry if their measurements are different. Measurements differ among women and are often different for a woman from one pregnancy to another.

If you see a doctor you don't normally see or if you see a new doctor, you may measure differently. This does not indicate a problem or that someone is measuring incorrectly. It's just that everyone measures a little differently.

Having the same person measure you on a regular basis can be helpful in following the growth of your baby. Within limits, changing measurements are a sign of fetal well-being and fetal growth. If they appear abnormal, it can be a warning sign. If you're concerned about your size and the growth of your pregnancy, ask your healthcare provider about it.

How Your Baby Is Growing and Developing

Your Baby's Skin

The skin covering your baby begins growing from two layers. These layers are the *epidermis*, which is on the surface, and the *dermis*, which is the deeper layer. By this point in your pregnancy, the epidermis is arranged in four layers. One of these layers contains epidermal ridges, which are responsible for surface patterns on fingertips, palms and soles. They are genetically determined.

The dermis lies below the epidermis. It forms projections that push upward into the epidermis. Each projection contains a small blood vessel (capillary) or a nerve. This deeper layer also contains large amounts of fat.

When a baby is born, its skin is covered by a white substance that looks like paste. Called *vernix*, it is secreted by the glands in the skin beginning around 20 weeks of pregnancy. Vernix protects your growing baby's skin from amniotic fluid.

Hair appears at around 12 to 14 weeks of pregnancy. It grows from the epidermis; hair ends (hair papillae) push down into the dermis. Hair is first seen on the fetus on the upper lip and eyebrow. It is usually shed around the time of birth and is replaced by thicker hair from new follicles.

Ultrasound Pictures

The illustration on page 192 shows an ultrasound exam (and an interpretive illustration of the ultrasound) in a pregnant woman at about 20 weeks' gestation. An ultrasound is often easier to understand when it is actually being done. The pictures you see are more like motion pictures.

Look closely at the illustration. Read the labels and try to visualize the baby inside the uterus. An ultrasound picture is like looking at a slice of an object. The picture you see is 2-dimensional.

An ultrasound done at this point in pregnancy is helpful for confirming or helping to establish your due date. If the ultrasound is done very early or very late (first or last 2 months), the accuracy of dating a pregnancy is not as good. If two or more fetuses are

A Visit with the Doctor

When Margaret had an ultrasound, she was disappointed—it didn't look like a baby to her. If you have an ultrasound exam and don't see everything or it doesn't make sense, don't feel bad. These images are difficult to interpret unless you've had extensive training and experience. Margaret was reassured to see the heartbeat and to see her baby move.

Body

Wall of uterus

Head

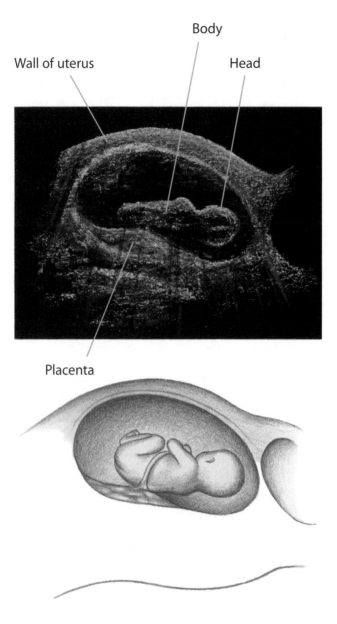

Placenta

Ultrasound of a baby at 20 weeks' gestation (fetal age—18 weeks).
The interpretive illustration may help you see more detail.

present, they can usually be seen. In many cases, fetal problems can also be seen at this time.

Percutaneous Umbilical Blood Sampling

Percutaneous umbilical blood sampling (PUBS), also called *cordocentesis*, is a test done on the fetus while it is still developing inside your uterus. The advantage of the test is that results are available in a few days. The disadvantage is that it carries a slightly higher risk of miscarriage than amniocentesis does.

Guided by ultrasound, a fine needle is inserted through the mother's abdomen into a tiny vein in the umbilical cord. A small sample of the baby's blood is removed for analysis. PUBS detects blood disorders, infections and Rh-incompatability.

The baby's blood can be checked before birth, and the baby can be given a blood transfusion, if necessary. This procedure can help prevent life-threatening anemia that may develop if the mother is Rh-negative and has antibodies that are destroying her baby's blood.

Changes in You

Stretching Abdominal Muscles

Your abdominal muscles are being stretched and pushed apart as your baby grows. Muscles are attached to the lower portion of your ribs and run vertically down to your pelvis. They may separate in the midline. These muscles are called the *rectus muscles*; when they separate, it is called a *diastasis recti*.

You will notice the separation most often when you are lying down and you raise your head, tightening your abdominal muscles. It will look like there is a bulge in the middle of your abdomen. You might even feel the edge of the muscle on either side of the bulge. It isn't painful and doesn't harm you or your baby. What you feel in the gap between the muscles is the uterus. You may feel the baby's movement more easily here.

If this is your first baby, you may not notice the separation at all. With each pregnancy, separation is often more noticeable. Exercising can strengthen these muscles, but you may still have the bulge or gap.

Following pregnancy, these muscles tighten and close the gap. The separation won't be as noticeable, but it may still be present. A girdle probably won't help get rid of the bulge or gap.

How Your Actions Affect Your Baby's Development

Sexual Relations

Pregnancy can be an important time of growing closer to your partner. As you get larger, sexual intercourse may become difficult because of discomfort for you. With some imagination and with different positions (ones in which you are not on your back and your partner is not directly on top of you), you can continue to enjoy sexual relations during this part of your pregnancy.

Tip for Week 20

An ultrasound test done at this point in pregnancy may make it possible to determine the sex of the baby, but the baby must cooperate. Sex is recognized by seeing the genitals. Even if the sex looks obvious, ultrasound operators have been known to be mistaken about a baby's sex.

If you feel pressure from your partner—either his concern about the safety of intercourse or requests for frequent sexual relations—discuss it openly with him. Don't be afraid to invite your partner to visit your healthcare provider with you to discuss these things.

If you're having problems with contractions, bleeding or complications, you and your partner should talk with your healthcare provider. Together you can decide whether you should continue to have sexual relations during your pregnancy.

Your Nutrition

Many women use artificial sweeteners to help cut calories. Aspartame and saccharin are the two most common artificial sweeteners added to foods and beverages. Aspartame (sold under the brand names Nutrasweet® and Equal®) may be the most popular artificial sweetener. It is used in many foods and beverages to help reduce calorie content. It is a combination of phenylalanine and aspartic acid, two amino acids.

There has been controversy as to the safety of aspartame. We advise you to substitute foods that do not contain the sweetener. At this point, we're unsure about its safety for pregnant women and their developing babies. If you suffer from phenylketonuria, you must follow a low-phenylalanine diet or your baby may be adversely affected. Phenylalanine in aspartame contributes to phenylalanine in the diet.

Saccharin is another artificial sweetener used in many foods and beverages. Although it is not used as much today as in the past, it still appears in many foods, beverages and other substances. The Center for Science in the Public Interest reports testing of saccharin does not indicate that it is safe to use during pregnancy. It would probably be better to avoid using this product while you're pregnant.

Don't use artificial sweeteners or food additives during pregnancy, if you can avoid them. It's probably best to eliminate any substance you don't really need from the foods you eat and the beverages you drink. Do it for the good of your baby.

You Should Also Know

Hearing Your Baby's Heartbeat

It may be possible to hear your baby's heartbeat with a stethoscope at 20 weeks. Before doctors had doppler equipment

> If you can't hear your baby's heartbeat with a stethoscope, don't worry. It's not always easy for a doctor who does this on a regular basis!

that enabled them to hear the heartbeat and ultrasound to see the heart beating, a stethoscope helped the listener hear the baby's heartbeat. This usually occurred after quickening for most women.

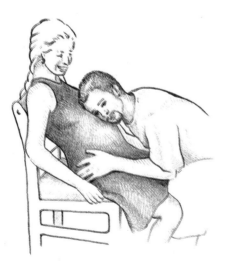

The sound you hear through a stethoscope may be different than what you are used to hearing at the doctor's office. The sound isn't loud. If you've never listened through a stethoscope, it may be difficult to hear at first. It does get easier as the baby gets larger and sounds are louder.

If you can't hear your baby's heartbeat with a

stethoscope, don't worry. It's not always easy for a doctor who does this on a regular basis!

If you hear a swishing sound (baby's heartbeat), you have to differentiate it from a beating sound (mother's heartbeat). A baby's heart beats rapidly, usually 120 to 160 beats every minute. Your heartbeat or pulse rate is slower, in the range of 60 to 80 beats a minute. Don't be afraid to ask your healthcare provider to help you distinguish the sounds.

Dad Tip

Around 20 weeks of pregnancy, your partner may have an ultrasound exam. Try to be present for this test. Ask your partner to consider your schedule when making the appointment for her ultrasound.

Week 21

Age of Fetus: 19 Weeks

How Big Is Your Baby?

Your baby is getting larger in this first week of the second half of your pregnancy. It now weighs about 10.5 ounces (300g), and its crown-to-rump length is about 7.2 inches (18cm). It is about the size of a large banana.

How Big Are You?

You can feel your uterus about half an inch (1cm) above your bellybutton. At the doctor's office, your uterus measures almost 8.5 inches (21cm) from the pubic symphysis. Your weight gain should be between 10 and 15 pounds (4.5 and 6.3kg).

By this week, your waistline is definitely gone. Your friends and relatives—and strangers, too—can tell you're pregnant. It would be hard to hide your condition!

How Your Baby Is Growing and Developing

The rapid growth rate of your baby has slowed. However, the baby continues to grow and to develop. Different organ systems within the baby are maturing.

The Fetal Digestive System
The fetal digestive system is functioning in a simple way. By the 11th week of pregnancy, the small intestine begins to contract and relax,

which pushes substances through it. The small intestine is capable of passing sugar from inside itself into the baby's body.

By 21 weeks of pregnancy, development of the fetal digestive system enables the fetus to swallow amniotic fluid. After swallowing amniotic fluid, the fetus absorbs much of the water in it and passes unabsorbed matter as far as the large bowel.

Fetal Swallowing

As mentioned above, your baby swallows before it is born. Using ultrasound, you can observe the baby swallowing at different stages of pregnancy. We have seen babies swallowing amniotic fluid as early as 21 weeks of pregnancy.

Why does a baby in the womb swallow? Researchers believe swallowing amniotic fluid may help growth and development of the fetal digestive system. It may condition the digestive system to function after birth.

Using ultrasound, you can observe the baby swallowing at different stages of pregnancy.

Studies have determined how much fluid a fetus swallows and passes through its digestive system. Evidence indicates babies at full term may swallow large amounts of amniotic fluid, as much as 17 ounces (500ml) in a 24-hour period.

Amniotic fluid swallowed by the baby contributes a small amount to its caloric needs. Researchers believe it may contribute essential nutrients to the developing baby.

Meconium

During your pregnancy, you may hear the term *meconium* and wonder what it means. It refers to undigested debris from swallowed amniotic fluid in the fetal digestive system. Meconium is a greenish black to light brown substance that your baby passes from its bowels several days or weeks before delivery, during labor or after birth.

Passage of meconium into the amniotic fluid may be caused by distress in the fetus. Meconium seen during labor may be an indication of fetal distress.

If a baby has had a bowel movement before birth and meconium is present in the amniotic fluid, the fetus may swallow the fluid. If baby inhales meconium into the lungs, it could develop pneumonia or pneumonitis. For this reason, if meconium is seen at delivery, an attempt is made to remove it from the baby's mouth and throat with a small suction tube.

Changes in You

In addition to your growing uterus, other parts of your body continue to change and to grow. You may notice swelling in your lower legs and feet, particularly at the end of the day. If you're on your feet a lot, you may notice less swelling if you're able to get off your feet and rest for a while during the day.

Blood Clots in the Legs

A serious complication of pregnancy is a blood clot in the legs or groin. Symptoms of the problem are swelling of the legs accompanied by leg pain and redness or warmth over the affected area in the legs.

The problem has many names, including *venous thrombosis, thromboembolic disease, thrombophlebitis* and *lower deep-vein thrombosis.* The problem is not limited to pregnancy, but pregnancy is a time when it is more likely to occur. This is due to the slowing of blood flow in the legs because of uterine pressure and changes in the blood and its clotting mechanisms.

Tip for Week 21

A good way to add calcium to your diet is to cook rice and oatmeal in skim milk instead of water.

The most probable cause of blood clots in the legs during pregnancy is decreased blood flow, also called *stasis.* If you have had a previous blood clot—in your legs or any other part of your body—tell your healthcare provider at the beginning of pregnancy. He or she needs to know this important information.

Deep-Vein Thrombosis

Superficial thrombosis and *deep-vein thrombosis* in the leg are different conditions. A blood clot in the superficial veins of the leg is not as serious. This condition is usually noted in veins close to the surface of the skin that can often be felt on the surface. This type of clot is treated with a mild pain reliever such as acetaminophen (Tylenol), elevation of the leg, support of the leg with an Ace™ bandage or support stockings and occasionally heat. If the condition doesn't improve rapidly, deep-vein thrombosis must be considered.

Deep-vein thrombosis is more serious; it requires diagnostic procedures and treatment. Symptoms of deep-vein thrombosis in the lower leg can differ greatly, depending on the location of the

clot and how bad it is. The onset of deep-vein thrombosis can be rapid, with severe pain and swelling of the leg and thigh.

With deep-vein thrombosis, the leg may occasionally appear pale and cool, but usually a portion of the leg is tender, hot and swollen. Often skin over the affected veins is red. There may even be streaks of red on the skin over veins where blood clots have occurred.

Squeezing the calf or leg may be extremely painful, and it may be equally painful to walk. One way to tell if you have deep-vein thrombosis is to lie down and flex your toes toward your knee. If the back of the leg is tender, it is a positive indication of this problem (Homan's sign). (This type of pain may also occur with a strained muscle or a bruise.) Check with your healthcare provider if this occurs.

Diagnostic studies of deep-vein thrombosis may be different for a pregnant woman than for a nonpregnant woman. In the nonpregnant woman, an X-ray may be accompanied by an injection of dye into leg veins to look for blood clots. This test is not usually performed on a pregnant woman because of exposure to radiation and the dye. Ultrasound is used to diagnose this problem in pregnant women. Most major medical centers offer it, but the test is not available everywhere.

Treatment of deep-vein thrombosis usually consists of hospitalization and heparin therapy. Heparin (a blood thinner) must be given intravenously; it cannot be taken as a pill. It is safe during pregnancy and is not passed to the fetus. A woman may be required to take extra calcium during pregnancy if she receives heparin. While heparin is being administered, the woman is required to stay in bed. The leg may be elevated and heat applied. Mild pain medicine is prescribed.

Recovery time, including hospitalization, may be 7 to 10 days. After this time, the woman continues taking heparin until delivery. Following pregnancy, she will need to continue taking a blood thinner for up to several weeks, depending on the severity of the clot.

If a woman has a blood clot during one pregnancy, she will likely need heparin during subsequent pregnancies. If so, heparin can be given by an in-dwelling I.V. catheter or by daily injections the woman administers to herself under her healthcare provider's supervision.

Another medication used to treat deep-vein thrombosis is warfarin, an oral medication. Warfarin (Coumadin®) is not given during pregnancy because it crosses the placenta and can be harmful to the baby. Warfarin is usually given to the woman after pregnancy to prevent blood clots. It may be prescribed for a few weeks or a few months, depending on the severity of the clot.

If you have had a blood clot in the past for any reason, pregnancy-related or not, see your healthcare provider early in pregnancy. Tell him or her about any problems you've had with blood clots at your first prenatal visit.

The greatest danger from deep-vein thrombosis is a pulmonary embolism, in which a piece of the blood clot breaks off and travels from the legs to the lungs. This is a rare problem during pregnancy and is reported in only 1 in every 3,000 to 7,000 deliveries. Although it is a serious complication in pregnancy, it can often be avoided with proper treatment.

How Your Actions Affect Your Baby's Development

Safety of Ultrasound

On page 202 is an illustration of an ultrasound exam, accompanied by an interpretive illustration. These show a baby inside a uterus; the mother-to-be also has a large cyst in her abdomen.

Many women wonder about the safety of ultrasound exams. Most medical researchers agree that ultrasound exams do not pose any significant risk to you or your baby. Researchers have looked for potential problems many times without finding evidence that the test causes any.

Ultrasound is an extremely valuable tool in diagnosing problems and answering some questions during pregnancy. Information that

Cyst in abdomen

Body

Head

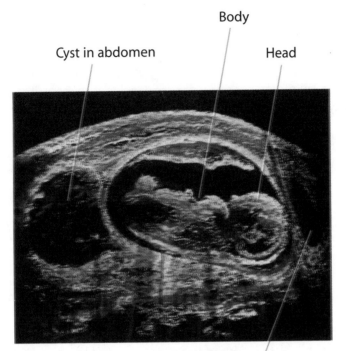

Mother's bladder

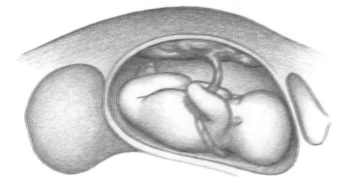

*Ultrasound is also used to detect problems.
In this ultrasound of a baby in-utero, there is a
cyst in the mother-to-be's abdomen. The interpretive
illustration clarifies the ultrasound image.*

ultrasound testing provides can be reassuring to the healthcare provider and the pregnant woman.

If your caregiver has recommended ultrasound for you and you're concerned about it, discuss it with him or her. Your caregiver may have an important reason for doing an ultrasound exam. It could affect the well-being of your developing baby.

Your Nutrition

Some women experience food cravings during pregnancy. Food cravings have long been considered a nonspecific sign of pregnancy. Craving a particular food can be both good and bad. If the food you crave is nutritious and healthful, eat it in  moderation. Don't eat food that isn't good for you. If you crave foods that are high in fat and sugar or loaded with empty calories, be careful. Take a little taste, but don't let yourself go. Try eating another food, such as a piece of fresh fruit or some cheese, instead of indulging in your craving.

We don't understand all the reasons a woman might crave a food while she's pregnant. We believe the hormonal and emotional changes that occur in pregnancy contribute to the situation.

On the opposite side of cravings is food aversion. Some foods that you have eaten without problems before pregnancy may now make you sick to your stomach. This is common. Again, we believe the hormones of pregnancy are involved. In this case, hormones affect the gastrointestinal tract, which can affect your reaction to some foods.

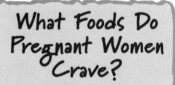

What Foods Do Pregnant Women Crave?

Recent research indicates three common cravings among pregnant women.

- 33% crave chocolate.
- 20% crave sweets of some sort.
- 19% crave citrus fruits and juices.

You Should Also Know

Will You Get Varicose Veins?

Varicose veins, also called *varicosities* or *varices*, occur to some degree in most pregnant women. There appears to be an inherited predisposition to varicose veins that can be made more severe by pregnancy, increased age and pressure caused by standing for long periods of time.

Varicose veins are blood vessels that are engorged with blood. They occur primarily in the legs but may also be present in the vulva. The change in blood flow and pressure from the uterus make varices worse, which causes discomfort.

In most instances, varicose veins become more noticeable and more painful as pregnancy progresses. With increasing weight (especially if you spend a lot of time standing), they will get worse.

Symptoms vary. For some, the main symptom is a blemish or purple-blue spot on the legs with little or no discomfort, except perhaps in the evening. Other women have bulging veins that require elevation at the end of the day.

Following pregnancy, swelling in the veins should go down, but varicose veins probably won't disappear altogether. Various

Treating Varicose Veins

Following these measures may help keep veins from swelling as much.

- Wear medical support hose; many types are available. Ask your doctor for a recommendation.
- Wear clothing that doesn't restrict circulation at the knee or the groin.
- Spend as little time on your feet as you can. Lie on your side or elevate your legs when possible. This enables veins to drain more easily.
- Wear flat shoes when you can.
- Don't cross your legs. It cuts off circulation and can make problems worse.

methods, including laser treatment, injection and surgery, can get rid of these veins; the surgery is called *vein stripping*. It would be unusual to operate on varicose veins during pregnancy, although it is a treatment to consider when you are not pregnant.

Dad Tip

It's not too early to talk about baby names. Sometimes couples have very different ideas about names for their child. There are lots of books available to help you. Do you plan to honor a close friend or relative by using their name? Will you use a family name? What problems could arise if you choose a peculiar, difficult-to-say or hard-to-spell name? What nicknames go with the name? Start thinking about it now, even if you decide you won't pick a name until after you meet your baby.

Notes

Week 22

How Big Is Your Baby?

Your baby now weighs about 12.25 ounces (350g). Crown-to-rump length at this time is about 7.6 inches (19cm).

How Big Are You?

Your uterus is now about 0.8 inch (2cm) above your bellybutton or almost 9 inches (22cm) from the pubic symphysis. You may feel "comfortably pregnant." Your enlarging abdomen is not too large and doesn't get in your way much. You're still able to bend over and to sit comfortably. Walking shouldn't be an effort. Morning sickness has probably passed, and you're feeling pretty good. It's kind of fun being pregnant now!

How Your Baby Is Growing and Developing

Your baby continues to grow; its body is getting larger every day. As you can see by looking at the illustration on page 208, your baby's eyelids and even the eyebrows are developed. Fingernails are also visible.

> **It's kind of fun being pregnant now!**

Liver Function
Your baby's organ systems are becoming specialized for their particular functions. Consider the liver. The function of the fetal liver

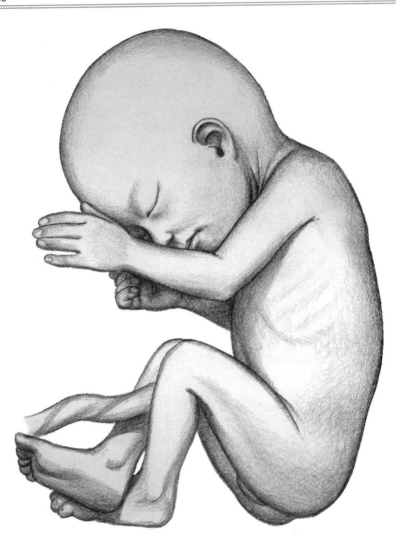

By the 22nd week of pregnancy (fetal age—20 weeks), your baby's eyelids and eyebrows are well developed. Fingernails have grown and now cover the fingertips.

is different from that of an adult. *Enzymes* (chemicals) are made in an adult liver that are important in various body functions. In the fetus, these enzymes are present but in lower levels than those present after birth.

An important function of the liver is the breakdown and handling of *bilirubin*. Bilirubin is produced by the breakdown of blood cells. The life span of a fetal red blood cell is shorter than that of an adult. Because of this, a fetus produces more bilirubin than an adult does.

The fetal liver has a limited capacity to convert bilirubin, then remove it from the fetal bloodstream. Bilirubin passes from fetal blood through the placenta to your blood. Your liver helps get rid of fetal bilirubin. If a baby is born prematurely, it may have trouble processing bilirubin because its own liver is too immature to get rid of bilirubin from the bloodstream.

A newborn baby with high bilirubin may exhibit *jaundice.* A baby with jaundice has a yellow tint to the skin and eyes. Jaundice is usually treated with phototherapy. Phototherapy uses light that penetrates the skin and destroys the bilirubin.

Jaundice in a newborn is typically triggered by the transition from bilirubin being handled by the mother's system to the baby handling it on its own. The baby's liver can't keep up. Jaundice is more likely to occur in an immature infant when the liver is not ready to take over this function. (For detailed information about your newborn, read our book *Your Baby's First Year Week by Week.)*

Changes in You

Fetal Fibronectin

In some cases, normal discomforts of pregnancy, such as lower-abdominal pain, dull backache, pelvic pressure, uterine contractions (with or without pain), cramping and a change in vaginal discharge may be confused with preterm labor. Until now, we have not had a reliable method of determining if a woman was truly at risk of delivering a preterm baby. A test is now available that can help doctors make this determination.

Fetal fibronectin (fFN) is a protein found in the amniotic sac and fetal membranes. However, after 22 weeks of pregnancy, fFN is not normally present until around week 38.

When it is present in the cervical-vaginal secretions of a pregnant woman after 22 weeks, it indicates increased risk for preterm delivery. If it is absent, risk of premature labor is low, and the woman probably won't deliver within the next 2 weeks.

The test is performed like a Pap smear. A swab of vaginal secretions is taken from the top of the vagina, behind the cervix. It is sent to the lab, and results are available within 24 hours.

Anemia in Pregnancy

Anemia is a common problem during pregnancy. If you suffer from anemia, treatment is important for you and your baby. If you are anemic, you won't feel well during pregnancy. You'll tire easily. You may experience dizziness.

What Is Anemia?

There is a fine balance in your body between the production of blood cells that carry oxygen to the rest of your body and the destruction of these cells. Anemia is the condition in which the number of red blood cells is low. If you are anemic, you have an inadequate number of red blood cells.

During pregnancy, the number of red blood cells in your bloodstream increases. The amount of *plasma* (the liquid part of the blood) also increases but at a higher rate. Your healthcare provider keeps track of these changes in your blood with a *hematocrit* reading. Your hematocrit is a measure of the percentage of the blood that is red blood cells. Your *hemoglobin* level is also tested. Hemoglobin is the protein component of red blood cells. If you are anemic, your hematocrit is lower than 37 and your hemoglobin is under 12.

A hematocrit determination is usually made at the first prenatal visit, along with other lab work. It may be repeated once or twice during pregnancy. It is done more often if you are anemic.

There is always some blood loss at delivery. If you're anemic when you go into labor, you are at higher risk of needing a blood transfusion after your baby is born. Follow your healthcare provider's advice about diet and supplementation if you suffer from anemia.

Looking Out for Iron Deficiency

Even with supplemental iron, some women develop iron-deficiency anemia during pregnancy. Several factors may make a woman more likely to have this condition in pregnancy:

- failure to take iron or failure to take a prenatal vitamin containing iron
- bleeding during pregnancy
- multiple fetuses
- previous surgery on the stomach or part of the small bowel (making it difficult to absorb an adequate amount of iron before pregnancy)
- antacid use that causes a decrease in absorption of iron
- poor dietary habits

Iron-Deficiency Anemia

The most common type of anemia seen in pregnancy is *iron-deficiency anemia*. During pregnancy, your baby uses some of the iron stores you have in your body. If you have iron-deficiency anemia, your body doesn't have enough iron left to make red blood cells because the baby has used some of your iron for its own blood cells.

Most prenatal vitamins contain iron, but it is also available as a supplement. If you are unable to take a prenatal vitamin, you may be given 300 to 350mg of ferrous sulphate or ferrous gluconate 2 or 3 times a day. Iron is the most important supplement to take. It is required in almost all pregnancies.

The goal in treating iron-deficiency anemia is to increase the amount of iron you consume. Iron is poorly absorbed through the gastrointestinal tract and must be taken on a daily basis. It can be given as an injection, but it's painful and may stain the skin.

Side effects of taking iron supplements include nausea and vomiting, with stomach upset. If this occurs, you may have to take a lower dose. Taking iron may also cause constipation.

If you cannot take an oral iron supplement, an increase in dietary iron from foods, such as liver or spinach, may help prevent anemia. Ask your healthcare provider for information on what types of foods you should include in your diet.

(continued)

Sickle Cell Anemia

For women who are dark-skinned and of Mediterranean or African descent, *sickle cell anemia* can cause significant problems during pregnancy. Anemia occurs in these cases because the bone marrow, which produces the body's red blood cells, cannot replace red blood cells as quickly as they are destroyed. In sickle cell anemia, the red blood cells produced are also abnormal, which can cause severe pain.

You may carry the trait for sickle cell anemia without having the disease. You could possibly pass the trait or the disease to your baby. Tell your healthcare provider of any family history of the disease.

A blood test easily detects the sickle cell trait. Sickle cell anemia can be diagnosed in the fetus with amniocentesis (discussed in Week 16) or chorionic villus sampling (discussed in Week 10).

Women with the sickle cell trait are more likely to have pyelonephritis (see Week 18) and bacteria in the urine during pregnancy. They are also susceptible to developing sickle cell anemia during pregnancy.

Women with sickle cell anemia may have repeated episodes of pain (sickle crises) throughout their lifetime. Pain in the abdomen or limbs is caused by the blockage of blood vessels by abnormal red blood cells. Episodes of pain may be severe and may require hospitalization for treatment with fluids and pain medication.

Hydroxurea has proved effective as treatment, but its use carries some risks. Because we do not have research data on long-term effects, pregnant women are advised not to use it.

Risks to a pregnant women with sickle cell disease are those of painful sickle crisis, infections and even congestive heart failure. Risks to the fetus include a high incidence of miscarriage and stillbirth, estimated to be as high as 50%. Even though the risks are greater, many women with sickle cell anemia have successful pregnancies.

Thalassemia

A type of anemia encountered less frequently is *thalassemia,* which occurs most often in Mediterranean populations. It is characterized by underproduction of part of the simple protein that makes up red blood cells, and anemia results. If you have a family history of thalassemia or know you have thalassemia, discuss it with your healthcare provider.

> **Even though the risks are greater, many women with sickle cell anemia have successful pregnancies.**

How Your Actions Affect Your Baby's Development

When You Feel "Under the Weather"

It's possible you could have diarrhea during pregnancy as well as viral infections, such as the flu. These problems may raise concerns for you.

- What can I do when I feel ill?
- What medication or treatment is acceptable?
- If I'm sick, should I take my prenatal vitamins?
- If I'm sick and unable to eat my usual diet, what should I do?

If you become sick during pregnancy, don't hesitate to call your healthcare provider's office. Get your caregiver's advice about a plan of action. He or she will be able to advise you about what medications you may be able to take to help you feel better. Even if it's only a cold or the flu, your caregiver wants to know when you're feeling ill. If any further measures are needed, your caregiver will recommend them.

> **Tip for Week 22**
>
> Drink extra fluids (water is best) throughout pregnancy to help your body keep up with the increases in your blood volume. You'll know you're drinking enough fluid when your urine looks like almost-clear water.

Is there anything you can do to help yourself? Yes, there is. If you have diarrhea or a possible viral infection, increase your fluid intake. Drink a lot of water, juice and other clear fluids, such as broth. You may find a bland diet without solid food helps you feel a little better.

Going off your regular diet for a few days won't be harmful to

you or your baby, but you do need to drink plenty of fluids. Solid foods may be difficult for you to handle and can make diarrhea a bigger problem. Milk products may also make diarrhea worse.

If diarrhea continues beyond 24 hours, call your healthcare provider. Ask which medications you can take for diarrhea during pregnancy.

Don't take any medication without consulting your healthcare provider first. Usually a viral illness with diarrhea is a short-term problem and won't last more than a few days. You may have to stay home from work or rest in bed until you feel better.

Your Nutrition

You need to drink water and other fluids during pregnancy—lots of it! Fluid helps your body process nutrients, develop new cells, keep up your blood volume and regulate body temperature. You may feel better during your pregnancy if you drink more water than you normally do.

Studies show that for every 15 calories your body burns, you need about 1 tablespoon of water. If you burn 2,000 calories a day, you need to drink about 2 quarts of water! Because your calorie needs increase during pregnancy, so does your need for water. Six to eight glasses a day is a good target. You can meet your goal of at least 2 quarts a day by sipping water or some other fluid throughout the day. If you decrease your consumption later in the day, you may save yourself some trips to the bathroom at night.

Some women wonder if they can drink other beverages besides water. Water is the best source of fluid; however, other fluid sources help meet your needs. You can drink milk, vegetable juice, fruit juice and some herbal teas. Eating vegetables and fruits, other milk products, meat and grain products also help you meet your fluid-consumption target. Avoid tea, coffee and cola—they may contain sodium and caffeine, which act as diuretics, which means they essentially increase your water needs.

> **Some of the common problems women experience during pregnancy may be eased by drinking water.**

Some of the common problems women experience during pregnancy may be eased by drinking water. Headaches, uterine cramping and bladder infections may be less of a problem for you when you drink lots of water.

Check your urine to see if you're drinking enough. If it is light yellow to clear, you're getting enough fluid. Dark yellow urine is a sign to increase your fluid intake. Don't wait till you get thirsty to drink something. By the time you get thirsty, you've already lost at least 1% of your body's fluids.

You Should Also Know

Appendicitis

Appendicitis can happen at any time, even during pregnancy. Pregnancy can make the diagnosis difficult because some of the symptoms are typical in a normal pregnancy, such as nausea and vomiting. Diagnosis is also difficult because as the uterus grows larger, the appendix moves upward and outward, so pain and tenderness are located in a different place than normal. See the illustration below.

Treatment for appendicitis is immediate surgery. This is major abdominal surgery, with a 3- or 4-inch incision, and it requires a few days in the hospital. Laparoscopy, with smaller incisions, is used in

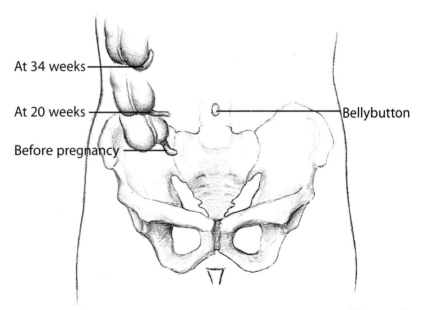

Location of the appendix during pregnancy

some situations, but laparoscopy may be more difficult to perform during pregnancy because of the enlarged uterus.

Serious complications can arise when an infected appendix ruptures. Most physicians believe it's better to operate and remove a "normal" appendix than to risk infection of the abdominal cavity if the infected appendix ruptures. Antibiotics are administered; many antibiotics are safe to use during pregnancy.

Dad Tip

When you ride in the car with your partner, ask if you can help her in any way. You may offer to assist her getting in and out of the car. You may propose trading vehicles (if you have more than one), if it's more comfortable for her to drive the other car. Ask if she needs help adjusting her seat belt or the car seat. Try to make riding and driving as easy and accessible as possible for her.

Week 23

How Big Is Your Baby?

By this week, your baby weighs almost 1 pound (455g)! Its crown-to-rump length is 8 inches (20cm). Your baby is about the size of a small doll.

How Big Are You?

Your uterus extends about 1.5 inches (3.75cm) above your bellybutton or about 9.2 inches (23cm) from the pubic symphysis. The changes in your abdomen are progressing slowly, but you definitely have a round appearance now. Your total weight gain should be between 12 and 15 pounds (5.5 and 6.8kg).

How Your Baby Is Growing and Developing

Your baby is continuing to grow. Its body is getting plumper, but its skin is still wrinkled because it will gain even more weight. See the illustration on page 218. Lanugo hair on the body occasionally turns darker at this time. The baby's face and body begin to assume more of the appearance of an infant at birth.

Pancreas Function
Your baby's pancreas is developing. This organ is important in hormone production, particularly insulin production; insulin is necessary for the body to break down and to use sugar.

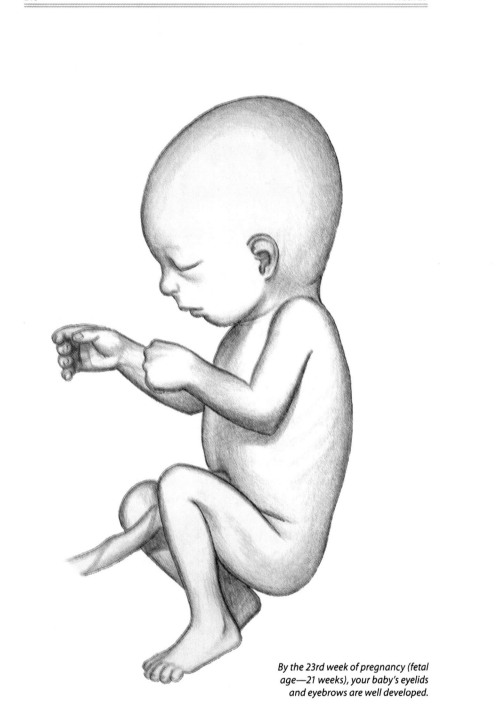

By the 23rd week of pregnancy (fetal age—21 weeks), your baby's eyelids and eyebrows are well developed.

When the fetus is exposed to high blood-sugar levels, the fetal pancreas responds by increasing the blood-insulin level. Insulin has been identified in a fetal pancreas as early as 9 weeks of pregnancy. Insulin in fetal blood has been detected as early as 12 weeks of pregnancy.

Insulin levels are generally high in the blood of babies born to diabetic mothers. That is one reason your doctor may monitor you for diabetes.

Changes in You

At this point, friends may comment on your size. They may say you must be carrying twins because you're so large. Or they may say you're too small for how far along you think you are. If these comments concern you, discuss them with your doctor.

Your doctor will measure you at every visit after this point. He or she is watching for changes in your weight gain and in the size of your uterus. Remember that women and babies are different sizes and grow at different rates. What's important for you is continual change and continual growth.

As your baby gets larger, the placenta gets larger. The amount of amniotic fluid also increases.

Loss of Fluid

As your pregnancy progresses, your uterus grows larger and gets heavier. In early pregnancy, it lies directly behind the bladder, in front of the rectum and the lower part of the colon, which is part of the bowel.

Later in pregnancy, the uterus sits on top of the bladder. As it increases in size, it can put a great deal of pressure on your bladder. You may notice times when your underwear is wet. You may be uncertain whether you have lost urine or if you are leaking amniotic fluid. It may be difficult to tell the difference between the two. However, when your membranes rupture, you usually experience a gush of fluid or a continual leaking from the vagina. If you experience this, call your doctor immediately!

Emotional Changes Continue

Do you find your mood swings are worse? Are you still crying easily? Do you wonder if you'll ever be in control again?

Don't worry. These emotions are typical at this point in your pregnancy. Most authorities believe they occur from the hormonal changes that continue throughout pregnancy.

There is little you can do about periods of moodiness. If you think your partner or others are suffering from your emotional outbursts, talk about it with them. Explain that these feelings are common in pregnant women. Ask them to be understanding. Then relax; try not to get upset about it. Feeling emotional is a normal part of being pregnant.

How Your Actions Affect Your Baby's Development

Diabetes in Pregnancy
Once a very serious problem during pregnancy, diabetes continues to be an important complication. Today, however, many diabetic women go through pregnancy safely with proper medical care and good nutrition—and by following their doctor's instructions.

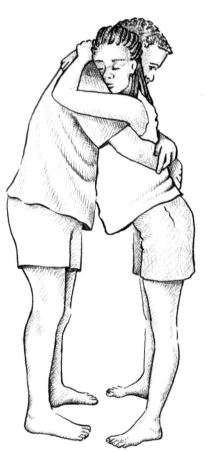

Diabetes is a condition defined as a lack of insulin in the bloodstream. Insulin is important for breaking down sugar and transporting it to the cells. If you do not have insulin, you will have high blood sugar and a high sugar content in your urine.

The condition can cause several medical problems, including kidney problems, eye problems and other blood or vascular problems, such as atherosclerosis or myocardial infarction (heart attack). These can be serious for you and your baby.

Before insulin was available, it was unusual for a diabetic woman to get pregnant. With the discovery of insulin and the development of various ways to monitor a fetus, it is uncommon to have a severe problem today. Survival rate of babies is good.

Pregnancy is well known for its tendency to reveal women who are predisposed to diabetes. Women who have trouble with high blood-sugar levels during pregnancy are more likely to develop diabetes in later life. Symptoms of diabetes include the following:

- more frequent urination
- blurred vision
- weight loss
- dizziness
- increased hunger

> **Today many diabetic women have safe pregnancies with proper medical care and good nutrition—and by following their doctor's instructions.**

It may be necessary to do blood tests to diagnose diabetes during pregnancy. In some areas, this testing is done routinely.

If you have diabetes or know members of your family have had diabetes in the past, tell your doctor. He or she will decide what course of action is best for you.

Gestational Diabetes

Some women develop diabetes only during pregnancy, called *gestational diabetes*. Gestational diabetes affects about 10% of all pregnancies. After pregnancy is over, nearly all women who experience this problem return to normal, and the problem disappears. However, if gestational diabetes occurs with one pregnancy, there is almost a 90% chance it will recur in subsequent pregnancies.

We believe gestational diabetes occurs for two reasons. One is the mother's body produces less insulin during pregnancy. The second is the mother's body can't use insulin appropriately. Both situations result in high blood-sugar levels.

A woman's weight when she was born may be an indicator of her chances of developing gestational diabetes. A study showed women who were in the bottom 10th percentile of weight when they were born were 3 to 4 times more likely to develop gestational diabetes during pregnancy.

If left untreated, gestational diabetes can be serious for you and your baby. You will both be exposed to a high concentration of sugar, which is not healthy for either of you. You might experience *polyhydramnios* (excessive amounts of amniotic fluid). This may cause premature labor because the uterus becomes overdistended.

A woman with gestational diabetes may have a long labor because the baby is quite large. Sometimes a baby cannot fit through the birth canal, and a Cesarean delivery is required.

If your blood-sugar level is high, you may experience more infections during pregnancy. The most common include those in the kidneys, the bladder, the cervix and the uterus.

Treatment of gestational diabetes includes regular exercise and increased fluid intake. Diet is essential in handling this problem. Your doctor will probably recommend a six-meal, 2,000- to 2,500-calorie per day eating plan. You may also be referred to a dietitian.

Your Nutrition

You may need to be careful with your sodium intake during pregnancy. Consuming too much sodium may cause you to retain water, which can cause swelling and bloating. Avoid foods that contain lots of sodium or salt, such as salted nuts, potato chips, pickles, and canned and processed foods.

Read food labels. They list the amount of sodium in a serving. Some books list the sodium content of foods without labels, such as fast foods. Check them out. You'll be surprised how many milligrams of sodium a fast-food hamburger contains!

Look at the chart on page 223, which lists some common foods and their sodium content. You can see foods that contain sodium do not always taste salty. Read labels, and check other available information before you eat!

You Should Also Know

Sugar in Your Urine

It is common for nondiabetic pregnant women to have a small amount of sugar in their urine. This occurs because of changes in sugar levels and how sugar is handled in the kidneys, which control the amount of sugar in your system. If excess sugar is present, you will lose it through the urine. Sugar in the urine is called *glucosuria*. It is common during pregnancy, particularly in the second and third trimesters.

Sodium Content of Various Foods

Food	Serving Size	Sodium Content (mg)
American cheese	1 slice	322
Asparagus	14.5-oz. can	970
Big Mac hamburger	1 regular	963
Chicken a la king	1 cup	760
Cola	8 oz.	16
Cottage cheese	1 cup	580
Dill pickle	1 medium	928
Flounder	3 oz.	201
Gelatin, sweet	3 oz.	270
Ham, baked	3 oz.	770
Honeydew melon	1/2	90
Lima beans	8.5-oz. can	1,070
Lobster	1 cup	305
Oatmeal	1 cup	523
Potato chips	20 regular	400
Salt	1 teaspoon	1,938

Many doctors test every pregnant woman for diabetes, usually around the end of the second trimester. Testing is particularly important if you have a family history of diabetes. Blood tests used to diagnose diabetes are a fasting-blood-sugar and glucose-tolerance test (GTT).

For a fasting-blood-sugar test, you eat the evening before the test. In the morning, before eating anything, you go to the lab and have the blood test done. A normal result indicates that diabetes is unlikely. An abnormal result is a high level of sugar in the blood, which needs further study.

Further study involves taking the glucose-tolerance test. You have to fast the night before this test. In the morning at the lab, you are

Tip for Week 23

Keep your consumption of sodium to 3 grams (3,000mg) or less a day. This may help you reduce fluid retention.

given a solution to drink that has a measured amount of sugar in it. It is similar to a bottle of soda pop but doesn't taste as good.

Before you drink the sugar solution, a fasting-blood-sugar test is done. After you drink the solution, blood is drawn at predetermined intervals; usually at 30 minutes, 1 hour and 2 hours and sometimes even 3 hours. Drawing the blood at intervals gives an indication of how your body handles sugar.

If you need treatment, your doctor will devise a plan for you.

Dad Tip

Are you also having pregnancy symptoms? Studies show that as many as 50% of all fathers-to-be experience physical symptoms of pregnancy when their partner is pregnant. *Couvade,* a French term meaning "to hatch," is used to describe the condition in a man. Symptoms for an expectant father may include nausea, weight gain and cravings for certain foods.

Week 24

How Big Is Your Baby?

By this week, your baby weighs about 1.2 pounds (540g). Its crown-to-rump length is about 8.4 inches (21cm).

How Big Are You?

Your uterus is now about 1.5 to 2 inches (3.8 to 5.1cm) above the bellybutton. It measures almost 10 inches (24cm) above the pubic symphysis.

How Your Baby Is Growing and Developing

Your baby is filling out. Its face and body look more like that of an infant at the time of birth. Although it weighs a little over 1 pound at this point, it is still tiny.

Role of the Amniotic Sac and Amniotic Fluid

By about the 12th day after fertilization, there is an early beginning of the amniotic sac. The baby grows and develops in the amniotic fluid inside the amniotic sac. (See the illustration on page 226.) Amniotic fluid has several important functions.

- It provides an environment in which the baby can move easily.
- It cushions the fetus against injury.
- Amniotic fluid regulates temperature for the baby.
- It provides a way of assessing the health and maturity of the baby.

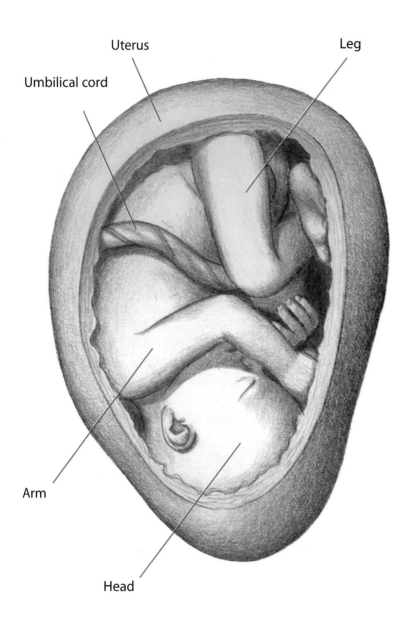

Uterus

Leg

Umbilical cord

Arm

Head

The fetus doesn't appear to have a great deal of room to move in the uterus by the 24th week. As the weeks pass, space gets even tighter!

Amniotic fluid increases rapidly from an average volume of 1.5 ounces (50ml) by 12 weeks of pregnancy to 12 ounces (400ml) at midpregnancy. Following the 24th week of pregnancy, the volume of amniotic fluid continues to increase as your due date approaches. There is a maximum of about 2 pints (1 liter) of fluid at 36 to 38 weeks' gestation.

Composition of amniotic fluid changes during pregnancy. During the first half of pregnancy, amniotic fluid is similar to maternal plasma (the fluid in blood without blood cells), except it has a much lower protein content. As pregnancy advances, fetal urine makes an increasingly important contribution to the amount of amniotic fluid present. Amniotic fluid also contains old fetal blood cells, lanugo hair and vernix.

The fetus swallows amniotic fluid during much of pregnancy. If it can't swallow amniotic fluid, you will develop a condition of excess amniotic fluid, called *hydramnios* or *polyhydramnios*. If the fetus swallows but doesn't urinate (for example, if the baby lacks kidneys), the volume of amniotic fluid surrounding the fetus may be very small. This is called *oligohydramnios*.

Amniotic fluid is important. It provides the baby space to move and allows it to grow. If there is an inadequate amount of amniotic fluid, the baby usually shows decreased growth.

Changes in You

Nasal Problems
Some women complain of stuffiness in their nose or frequent nosebleeds during pregnancy. Some researchers believe these symptoms occur because of changes in circulation due to hormonal changes during pregnancy. This can cause the mucous membranes of your nose and nasal passageways to swell and to bleed more easily.

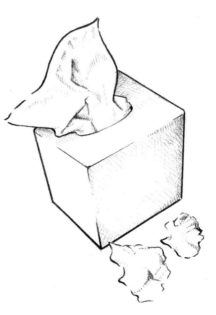

Don't try different medications, such as decongestants or nasal sprays. Many of these are combinations of several medications and may be ill-advised during pregnancy.

It may help to use a humidifier, particularly during the winter months when heating may dry out the air. Some women get relief from increasing their fluid intake and using a gentle lubricant, such as petroleum jelly. As for other relief, you may have to wait until your baby is born to breathe normally through your nose again.

How Your Actions Affect Your Baby's Development

What Your Baby Can Hear
Can a growing baby hear sounds while it's inside the uterus? From various research studies, we know that sounds can penetrate amniotic fluid and reach your baby's developing ears.

If you work in a noisy place, you may want to request a quieter area during your pregnancy. From data gathered in some studies, it is believed that chronic loud noise and short, intense bursts of sound may cause hearing damage before and after birth.

It's OK to expose your growing baby to loud noises, such as a concert, every once in a while. But if you are repeatedly exposed to noise that is so loud it forces you to shout, there may be potential danger to your baby.

Your Nutrition

Many pregnant women are concerned about eating out. Some want to know if they can eat certain types of food, such as Mexican, Vietnamese, Thai or Greek food. They're concerned that spicy foods could be harmful to the baby. It's OK to eat out, but you might find certain foods don't agree with you.

The best types of food to eat at restaurants are those you tolerate well at home. Fish, fresh vegetables and salads are usually good choices. Restaurants that feature spicy foods or unusual cuisine may cause stomach or intestinal distress. You may even notice an increase in weight from water retention after eating at a restaurant.

During pregnancy, avoid restaurants that serve highly salted food, food high in sodium or food loaded with calories and fat, such as gravies, fried food, junk food and rich desserts. It may be difficult to control your calorie intake at specialty restaurants.

Another challenge of eating out is maintaining a healthy diet when you work. It may be

> The best types of food to eat at restaurants are those you tolerate well at home.

necessary to go to business lunches or to travel for your company. Be selective. If you can choose off the menu, look for healthy or low-fat choices. You may ask about preparation—maybe a dish can be steamed instead of fried. On a business trip, take along some of your own food. Choose healthy nonperishables, such as fruits and vegetables that don't need refrigeration.

You Should Also Know

An Incompetent Cervix

An *incompetent cervix* refers to the painless premature dilatation of the cervix, which usually results in delivery of a premature baby. It can be an important problem during pregnancy.

Dilatation or stretching of the cervix goes unnoticed by the woman until the baby is delivering; it often occurs without warning. Diagnosis is usually made after one or more deliveries of a premature infant without any pain before delivery.

The cause of cervical incompetence is usually unknown. Some medical researchers believe it occurs because of previous trauma to the cervix, such as dilatation and curettage (D&C) for an abortion or a miscarriage. It may also occur after cervical surgeries.

Usually the cervix doesn't dilate like this before the 16th week of pregnancy. Before this time, the products of conception are not heavy enough to cause the cervix to dilate and to thin out.

A pregnancy that is lost from an incompetent cervix is completely different from a miscarriage. A miscarriage during the first trimester is common. Incompetent cervix is a relatively rare complication early in pregnancy.

Treatment for an incompetent cervix is usually surgical. The weak cervix is reinforced with a suture that sews the cervix shut.

If this is your first pregnancy, there is no way you can know whether you have an incompetent cervix. If you have had problems in

Tip for Week 24

Overeating and eating before going to bed at night are two major causes of heartburn. Eating five or six small, nutritious meals a day instead of three large ones may make you feel better.

the past or have had premature deliveries and have been told you might have an incompetent cervix, share this important information with your healthcare provider.

Dad Tip

Now is a good time to find out about prenatal classes in your area. Find out how many classes there are, when and where to register and the registration cost. You may be able to take classes at the hospital or birthing center where you plan to deliver. Try to complete the classes at least 1 month before your baby is due.

Week 25

How Big Is Your Baby?

Your baby now weighs about 1.5 pounds (700g), and crown-to-rump length is about 8.8 inches (22cm). These are average lengths and weights and vary from one baby to another and from one pregnancy to another.

How Big Are You?

Look at the illustration on page 232. By this week of pregnancy, your uterus has grown quite a bit. When you look at a side view, you're obviously getting bigger.

The measurement from the pubic symphysis to the top of your uterus is about 10 inches (25cm). If you saw your healthcare provider when you were 20 or 21 weeks pregnant, you have probably grown about 1.5 inches (4cm). At this point, your uterus is about the size of a soccer ball.

The top of the uterus is about halfway between your bellybutton and the lower part of your sternum. (The sternum is the bone between your breasts where the ribs come together.)

How Your Baby Is Growing and Developing

Survival of a Premature Baby
It may be hard to believe, but if your baby were delivered at this time, it would have a chance of surviving. Some of the greatest

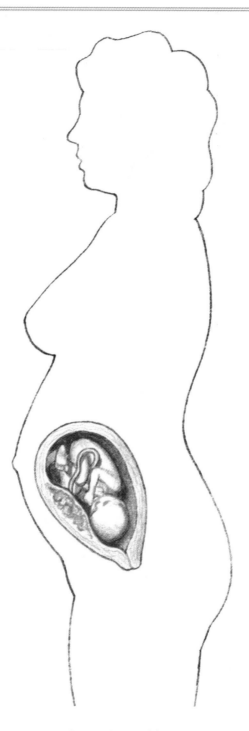

Comparative size of the uterus at 25 weeks of pregnancy (fetal age—23 weeks). The uterus can be felt about 2 inches (5cm) above your umbilicus (bellybutton).

Is It a Boy? Is It a Girl?

One of the most common questions parents-to-be ask is, "What is the sex of our baby?" Amniocentesis can reveal the sex of the baby by chromosome study. Ultrasound examination can also be used to determine the sex of the baby, but it may be inaccurate. Don't get your heart set on a particular sex if ultrasound is used. For many people, not knowing is part of the fun of having a baby.

Some people believe a baby's heartbeat rate can indicate its sex. A normal heart rate for a baby ranges from 120 to 160 beats a minute. Some believe a fast heartbeat indicates a girl, and a slow heartbeat indicates a boy. Unfortunately, there is no scientific proof of this. Don't pressure your healthcare provider to guess based on this method because it is only a guess.

A more reliable source might be a mother, mother-in-law or someone who can look at you and tell by how you're carrying the baby if it is a boy or girl. Although we make this statement with our tongues placed firmly in our cheeks, many people believe it's true. Some people claim they're never wrong about guessing or predicting the sex of a baby before birth. Again, there is no scientific basis for this.

Your healthcare provider is more concerned about your health and well-being and that of your baby. He or she will concentrate on making sure you and your baby, whether it's a boy or girl, are progressing through pregnancy safely and that you both get through pregnancy, labor and delivery in good health.

advances in medicine have been in the care of the premature baby. No one wants a baby to deliver this early, but with new treatment methods, such as ventilators, monitors and medication, a baby does have a chance of living.

The baby weighs less than 2 pounds and is extremely small. Survival is difficult for an infant delivered this early. The baby would probably spend several months in the hospital, with risks of infection and other possible complications.

Changes in You

Abdominal Itching

As your uterus has grown and filled your pelvis, your abdominal skin and muscles have stretched. Itchiness is a fairly natural consequence. Lotions are OK to use to help reduce itching. Try not to scratch and irritate your skin—that can make it worse! (See also Your Skin, page 130.)

How Your Actions Affect Your Baby's Development

Falling and Injuries from Falls

A fall is the most frequent cause of minor injury during pregnancy. Fortunately, a fall is usually without serious injury to the baby or mother. The uterus is well protected in the abdomen inside the bony pelvis. The baby is protected against injury by the cushion of amniotic fluid surrounding it. Your uterus and abdominal wall also offer some protection.

If You Fall

If you fall, contact your healthcare provider; he or she may want to examine you. You may feel reassured if you are monitored and your baby's heartbeat is checked. The baby's movement after a fall can be reassuring.

Minor injuries to the abdomen are treated in the usual fashion, as though you were not pregnant. However, avoid X-rays if possible. Ultrasound evaluation may be important after a fall. This is judged on an individual basis, depending on the severity of your symptoms and your injury.

Take Care to Avoid Falls

Remember your balance and mobility change as you grow larger during pregnancy. Be careful during the winter when parking lots and sidewalks may be wet or icy. Many pregnant women also fall on stairs. Always use the handrail.

> **Tip for Week 25**
>
> Pregnancy can be a time of communication and personal growth with your partner. Listen when he talks. Let him know he is an important source of emotional support for you.

Signs to Watch for after a Fall

Some signs can alert you to a problem after a fall:

- bleeding
- a gush of fluid from the vagina, indicating rupture of membranes
- severe abdominal pain

Placental abruption (discussed in Week 33) is one of the most serious events that can occur because of a fall or injury. With placental abruption, the placenta prematurely separates from the uterus. Another significant injury is a broken bone or an injury that immobilizes you. (See the discussion below.)

Slow down a little as you get larger; you won't be able to get around as quickly as you normally do. With the change in your balance, plus any dizziness you may experience, it's important to be vigilant about trying to avoid falling.

Treating Broken Bones

Sometimes a fall or accident causes a broken bone, which may require X-rays and surgery. Treatment cannot be delayed until after pregnancy; the problem must be dealt with immediately. If you find yourself in such a situation, insist your OB/GYN be contacted before any test or treatment is done.

If X-rays are required, your pelvis and abdomen must be shielded. If they cannot be shielded, the need for the X-ray must be weighed against the risks it poses to the baby.

Anesthesia or pain medication may be necessary with a simple break that requires setting or pinning. It is best for you and the baby to avoid general anesthesia if possible. You may need pain medication, but keep its use to a minimum.

If general anesthesia is required to repair a break, the baby should be monitored closely. You may not have a lot of choice in the matter. Your surgeon and OB/GYN will work together to provide the best care for you and your baby.

Your Nutrition

Pregnancy increases your need for vitamins and minerals. It's best if you can meet most of these needs through the foods you eat. However, being realistic, we know that's difficult for many women. That's one reason your healthcare provider prescribes a prenatal vitamin for you—to help you meet your nutritional needs.

Some women do need extra help during pregnancy—supplements are often prescribed for them. These pregnant women include teenagers (whose bodies are still growing), severely underweight women, women who ate a poor diet before conception and women who have previously given birth to multiples. Women who smoke or drink heavily need supplements, as do some who have a chronic medical condition, those who take certain medications and those who have problems digesting cow's milk, wheat and other essential foods. In some cases, vegetarians may need supplements.

> ### Caution!
> **Never take any supplements without your caregiver's approval and consent!**

Your healthcare provider will discuss the situation with you. If you need more than a prenatal vitamin, he or she will give you advice. Caution: Never take any supplements without your caregiver's approval and consent! (See Your Nutrition in Week 27.)

You Should Also Know

Thyroid Disease

Thyroid problems and thyroid disease can affect your pregnancy. Thyroid hormone is made in the thyroid gland; this hormone affects your entire body and is important in your metabolism.

Thyroid-hormone levels may be high or low. High levels of thyroid cause a condition called *hyperthyroidism*; low levels cause *hypothyroidism*. Women who have a history of miscarriage or premature delivery or who have problems around the time of delivery may have problems with their thyroid-hormone levels.

Symptoms of thyroid disease may be hidden by pregnancy. Or you may notice changes during pregnancy that cause you and your healthcare provider to suspect the thyroid is not functioning properly. These changes could include an enlarged thyroid, changes in your pulse, redness of the palms and warm, moist palms. Because thyroid-hormone levels can change during pregnancy (because of pregnancy), your healthcare provider must be careful interpreting lab results about this hormone while you're pregnant.

The thyroid is tested primarily by blood tests (a thyroid panel), which measure the amount of thyroid hormone produced. The tests also measure levels of another hormone, *thyroid-stimulating hormone* (TSH), made at the base of the brain. Another test, an X-ray study of the thyroid (radioactive iodine scan), should not be done during pregnancy.

If you have hypothyroidism, thyroid replacement (thyroxin) is prescribed. It is believed to be safe during pregnancy. Your healthcare provider may check the level during pregnancy with a blood test to make sure you are receiving enough of the hormone.

If you have hyperthyroidism, the medication propylthiouracil is used for treatment. It does pass through the placenta to the baby. Your healthcare provider will prescribe the lowest possible amount to reduce risk to your baby. Blood testing during pregnancy is necessary to monitor the amount of medication needed. Iodide is another medication used for hyperthyroidism. Avoid iodide during pregnancy because of harmful effects to a developing baby.

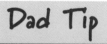

Dad Tip

Offer to do the shopping. This may be an unsettling prospect for some men, but cell phones have made men better shoppers. Even if you don't shop solo, go with your partner to lift and to carry her purchases.

After delivery, it's important to test the baby and to watch for signs of thyroid problems related to the medications prescribed during pregnancy. If you have a past history of problems with your thyroid, if you are now taking medication or if you have taken medication in the past for your thyroid, tell your healthcare provider. Discuss treatment during pregnancy.

Notes

Week 26

How Big Is Your Baby?

Your baby now weighs almost 2 pounds (910g). By this week, its crown-to-rump length is around 9.2 inches (23cm). See the illustration on page 240. Your baby is beginning to put on weight.

How Big Are You?

The measurement of your uterus is about 2.5 inches (6cm) above your bellybutton or nearly 10.5 inches (26cm) from your pubic symphysis. During this second half of pregnancy, you will grow about 0.4 inch (1cm) each week. If you have been following a nutritious, balanced meal plan, your total weight gain is probably between 16 and 22 pounds (7.2 to 9.9kg).

How Your Baby Is Growing and Developing

By now you have heard your baby's heartbeat at several visits. Listening to your developing baby's heartbeat is reassuring.

Heart Arrhythmia
When listening to your baby's heartbeat during pregnancy, you may be startled to hear a skipped beat. An irregular heartbeat is called an *arrhythmia*. This is best described by regular pulsing or pounding with an occasional skipped or missed heartbeat. Arrhythmias in a fetus are not unusual.

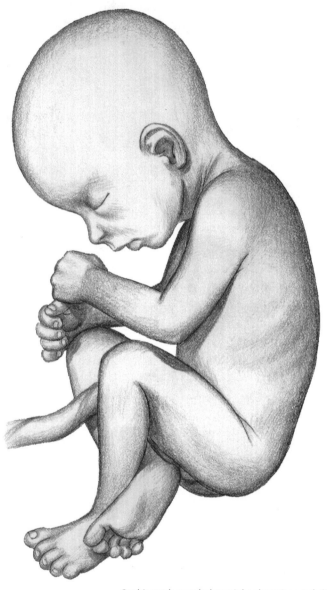

By this week, your baby weighs about 2 pounds (910g).
It is now putting on some weight and filling out.

There are many causes of fetal arrhythmias. An arrhythmia may occur as the heart grows and develops. As the heart matures, the arrhythmia often disappears. It may occur in the fetus of a pregnant woman who has lupus.

If an arrhythmia is discovered before labor and delivery, you may require fetal heart-rate monitoring during labor. (See Weeks 34 and 38.)

When an arrhythmia is detected during labor, it may be desirable to have a pediatrician present at the time of delivery. He or she will make sure the baby is all right and is treated right away if a problem exists.

Changes in You

You are getting bigger as your uterus, placenta and baby grow larger. Discomforts such as back pain, pressure in your pelvis, leg cramps and headaches may occur more frequently.

Time is passing quickly. You are approaching the end of the second trimester. Two-thirds of the pregnancy is behind you; it won't be long until your baby is born.

How Your Actions Affect Your Baby's Development

Home Uterine Monitoring

Home uterine monitoring is used to identify women with premature labor. Conditions associated with premature delivery include a previous preterm delivery, infections, premature rupture of membranes, pregnancy-induced hypertension and multiple fetuses.

Home uterine monitoring combines recording uterine contractions with daily telephone contact with the healthcare provider. A recording of contractions is transmitted from the woman's home by telephone to a center where contractions can be evaluated. Thanks to personal computers, your caregiver may be able to view the recordings at his or her own home.

Cost for home monitoring varies but runs between $80 and $100 a day; some insurance companies cover it. The cost of home monitoring can often be justified if a premature delivery is prevented—it saves thousands of dollars in the care of a premature baby (sometimes more than $100,000).

Not everyone agrees that home monitoring is beneficial or cost-effective. It may be difficult to identify all the patients who need this type of monitoring. The need for home uterine monitoring should be considered on an individual basis. Discuss this option with your physician if you have experienced preterm labor in the past or have other risk factors for preterm labor.

Your Nutrition

You're in the last week of your second trimester of pregnancy. About this time, you may be having a harder time with your food plan than you had earlier

in your pregnancy. You may be bored with the foods you've been eating. Your baby is getting larger, and you don't seem to have as much room for food. Heartburn or indigestion may also be problems now.

Don't give up on good nutrition! It's important to continue to pay attention to what you eat. Be vigilant so you continue to provide your baby the best nutrition it needs before its birth.

Every day, try to eat one serving of a dark green leafy vegetable, a serving of food or juice rich in vitamin C, and one serving of a food rich in vitamin A (many foods that are yellow, such as yams, carrots and cantaloupes, are good sources of vitamin A). Remember to keep up your fluid intake.

A Balanced Meal Plan

Breads, cereals, rice, pasta and grains, 6 to 11 servings—1 slice of bread, ½ bun, ½ English muffin or bagel, ½ cup cooked pasta, rice or hot cereal, 4 crackers, ¾ cup cooked cereal

Fruit, 2 to 4 servings—¼ cup dried fruit, ½ cup fresh, canned or cooked fruit, ¾ cup juice

Vegetables, 3 to 5 servings—½ cup cooked vegetables, 1 cup leafy salad vegetables, ¾ cup juice

Protein sources, 2 to 3 servings—2 to 3 ounces of cooked poultry, meat or fish, 1 cup cooked beans, ¼ cup seeds or nuts, ½ cup tofu, 2 eggs

Dairy products, 4 servings—1 cup milk (any type), a cup yogurt, 1½ ounces cheese, 1½ cups of cottage cheese, 1½ cups frozen yogurt or ice cream

Fats, oils and sweets—limit intake of these food products and concentrate on nutritious, healthy foods

You Should Also Know

Seizures

A history of seizures—before pregnancy, during a previous pregnancy or during this pregnancy—is information you must share with your healthcare provider. Another term for seizure is *convulsion*.

Seizures can and usually do occur without warning. A seizure indicates an abnormal condition related to the nervous system, particularly the brain. During a seizure, a person often loses body control. The serious nature of this problem during pregnancy is compounded because of concern about the baby's safety.

Doctors describe different types of seizures. Seizures involving the entire body are called *grand mal* seizures. A grand mal seizure begins with the sudden loss of consciousness; the person usually falls to the ground. Arms and legs often twitch, and sometimes the person loses bladder and bowel control at the same time. Following a seizure, the person may be in a state of recovery that can last for several minutes. As it passes, there can be mental confusion, headache and drowsiness.

> **Tip for Week 26**
>
> Lying on your side (your left side is best) when you rest provides the best circulation to your baby. You may not experience as much swelling if you rest on your left side during the day.

Another type of seizure is a *petit mal* seizure. This type also comes without warning. It is noted for its short duration and minimal movement of arms or legs. It usually involves a loss of consciousness that lasts only a few seconds. Other types of seizures can also occur. They are not within the scope of this book.

If you have never had a problem with seizures, know that a short episode of dizziness or lightheadedness is *not* usually a seizure. Seizures are usually diagnosed by someone observing the seizure and noting the symptoms previously mentioned. An electroencephalogram (EEG) may be needed to diagnose a seizure. (See Week 31 for discussion on seizures as they relate to eclampsia.)

Medication to Control Seizures

If you take medication for seizure control or prevention, share this important information with your healthcare provider at the beginning of pregnancy. Medication can be taken during pregnancy to control seizures, but some medications are safer than others.

For example, Dilantin® can cause birth defects in a baby, which include facial problems, microcephaly (a small head) and developmental delay. Other medications are used during pregnancy for seizure prevention. One of the more common is phenobarbital, but there is some concern about the safety of this medication.

Seizures during pregnancy or at any other time require serious discussion with your healthcare provider and increased monitoring during pregnancy. If you have questions or concerns about a history of possible seizures, talk to your caregiver about them.

Dad Tip

About now, your partner may not feel very attractive. Take her on a date—go to dinner and a movie! Tell her she's beautiful. Take a full-view picture of her as a remembrance of how lovely she is now.

Third Trimester Journal

Questions to ask at my next doctor's visit: _____

_____

_____

_____

_____

_____

Baby gear to get (car seat, crib, diapers):

_____

_____

_____

_____

_____

What to pack for the hospital:

_____

_____

_____

_____

_____

Backup names and numbers if my partner isn't available when I go into labor:

_____

_____

_____

_____

Baby names:

Girl _____   Boy _____

_____   _____

_____   _____

_____   _____

_____   _____

_____   _____

_____   _____

Notes:_____

_____

_____

_____

_____

Week 27

How Big Is Your Baby?

This week marks the beginning of the third trimester. In addition to weight and crown-to-rump length, we're adding total length of your baby's body from head to toe. This will give you an even better idea of how big your baby is during this last part of your pregnancy.

Your baby now weighs a little more than 2 pounds (1kg), and crown-to-rump length is about 9.6 inches (24cm) by this week. Total length is 15.3 inches (34cm). See the illustration on page 250.

How Big Are You?

Your uterus is about 2.8 inches (7cm) above your bellybutton. If measured from the pubic symphysis, it is more than 10.5 inches (27cm) from the pubic symphysis to the top of the uterus.

How Your Baby Is Growing and Developing

Eye Development
Eyes first appear around day 22 of development in the embryo (about 5 weeks' gestation). In the beginning, they look like a pair of shallow grooves on each side of the developing brain. These grooves continue to develop and eventually turn into pockets called *optical vesicles*. The lens of each eye develops from the ectoderm. (We discuss ectoderm in Week 4.)

Early in development, eyes are on the side of the head. They move toward the middle of the face between 7 and 10 weeks of gestation.

At about 8 weeks' gestation, blood vessels form that lead to the eye. During the 9th week of gestation, the pupil forms, which is the round opening in the eye. By the 8th or 9th week of gestation, the nerve connection from the eyes to the brain begins to form. This nerve is called the optic nerve.

Eyelids that cover the eyes are fused (connected together) at around 11 to 12 weeks. They remain fused until about 27 to 28 weeks of pregnancy, when they open.

The retina, at the back of the eye, is light-sensitive. It is the part of the eye where light images come into focus. It develops its normal layers by about the 27th week of pregnancy. These layers receive light and light information, and transmit it to the brain for interpretation—what we know as sight.

Congenital Cataracts

A congenital cataract is an eye problem that may occur at birth. Most people believe cataracts occur only in old age, but that's a misconception. They can appear in a newborn baby! Instead of being transparent or clear, the lens that focuses light onto the back of the eye is opaque or cloudy. This problem is usually caused by a genetic predisposition (it is inherited). However, it has been found in children born to mothers who had German measles (rubella) around the 6th or 7th week of pregnancy.

Microphthalmia

Another congenital eye problem is microphthalmia, in which the overall size of the eye is too small. The eyeball may be only two-thirds its normal size. This abnormality often occurs with other abnormalities of the eyes. It frequently results from maternal infections while the baby is developing inside the uterus, such as cytomegalovirus (CMV) or toxoplasmosis.

Changes in You

Feeling Your Baby Move

Feeling your baby move (quickening) is one of the more precious parts of pregnancy. Before you feel the baby move, you probably

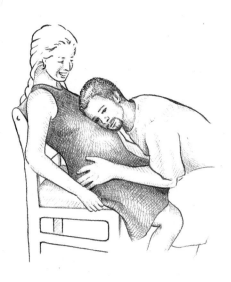

had a positive pregnancy test and heard the baby's heartbeat at your healthcare provider's office.

Feeling life inside you can be the beginning of your bonding with your baby. Many women feel they begin to relate to the baby and its personality before delivery by feeling the baby's movements. This movement is usually reassuring and a sensation most pregnant women enjoy. Your partner can experience and enjoy the baby's movements by feeling your abdomen when the baby is active.

Movement of your baby can vary in intensity. It can range from a faint flutter, sometimes described as a feeling of a butterfly or a gas bubble in early pregnancy, to brisk motions or even painful kicks and pressure as your baby gets larger.

Women often ask how often a baby should move. They want to know if they should be concerned if the baby moves too much or doesn't move enough. These are hard questions to answer because your sensation is different from that of another woman. The movement of each baby you carry may be different. It is usually more reassuring to have a baby move frequently. But it isn't unusual for a baby to have quiet times when there is not as much activity.

> **Your partner can experience and enjoy the baby's movements by feeling your abdomen when the baby is active.**

If you've been on the go, you may not have noticed the baby move because you've been active and busy. It may help to lie on your side to notice if the baby is moving or is still. Many women report that their baby is much more active at night, keeping them awake and making it hard to sleep.

If your baby is quiet and not as active as what seems normal or what you expected, discuss it with your healthcare provider. You can always visit your caregiver to hear the baby's heartbeat if the baby hasn't been moving in its usual pattern. In most instances, there is nothing to worry about.

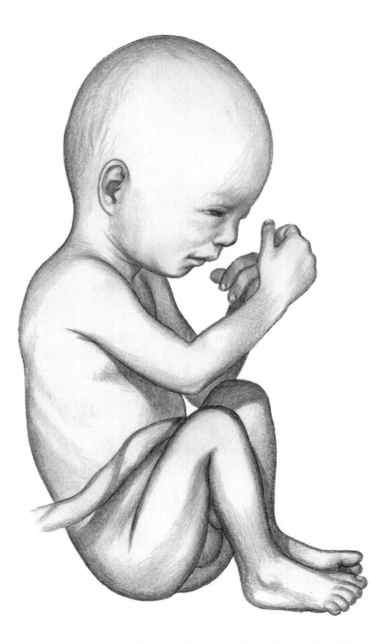

*Around this time, your baby's eyelids open. Your baby begins
opening and closing its eyes while still inside your uterus.*

A Visit with the Doctor

Jane asked me at her office visit why she was having "sharp, stabbing pains" under her ribs. I told her this was normal for some women. I advised her the best thing she could do was to lie on her side to relieve pressure in the area that was painful. If she felt pressure under her right ribs, for example, she should lie on her left side.

Pain under Your Ribs

Some women complain of pain under their ribs and in their lower abdomen when their baby moves. This type of pain isn't an unusual problem, but it may cause enough discomfort to concern you. The baby's movement has increased to a point where you will probably feel it every day, and movements are getting stronger and harder. At the same time, your uterus is getting larger and putting more pressure on all your organs. Your growing, expanding uterus presses on the small bowel, bladder and rectum.

If the pressure really is pain, don't ignore it. You need to discuss it with your healthcare provider. In most cases, it isn't a serious problem.

How Your Actions Affect Your Baby's Development

Will Working at a Computer Terminal Hurt Your Baby?

Many women are concerned about working in front of a computer screen. Currently nothing suggests that working at a computer terminal is likely to harm your unborn baby.

If you work at a computer terminal (or at a typewriter), consider the way you sit and how long you sit. Sit in a chair that offers good support for your back and legs. Don't slouch or cross your legs when sitting. Be sure to get up and walk around at least once every 15 minutes—you need to keep good circulation in your legs.

Prenatal Classes

When should you think about signing up for prenatal classes? Even though it's just the beginning of the third trimester, it isn't too early to think about and register for these classes now. It's a good idea to get signed up for classes so you can take them before you get to the end of your pregnancy. By doing this, you'll have time to practice what you learn. You won't be just beginning your classes when you deliver!

Why Should You Take Prenatal Classes?

During pregnancy, you have probably been learning what's going to happen at delivery by talking with your healthcare provider and by asking questions. You have also learned what lies ahead from reading materials given to you by your caregiver, from other books, such as *Your Pregnancy: Every Woman's Guide, Your Pregnancy Questions & Answers* or *Your Pregnancy after 30*, or from pamphlets. Childbirth classes offer yet another way to learn about this important part of pregnancy. They help you prepare for labor and delivery.

Who Goes to Prenatal Classes?

Classes are usually held for small groups of pregnant women and their partners or labor coaches. This is an excellent way to learn. You can also interact with other couples and ask questions. You'll discover that other women are concerned about many of the same things you are, such as labor and pain management. It's good to know you aren't the only one thinking about what lies ahead.

Prenatal classes are not only for first-time pregnant women. If you have a new partner, if it has been a few years since you've had a baby, if you have questions or if you would like a review of what lies ahead, a prenatal class can help you.

These classes may reduce any worry or concern you and your partner feel about labor and delivery. And they'll help you enjoy the birth of your baby even more.

Tip for Week 27

Childbirth-education classes are not just for couples. Classes are often offered for single mothers or for pregnant women whose partners cannot come to classes. Ask your physician about classes for you.

Where Do You Take the Classes?

Childbirth classes are offered in various settings. Most hospitals that deliver babies offer prenatal classes, often taught by the labor-and-delivery nurses or by a midwife. Other types of classes have different degrees of involvement.

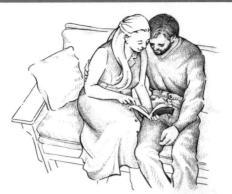

This means the time commitment or depth of the subject covered is different for each of the various classes that may be available. Ask your doctor or your doctor's nurse about classes they recommend. They can help you decide which type of class would be best for you.

What Will You Learn?

Classes are intended to inform you and your partner or labor coach about pregnancy, what happens at the hospital and what happens during labor and delivery. Some couples find classes are a good opportunity to get a partner more involved and to help make him feel more comfortable with the pregnancy. This may give him the opportunity to take a more active part at the time of labor and delivery, as well as during the rest of the pregnancy.

More Reasons to Take Prenatal Classes

By meeting in class on a regular basis, usually once a week for 4 to 6 weeks, you can learn about many things that concern you. Classes often cover a wide range of subjects, including the following areas.

- Will you need an episiotomy?
- Will you need an enema?
- When is a fetal monitor necessary?
- What's going to happen when you reach the hospital?
- Is an epidural or some other type of anesthesia right for you?

These are important questions. Discuss them with your doctor if they are not answered in your childbirth-education classes.

Infant-Restraint Seats

It isn't too early to think about infant- and child-restraint systems. Some people believe they can hold their baby safely in an accident. Others say their child won't sit still in a restraint.

In an accident, an unrestrained child becomes a missile. The force of a crash can literally pull a child out of an adult's arms! One study showed *more than 30 deaths a year* occur to unrestrained infants going home from the hospital after birth. In nearly all cases, if the baby had been in an approved infant-restraint system, he or she would have survived the accident.

Start early to teach your child safety. If you always place your child in a restraint system in the car, it will become a natural thing to do. You can increase your child's acceptance of a restraint if you wear seat belts, too!

Many states now have infant-restraint laws. Call your local police department or hospital for further information.

Many hospitals require you to take your baby home from the hospital in an approved infant-restraint system. If you want additional information, a pediatrician or the American Academy of Pediatrics can provide a list of safe child- and infant-restraint systems. Consumer magazines rate them quite frequently. Check your local library.

Your Nutrition

Some important vitamins you may need during pregnancy include vitamin A, vitamin B and vitamin E. Let's examine each vitamin and how it helps you during pregnancy.

Vitamin A—This vitamin is essential to human reproduction. Fortunately, deficiency in North America is not common. What is of more concern today is the excessive use of the vitamin before conception and in early pregnancy. (This discussion concerns only the retinol forms of vitamin A, usually derived from fish oils. The beta-carotene form, of plant origin, is believed to be safe.)

The RDA (recommended dietary allowance) is 2,700IU (international units) for a woman of childbearing age. The maximum dosage is 5,000IU. Pregnancy does not change these requirements. You probably get the vitamin A from the foods you eat, so supplementation during pregnancy is not recommended.

Vitamin B—B vitamins important to you in pregnancy include B_6, B_9 (folic acid) and B_{12}. They influence the development of your baby's nerves and the formation of blood cells. If you don't take in enough B_{12} during pregnancy, you could develop anemia. Good food sources of B vitamins include milk, eggs, tempeh, miso, bananas, potatoes, collard greens, avocados and brown rice.

Exercise Software

Do you need to be reminded to stop and exercise during the day? Now there's software you can load onto your computer to help you keep in shape. The program, StretchWare™, is available from Shelter Publications and can lead you through many different routines. You can work your hands, shoulders, lower back, legs or neck—each routine is fast and easy.

Vitamin E—This is an important vitamin during pregnancy because it helps metabolize fats and helps build muscles and red-blood cells. You can usually get enough of this vitamin if you eat meat. Vegetarians and pregnant women who can't eat meat may have a harder time getting enough vitamin E. Foods rich in the vitamin include olive oil, wheat germ, spinach and dried fruit. You may want to check with your healthcare provider or read the label on your prenatal vitamin to see if it supplies 100% of the RDA.

Be cautious about every substance you take during pregnancy. If you have questions, discuss them with your healthcare provider.

You Should Also Know

Systemic Lupus Erythematosus (SLE)

Some women have conditions before pregnancy that require them to take medication for the rest of their lives. They are often concerned about the effects medication may have on their developing babies. One such condition is *systemic lupus erythematosus* (SLE).

Many young women have lupus and take steroids to control the problem. They want to know if medication they take can harm their baby. Should they continue to take steroids during pregnancy?

Lupus is an autoimmune disorder of unknown cause that occurs most often in young or middle-aged women. (Women have lupus much more frequently than men—about nine women to every man.) Those who have lupus have a large number of antibodies in their bloodstream.

These antibodies are directed toward the woman's own tissues, which causes problems.

The diagnosis of SLE is made through blood tests, which look for the suspect antibodies. Blood tests done for lupus are a lupus antibody test and an antinuclear antibody test.

Antibodies can be directed to various organs in the body and may actually damage an organ. Affected organs include joints, skin, kidneys, muscles, lungs, the brain and the central nervous system. The most common symptom of lupus is joint pain, which is often mistaken for arthritis. Other symptoms include lesions, rashes or sores on the skin, fever and hypertension.

We don't have a cure for lupus. Systemic lupus erythematosus is generally unaffected by pregnancy. However, miscarriage, premature delivery and complications around the time of delivery are slightly increased in a woman with lupus.

If kidneys were involved and there was kidney damage during the flareups, you must be on the lookout for kidney problems during pregnancy.

Steroids, short for corticosteroids, are generally prescribed to treat lupus. The primary medication used is prednisone. It is usually prescribed on a daily basis. It may be unnecessary to take prednisone every day, unless complications from lupus occur during pregnancy.

Dad Tip

Offer to do chores that may be more difficult for your partner now. Cleaning the bathtub or the toilet can be a big help. You can add to her safety by putting away anything that belongs in a high or difficult-to-reach location.

Week 28

How Big Is Your Baby?

Your baby weighs about 2.4 pounds (1.1kg). Crown-to-rump length is close to 10 inches (25cm). Total length is 15.75 inches (35cm).

How Big Are You?

Your uterus is now well above your umbilicus. Sometimes this growth seems gradual. At other times, it may seem as though changes happen rapidly, as if overnight.

Your uterus is about 3.2 inches (8cm) above your bellybutton. If you measure from the pubic symphysis, it is about 11 inches (28cm) to the top of the uterus. Your weight gain by this time should be between 17 and 24 pounds (7.7 and 10.8kg).

How Your Baby Is Growing and Developing

Until this time, the surface of the baby's developing brain has appeared smooth. At around 28 weeks of pregnancy, the brain forms characteristic grooves and indentations on the surface. The amount of brain tissue also increases.

Your baby's eyebrows and eyelashes may be present. Hair on the baby's head is growing longer. The baby's body is becoming plumper and rounder. It's beginning to fill out a little because of increased fat underneath the skin. Before this time, the baby had a thin appearance.

Placenta

Cord

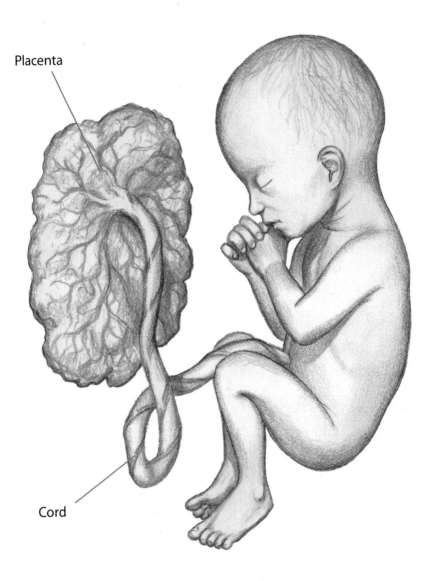

The placenta, shown here with the fetus, carries oxygen and nutrients to the growing baby. It is an important part of pregnancy.

Your baby now weighs about 2.4 pounds (1,100g). This is an amazing growth compared to just 11 weeks ago, when it weighed only about 3.5 ounces (100g) at 17 weeks of pregnancy. Your baby has increased its weight more than 10 times in 11 weeks! In the last 4 weeks, from the 24th week of your pregnancy to this week, its weight has doubled. Your baby is growing rapidly!

Changes in You

The Placenta

The placenta plays a critical role in the growth, development and survival of the baby. The illustration on the opposite page shows the fetus attached to the umbilical cord, which attaches to the placenta.

Two important cell layers, the *amnion* and the *chorion*, are involved in the development of the placenta and the amniotic sac. Development and function of the cell layers is complicated, and their description is beyond the scope of this book. However, the amnion is the layer around the amniotic fluid in which the fetus floats.

The placenta begins to form with *trophoblastic cells*. These cells grow through the walls of maternal blood vessels and establish contact with your bloodstream without your blood or fetal blood mixing. (Fetal circulation is separate from your circulation.) These cells grow into the blood vessels without making a vascular connection (or opening) between the blood vessels. But fetal blood flow in the placenta is close to your blood flow in the placenta.

We have closely followed your baby's weight gain in this book. The placenta is also growing at a rapid rate. At 10 weeks' gestation, the placenta weighed about 0.7 ounce (20g). Ten weeks later, at 20 weeks' gestation, it weighs almost 6 ounces (170g). In another 10 weeks, the placenta will have increased to 15 ounces (430g). At full term, 40 weeks, it can weigh almost 1.5 pounds (650g)!

Fetal blood vessels and the developing placenta begin connecting as early as the 2nd or 3rd week of development. During the 3rd week of gestation, projections (villi) at the base of the placenta become firmly attached to the underlying layer of the uterus.

Villi are important during pregnancy. The space around the villi (intervillus space) becomes honeycombed with maternal blood vessels. The villi absorb nutrients and oxygen from the maternal blood; these are transported to the growing baby through the umbilical vein in the umbilical cord. Waste products from the baby are brought through the umbilical arteries to the intervillus space and are transferred to the maternal bloodstream. In this way, the baby gets rid of waste products.

What Does the Placenta Do?

The placenta is involved in moving oxygen and carbon dioxide to and from the baby. It is also involved in nutrition and the excretion of waste products from the baby.

In addition to these functions, the placenta has an important hormonal role. It produces human chorionic gonadotropin (HCG) (discussed in Week 5). This hormone is found in your bloodstream in measurable amounts within 10 days after fertilization. Pregnancy tests check HCG levels to determine if a woman is pregnant. The placenta also begins making the hormones estrogen and progesterone by the 7th or 8th week of pregnancy.

What Does the Placenta Look Like?

At full term, a normal placenta is flat and has a cakelike, round or oval appearance. It is about 6 to 8 inches (15 to 20cm) in diameter and 0.8 to 1.2 inches (2 to 3cm) thick at its thickest part. It weighs between 17.5 and 24 ounces (500 to 650g) on average.

Placentas vary widely in size and shape. A placenta that is too large (placentamegaly) can be found when a woman is infected with syphilis or when a baby has erythroblastosis (Rh-sensitization). Sometimes it occurs without any obvious explanation. A small placenta may be found in normal pregnancies but may also be found with intrauterine-growth retardation.

The part of the placenta that attaches to the wall of the uterus has a beefy or spongy appearance. The fetal side of the placenta, the side closest to the baby inside the amniotic sac, is smooth. It is covered with amniotic and chorionic membranes.

> **Tip for Week 28**
>
> Even though delivery is several weeks away, it is not too early to begin making plans for the trip to the hospital. This includes knowing how to reach your partner (keep all of his phone numbers with you). Also consider what you will do if he isn't near enough to take you. Who are potential drivers? How do you get a hold of them?

The placenta is a red or reddish brown color. Around the time of birth, the placenta may have white patches on it, which are calcium deposits.

In multiple pregnancies, there may be more than one placenta. Or there may be one placenta with more than one umbilical cord coming from it. Usually with twins, there are two amniotic sacs, with two umbilical cords running to the fetuses from one placenta.

The umbilical cord, which is the attachment from the placenta to the baby, contains two umbilical arteries and one umbilical vein, which carry blood to and from the baby. It is about 22 inches (55cm) long. The cord is usually white.

A few women experience problems involving the placenta during pregnancy. These include placental abruption (see Week 33) and placenta previa (see Week 35). After delivery, a retained placenta is sometimes a problem (see Week 38).

How Your Actions Affect Your Baby's Development

Dealing with Maternal Asthma

Asthma is a respiratory illness characterized by an increased responsiveness or sensitivity to stimulation of the trachea and the bronchi, both important to breathing. Problems with asthma are manifested by difficulty breathing, shortness of breath, coughing and wheezing. (Wheezing is a noise like a whistling or a hissing made as air moves through narrowed airways.)

Asthma comes and goes, with acute worsening of symptoms interspersed with symptom-free periods. It affects about 2% of the population in the United States and Canada. It is equally common in other countries.

A Visit with the Doctor

Leeanne was concerned about her asthma and wanted to know what she could do for it that didn't require medication. I told her that many women have found they can help themselves with their asthma during pregnancy fairly easily. Maintaining good hydration by drinking a lot of liquid seems to help many women.

It may occur at any age, but about 50% of all asthma cases occur before age 10. Another 33% of the cases occur by age 40. Pregnancy does not seem to cause any consistent, predictable problem with asthma. Some pregnant women appear to get better during pregnancy, while others remain about the same. A few get worse.

Treating Asthma Attacks

Most pregnant women with asthma can have a safe pregnancy, labor and delivery. If a woman has severe asthma attacks when she isn't pregnant, she may have severe attacks during pregnancy.

In general, the treatment plan used before pregnancy will probably continue to be helpful. This includes medications prescribed for asthma before or during pregnancy.

During pregnancy, oxygen consumption increases by about 25%. Your baby needs oxygen to grow and to develop. That's why asthma treatment is so important while you're pregnant.

Asthma medication, such as terbutaline, and steroids, such as hydrocortisone or methylprednisolone, can be used during pregnancy. Aminophylline or theophyline may also be used.

Your Nutrition

You may be wondering what kinds of foods to eat and what to delete from your diet during pregnancy. Below is a chart that offers you some guidance.

What Kinds of Foods Do I Eat?

Foods to Eat	Servings per Day
Dark green or dark yellow fruits and vegetables	1
Fruits and vegetables with vitamin C (tomatoes, citrus)	2
Other fruits and vegetables	2
Whole-grain breads and cereals	6 to 11
Dairy products, including milk	4
Protein sources (meat, poultry, eggs, fish)	2
Dried beans and peas, seeds and nuts	2
Foods to Eat in Moderation	
Caffeine	200mg
Fat	limited amounts
Sugar	limited amounts
Foods to Avoid	
Anything containing alcohol	Food additives, when possible

You Should Also Know

Additional Testing
Twenty-eight weeks of gestation is a time when many doctors initiate or repeat certain blood tests or procedures. Glucose-tolerance testing for diabetes may also be done at this time.

> **If you are Rh-negative, you will probably receive an injection of RhoGAM at this point in your pregnancy. This injection keeps you from becoming sensitized if your baby's blood mixes with yours. The RhoGAM protects against sensitization until the time of delivery.**

How Is the Baby Lying?
It is common at this point in pregnancy to ask your healthcare provider which way the baby is lying. Is the baby head first? Is it bottom first (breech)? Is the baby lying sideways?

It's difficult—usually impossible—at this point in pregnancy to tell just by feeling your abdomen how the baby is lying and if it is coming bottom first, feet first or head first. The baby changes position during pregnancy and may continue to change its position for another month.

It doesn't hurt to try to feel the abdomen to see where the head or other parts are located. In another 3 to 4 weeks, the baby's head will be harder; it will be easier at that time for your healthcare provider to determine how the baby is lying (called *presentation of the fetus*).

Dad Tip

Your partner has been feeling the baby move for 2 or 3 months. Around this time, you may be able to feel it, too! Gently place your hand on her abdomen, and leave it there for a while. Your partner can tell you when the baby is moving.

Notes

Week 29

How Big Is Your Baby?

By this time, your baby weighs about 2.7 pounds (1.25kg). Crown-to-rump length is 10.4 inches (26cm). Total fetal length is 16.7 inches (37cm).

How Big Are You?

Measuring from your bellybutton, your uterus is about 3.5 to 4 inches (7.6 to 10.2cm) above it. Your uterus is about 11.5 inches (29cm) above the pubic symphysis. If you saw your healthcare provider 4 weeks ago, around the 25th week of pregnancy, you probably measured about 10 inches (25cm) at that time. You've grown about 1.5 inches (4cm) in 4 weeks. Your total weight gain by this week should be between 19 and 25 pounds (8.55 and 11.25kg).

How Your Baby Is Growing and Developing

Fetal Growth
Week by week, we've noted the change in your baby's size as pregnancy progresses. We use average weights to give you an idea of about how large your baby is at a particular time. However, these are only averages; babies vary greatly in size and weight.

Because growth is rapid during pregnancy, infants born prematurely may be tiny. Even a few weeks' less time in the uterus can have a dramatic effect on the size of your baby. The baby continues to grow after 36 weeks of gestation, but at a slower rate.

A couple of interesting factors about birthweight have been identified.

- Boys weigh more than girls.
- Birthweight of an infant increases with the increasing number of pregnancies you have or the number of babies you deliver.

These are general statements and don't apply to everyone, but they appear to apply in many cases. The average baby's birthweight at full term is 7 to 7.5 pounds (3.28kg to 3.4kg).

How Mature Is Your Baby?

A baby born between the 38th and 42nd weeks of pregnancy is a *term baby* or *full-term infant*. Before the 38th week, the term preterm can be applied to the baby. At 42 weeks of pregnancy, and after this time, *postterm* is used. *Postdate* is a newer term that some doctors use.

When a baby is born before the end of pregnancy, many people use the terms premature and preterm interchangeably. There is a difference. An infant that is 32 weeks gestational age but has mature pulmonary or lung function at the time of birth is more appropriately called a preterm infant than a premature infant. Premature best describes an infant that has immature lungs at the time of birth.

> **Nearly twice the number of preterm infants survive today than 40 years ago.**

Premature Babies

Premature birth increases the risk of problems in the baby. It also increases the risk of fetal death. Babies born prematurely usually weigh less than 5.5 pounds (2.5kg).

The illustration on page 270 shows a premature baby with several leads attached to its body to monitor its heart rate. Many other attachments are used, such as I.V.s, tubes, and masks that provide oxygen.

In 1950, the neonatal death rate was about 20 per 1,000 live births. Today, the rate is less than 10 per 1,000 live births. Nearly twice the number of preterm infants survive today than 40 years ago.

The decreasing death rate applies primarily to infants delivered during the third trimester (27 weeks or more of gestation) who weigh at least 2.2 pounds (1kg) and are without birth defects. When gestational age and birthweight are below these levels, the death rate increases.

Better methods of caring for premature babies have contributed to higher survival statistics. Today, infants born as early as 25 weeks of pregnancy can survive. However, the long-term survival and quality of life for these babies remains to be seen as they grow older.

What is the survival rate for premature babies? The most recent information indicates that for infants who weighed 1.1 pound (500g) to 1.5 pounds (700g), the survival rate is about 43%. For babies weighing between 1.5 pounds and 2.2 pounds (1kg), the survival rate is about 72%. These rates vary from hospital to hospital.

The average hospital stay for premature babies ranges from 125 days for infants weighing between 1.3 and 1.5 pounds (600 and 700g) to 76 days for babies in the 2- to 2.2-pound (900g to 1kg) birthweight range.

Any discussion of survival rates must include the frequency rate of disabilities these premature babies suffer. In the lower birthweight range, many babies who survived had disabilities. Higher-weight babies also had disabilities, but statistics for this group were much lower.

It's usually best for the baby to remain in the uterus as long as possible, so it can grow and develop fully. Occasionally it is best for

Causes of Premature Labor

In most cases, the cause of premature labor is unknown. Causes we do understand include the following:

- a uterus with an abnormal shape
- multiple fetuses
- polyhydramnios or hydramnios
- placental abruption or placenta previa
- premature rupture of membranes
- an incompetent cervix
- abnormalities of the fetus
- fetal death
- retained IUD
- abortion performed late in previous pregnancy
- serious maternal illness
- incorrect estimate of gestational age

the baby to be delivered early, such as when the fetus is not receiving adequate nutrition.

Finding the cause of premature labor and delivery may be difficult. An attempt is always made to determine what causes preterm labor before active labor begins. In this way, treatment may be more effective. One test, called *SalEst*, can help determine if a woman might go into premature labor. The test measures levels of the hormone estriol in a pregnant woman's saliva. Research has shown that there is often a surge in this chemical several weeks before early labor. A positive result means a woman has a 7 times higher chance of delivering her baby before the 37th week of pregnancy.

Some difficult questions that must be answered when premature labor begins include those below.

- Is it better for the infant to be inside the uterus or to be delivered?
- Are the dates of the pregnancy correct?
- Is this really labor?

Intrauterine-Growth Retardation

Intrauterine-growth retardation (IUGR) refers to a fetus that does not grow as fast as it should while in the uterus. A baby suffering from IUGR has a higher risk of serious problems. (We discuss IUGR in depth in Week 31.)

The word "retardation" may cause a mother-to-be some concern. Retardation in this sense doesn't apply to the development or function of the baby's brain. It means the total growth and overall size of the baby are inappropriately small; growth and size are considered to be retarded.

Changes in You

Treatment of Premature Labor

Can anything be done about premature labor? Yes—we now treat premature labor in several different ways.

The treatment most often used for premature labor is bed rest. A woman is advised to stay in bed and lie on her side. (Either side is OK.) Not everyone agrees on this treatment, but bed rest is often successful in stopping contractions and premature labor. If this happens to you, it may mean you can't go to work or continue many activities. It's worth it to try bed rest if you can avoid premature delivery of your baby.

Beta-adrenergic agents, also called *tocolytic agents*, may be used to suppress labor. Beta-adrenergics are muscle relaxants. They relax the uterus and decrease contractions. (The uterus is mainly muscle, which is active in pushing the baby out through the cervix during labor.) At this time, only ritodrine (Yutopar®) is approved by the FDA to treat premature labor.

Ritodrine is given in three different forms: as an I.V., as an intramuscular injection and as a pill. It is usually initially given intravenously and may require a hospital stay of a couple of days or more.

When premature contractions stop, you can be switched to oral medications, which you take every 2 to 4 hours. Ritodrine is approved for use in pregnancies over 20 weeks' and under 36 weeks'

Maternal Side Effects of Ritodrine

- tachycardia (rapid heartbeat)
- hypotension (the feeling of apprehension or fear)
- chest tightness or chest pain
- changes in the electrocardiogram (record of the heart's electrical activity)
- pulmonary edema (fluid in the lungs)
- maternal metabolic problems, including increased blood sugar, low blood potassium and even acidosis of the blood, similar to a diabetic reaction
- headaches
- vomiting
- shaking
- fever
- hallucinations

Similar problems probably occur in the baby. Low blood-sugar levels have been seen in babies after birth in some mothers who took ritodrine before delivery. Rapid heartbeat is also commonly seen in these babies.

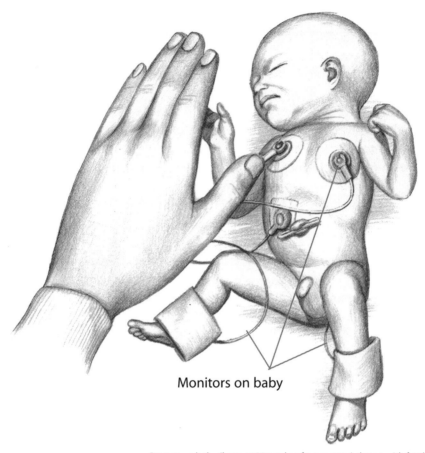

Monitors on baby

*Premature baby (born at 29 weeks of pregnancy) shown with fetal
monitors attached to it. Note size of adult hand in comparison.*

gestation. In some cases, medication is used without giving an I.V.
first. This is done most often in women with a history of premature
labor or for a woman with multiple pregnancies.

Terbutaline is also frequently used as a muscle relaxant.
Although it has been shown to be an effective medication, it has not
been approved for this use by the FDA. Terbutaline side effects are
similar to those of ritodrine (see the box on page 269).

Magnesium sulfate is used to treat pre-eclampsia (see Week
31 for information on pre-eclampsia). We have known for quite
a while that magnesium sulfate can also be used to help stop
labor. This medication is most often given through an I.V. and
requires hospitalization. However, it is occasionally given as an oral
preparation, without hospitalization. Your healthcare provider must
monitor you frequently if he or she prescribes magnesium sulfate.

Sedatives or narcotics may be used in early attempts to stop labor. This may consist of an injection of morphine or meperidine (Demerol). This is not a long-term solution but may be effective in initially stopping labor.

Benefits of Stopping Premature Labor
Benefits of stopping premature labor include reducing the risks of fetal problems and problems related to premature delivery. If you experience premature labor, you may need to see your healthcare provider frequently. Your caregiver will probably monitor your pregnancy with ultrasound or nonstress tests.

How Your Actions Affect Your Baby's Development

Most of our discussion this week has been devoted to the premature infant and treatment of premature labor. If you are diagnosed as having premature labor and your healthcare provider prescribes bed rest and medications to stop it, follow his or her advice!

If you're concerned about your healthcare provider's instructions, discuss them with him or her. If you're told not to work or to reduce your activities and you ignore the advice, you're taking chances with your well-being and your unborn baby's. It isn't worth taking risks. Don't be afraid to ask for another opinion or the opinion of a perinatologist if you experience premature labor.

Your Nutrition

We hope you have been listening to your body during your pregnancy. You rest when you're tired. You go to the bathroom when you first feel the urge. You pay attention to any new discomforts. You may also listen to your body when it comes to food and drink. When you feel hungry or thirsty, you eat or drink something. Eating smaller, more-frequent meals provides a constant supply of nutrients to your growing baby.

Keep nourishing snacks near at hand. Raisins, dried fruit and nuts are good choices when you're on the go. Know what time of day or night hunger strikes you the hardest. Be prepared.

You can be different, if you want to be. Eat spaghetti for breakfast and cereal for lunch if that's what appeals to you. Don't force yourself to eat something that turns you off. There's always an alternative. As long as you eat nourishing food and pay attention to the types of foods you eat, you are helping yourself and your growing baby.

You Should Also Know

Group-B Streptococcus Infection

Group-B streptococcus (GBS) infection rarely causes problems in adults but can cause life-threatening infections in newborns. GBS is often transmitted from person to person by sexual contact. In women, GBS is most often found in the vagina or rectum. It is possible to have GBS in your system and not be sick or have any symptoms.

> **Dad Tip**
>
> After the baby is born, you may be able to take time off to help out at home and to be part of your baby's early development. The Family and Medical Leave Act of 1993 was passed to help people take time off to care for family members. Ask your employer or supervisor now if it applies to you. If it does, and you plan to take time off, begin making arrangements in the next few weeks.

The Centers for Disease Control, the American College of Obstetricians and Gynecologists and the American Academy of Pediatrics have developed recommendations aimed at preventing this infection in newborns. One recommendation is that all women who have risk factors be treated for GBS. Risk factors include the following:

- a previous infant with GBS infection
- preterm labor
- ruptured membranes for more than 18 hours
- a temperature of 100.4F (38C) immediately before or during childbirth

The second recommendation is that a GBS culture be taken from the rectal and vaginal areas of all pregnant women at 35 to 37 weeks' gestation. Antibiotics, such as penicillin or ampicillin, are given during labor to patients with a positive culture.

Week 30

How Big Is Your Baby?

At this point in your pregnancy, your baby weighs about 3 pounds (1.35kg). Its crown-to-rump length is a little over 10.8 inches (27cm), and total length is 17 inches (38cm).

How Big Are You?

Measuring from your bellybutton, your uterus is about 4 inches (10cm) above it. From the pubic symphysis, the top of your uterus measures about 12 inches (30cm).

It may be hard to believe you still have 10 weeks to go! You may feel like you're running out of room as your uterus grows up under your ribs. However, your fetus, placenta and uterus, along with the amniotic fluid, will continue to get larger.

The average weight gain during pregnancy is 25 to 35 pounds (11.4 to 15.9kg). About half of this weight is concentrated in the growth of the uterus, the baby and the placenta, and in the volume of amniotic fluid. This growth is mostly in the front of

> It may be hard to believe you still have 10 weeks to go!

your abdomen and in your pelvis, where it is noticeable to you. You may experience increasing discomfort in your pelvis and abdomen as pregnancy progresses. At this point, you should be gaining about a pound a week.

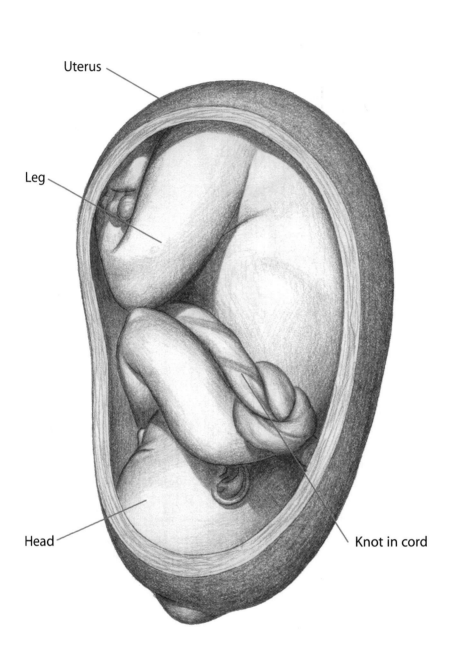

This fetus has a knot in its umbilical cord.

How Your Baby Is Growing and Developing

Umbilical-Cord Knots
The illustration this week (opposite page) shows a fetus and its umbilical cord. Can you see the knot in the cord? You may wonder how a knot like this can occur. We do not believe the cord grows in a knot.

A baby is usually quite active during pregnancy. We believe these knots occur as the baby moves around in early pregnancy. A loop forms in the umbilical cord; the baby moves through the loop, and a knot results. Your actions do not cause or prevent this kind of complication, which is very serious. A knot in the umbilical cord does not occur often.

Changes in You

Rupture of Membranes
The membranes around the baby that contain the amniotic fluid are called the *bag of waters*. They usually do not break until just before labor begins, when labor begins or during labor. But that isn't always the case.

After your water breaks, you need to take certain precautions. The membranes of pregnancy help protect your baby from infection. When your water breaks and you leak fluid, your risk of infection increases. An infection could be harmful to your baby. Call your healthcare provider immediately when your water breaks.

How Your Actions Affect Your Baby's Development

Bathing during Pregnancy
Many women wonder if bathing in the latter part of pregnancy will in some way harm their baby. Most doctors believe it's safe to bathe throughout pregnancy. They may caution you to be careful as you get in or out of the bathtub. And be sure the bath water is not too hot. Most will not tell you to  avoid a bath while you're pregnant. However, if you think your water has broken, avoid a tub bath.

Women also want to know how they'll recognize it if their water breaks while they are in

> **Most doctors believe it's safe to bathe throughout pregnancy.**

the tub. When your water breaks, you'll usually notice a gush of water followed by slow leakage. If your water breaks while you're in the tub, you may not notice the initial gush of fluid. However, you'll probably notice the leakage of fluid, which can last for quite a while.

Your Nutrition

Some women ask if herbal teas are safe to drink during pregnancy. Many have heard that some herbal teas can be beneficial to a pregnant woman. Many herbal teas are safe to use; some are not. Herbal teas you can use safely include chamomile, dandelion, ginger root, nettle leaf, peppermint and red raspberry. See the chart below for their benefits.

You should not use some herbal teas while you're pregnant. Studies indicate herbal teas to avoid include blue cohosh, black cohosh, penny-royal leaf, yarrow, goldenseal, feverfew, psillium seed, mugwort, comfrey, coltsfoot, juniper, rue, tansy, cottonroot bark, large amounts of sage, senna, cascara sagrada, buckthorn, fern, slippery elm and squaw vine.

Herbal Tea Benefits

chamomile	aids digestion
dandelion	helps with swelling and can soothe an upset stomach
ginger root	helps with nausea and nasal congestion
nettle leaf	rich in iron, calcium and other vitamins and minerals
peppermint	relieves gas pains and calms the stomach
red raspberry	helps with nausea and stabilizes hormones

You Should Also Know

Pregnancy is a happy time for most women, filled with anticipation and excitement. Occasionally, however, serious problems can occur. Cancer in pregnancy is one serious complication that rarely occurs.

This discussion is included not to scare you but to provide you with information. It is not a pleasant subject to discuss, especially at this time. However, every woman should have this information available. Its inclusion in this book is twofold:

- to increase your awareness of this serious problem
- to provide you with a resource to help you formulate questions for a dialogue with your healthcare provider if you wish to discuss it

Cancer before Pregnancy

If you are now pregnant and you have had cancer in the past, tell your healthcare provider as soon as you discover you are pregnant. He or she may need to make decisions about individualized care for you during pregnancy.

> **Tip for Week 30**
>
> Good posture can help relieve lower-back stress and eliminate some backache discomfort. Maintaining good posture may take some effort, but it's worth it if it relieves your pain.

Cancer in Pregnancy

The occurrence of cancer at any time is stressful. When cancer occurs during pregnancy, it is even more stressful. The doctor must consider how to treat the cancer, but he or she is also concerned about the developing baby.

The way in which these issues are handled depends on when cancer is discovered. A woman's concerns may include the following.

- Will the pregnancy have to be terminated so the cancer can be treated?
- Will medications used for treatment harm the baby?
- Will the malignancy or therapy used to treat the malignancy affect the baby or be passed to the baby?
- Should therapy be delayed until after delivery or after termination of the pregnancy?

Fortunately, many cancers in women occur after the reproductive years, which lowers the likelihood of cancer during pregnancy. Cancer during pregnancy is a rare occurrence and must be treated on an individual basis.

Some cancers found during pregnancy include breast tumors, leukemia and lymphomas, melanomas, gynecologic cancers (cancer of the female organs, such as the cervix, uterus and ovaries) and bone tumors.

Tremendous changes affect your body during pregnancy. Researchers suggest that these changes can affect the possible discovery of cancer during pregnancy.

- Some believe cancers influenced by the increased hormone levels during pregnancy may increase in frequency during pregnancy.
- Increased blood flow, with accompanying changes in the lymphatic system, may contribute to the transfer of cancer to other parts of the body.
- Anatomical and physiological changes of pregnancy (growth of the abdomen and changes in the breast) can make it difficult to find or to diagnose an early cancer.

These three beliefs about cancer during pregnancy appear to have some validity but this varies widely depending on the cancer and the organ involved.

Breast Cancer

Breast cancer is rare in women younger than 35. Fortunately, it is an uncommon complication of pregnancy.

During pregnancy, it may be harder to find breast cancer because of changes in the breasts, such as tenderness, increased size and even lumpiness. Of all women who have breast cancer, about 2% are pregnant at the time of diagnosis. Most evidence indicates pregnancy does not increase the rate of growth or spread of a breast cancer.

Treatment of breast cancer during pregnancy varies and must be individualized. It may require surgery, chemotherapy or radiation; a combination of all these treatments may be used. (For more information, see Week 13.)

Pelvic Cancers

Cervical cancer is believed to occur about once in every 10,000 pregnancies. However, about 1% of the women who have cancer of the cervix are pregnant when it is diagnosed. Cancer of the cervix is curable, particularly if it is found and treated in its early stages.

Malignancies of the vulva, the tissue surrounding the opening to the vagina, have also been reported during pregnancy. But only a few cases have occurred.

Other Cancers in Pregnancy

Hodgkin's disease (a form of cancer) commonly affects young people. It is now being controlled for long periods with radiation and chemotherapy. The disease occurs in about 1 of every 6,000 pregnancies. Pregnancy does not appear to have a negative effect on the course of Hodgkin's disease.

Pregnant women who have leukemia have demonstrated an increased chance of premature labor. They may also experience an increase in bleeding after pregnancy. Leukemia is usually treated with chemotherapy or radiation therapy.

Melanoma may occur during pregnancy. A melanoma is a cancer derived from skin cells that produce *melanin* (pigment). A malignant melanoma spreads through the body. Pregnancy may cause symptoms or problems to worsen. A melanoma can spread to the placenta and to the baby.

Bone tumors are rare during pregnancy. However, two types of benign (noncancerous) bone tumors can affect pregnancy and delivery. These tumors, *endochondromas* and *benign exostosis*, can involve the pelvis; tumors may interfere with labor. The possibility of having a Cesarean delivery is more likely with these tumors.

Dad Tip

Now's the time to think about changing your work schedule so you can be around home more during the last part of the pregnancy and after baby is born. Nearly all parents wish they were able to spend more time at home. If you travel a great deal, you may need to alter your schedule so you can be home the last part of the pregnancy. Babies come on their own schedule. If you want to be present for the delivery, plan ahead!

Notes

Week 31

How Big Is Your Baby?

Your baby continues to grow. It weighs about 3.5 pounds (1.6kg), and crown-to-rump length is 11.2 inches (28cm). Its total length is 18 inches (40cm).

How Big Are You?

Measuring from the pubic symphysis, it is now a little more than 12 inches (31cm) to the top of the uterus. From your bellybutton, it is about 4.4 inches (11cm).

At 12 weeks' gestation, the uterus was just filling the pelvis. As you can see in the illustration on page 284, by this week the uterus fills a large part of your abdomen.

Your total pregnancy weight gain by this time should be between 21 and 27 pounds (9.45 and 12.15kg).

How Your Baby Is Growing and Developing

Intrauterine-Growth Retardation
Intrauterine-growth retardation (IUGR) indicates a newborn infant is small for its gestational age. By definition, its birthweight is below the 10th percentile (in the lowest 10%) for the baby's gestational age. This means 9 out of 10 babies of normal growth are larger.

When gestational age is appropriate—meaning dates are correct and the pregnancy is as far along as expected—and weight falls below the 10th percentile, there is reason for concern. Growth-retarded infants have a higher rate of death and injury than infants in the normal-weight range.

Diagnosing and Treating IUGR

Diagnosing IUGR can be difficult. One reason your healthcare provider measures you at each visit is to see how your uterus is growing. A problem is usually found by measuring the uterus over a period of time and finding no change. If you measured 10.8 inches (27cm) at 27 weeks' gestation and at 31 weeks' you measure only 11 inches (28cm), your caregiver might become concerned about IUGR and order tests.

Diagnosis of this type of problem is one important reason to keep all your prenatal appointments. You may not like being weighed at every appointment, but it helps your caregiver see that your pregnancy is growing and the baby is getting bigger.

Intrauterine-growth retardation can be diagnosed or confirmed by ultrasound. Ultrasound may also be used to assure that the baby is healthy and no malformations exist that must be taken care of at birth.

When IUGR is diagnosed, avoid doing anything that could make it worse. Stop smoking. Improve your nutrition. Stop using drugs and alcohol.

Bed rest is another treatment. Resting enables the baby to receive the best blood flow, and better blood flow is the best chance it has to improve growth. If maternal disease causes IUGR, treatment involves improving the mother's general health.

An infant with intrauterine-growth retardation is at risk of dying before delivery. Avoiding this may involve delivering the baby before it is full term. Infants with IUGR may not tolerate labor well; a C-section is more likely because of fetal distress. The baby may be safer outside the uterus than inside in some cases.

Causes of IUGR

What causes intrauterine-growth retardation? Below are some conditions that increase the chance of intrauterine-growth retardation or a small fetus.

- **Tobacco.** Smoking and other tobacco use inhibits the baby's growth. The more cigarettes smoked, the greater the impairment and the smaller the baby.

- **Poor weight gain in the mother-to-be.** A woman of average size or smaller who doesn't gain enough weight may have a growth-retarded baby. This is one of the reasons that good nutrition and a healthful diet are so important during pregnancy. Do not attempt to restrict normal weight gain during pregnancy. Research indicates that when calories are restricted to under 1,500 a day for an extended time, IUGR may result.

- **Maternal blood-flow problems.** Pre-eclampsia and high blood pressure (hypertension) can have a marked effect on fetal growth.

- **Kidney disease.**

- **Altitude.** Women who live at high altitudes are more likely to have babies that weigh less than those born to women who live at lower altitudes.

- **Alcoholism and drug use.**

- **Multiple fetuses**.

- **Infections in the fetus.** Cytomegalovirus, rubella or other infections may restrict fetal growth.

- **Maternal anemia.** However, not every authority accepts maternal anemia as a cause of intrauterine-growth retardation. (Anemia is discussed in depth in Week 22.)

- **Abnormalities of the umbilical cord or placenta.** Abnormalities may cause inhibited growth because the baby receives less nutrition during pregnancy.

- **History of IUGR.** A woman who has delivered a growth-retarded infant may be more likely to do so again in subsequent pregnancies.

Other reasons for a small baby, unrelated to IUGR, include the fact that a woman who is small might have a small baby; prolonged pregnancy can lead to an undernourished, smaller baby; and a malformed or abnormal fetus may also be smaller, especially when chromosomal abnormalities are present.

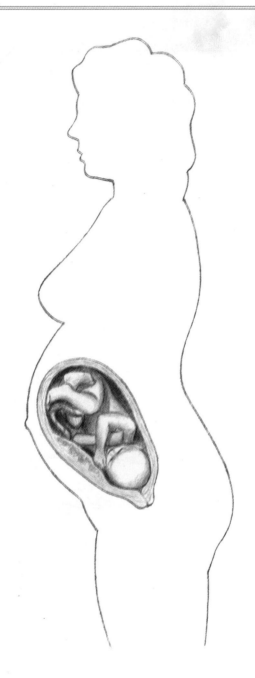

Comparative size of the uterus at 31 weeks of pregnancy (fetal age—29 weeks). The uterus can be felt about 4.4 inches (11cm) above the bellybutton.

A Visit with the Doctor

Margo couldn't get her shoes on after she'd been up for a couple of hours, and her rings were getting tight. She thought something might be wrong. I told her that some swelling is normal in most pregnancies and that wearing tight-fitting clothing that restricts blood flow can produce a problem in blood return from the arms and legs. Sure enough, she said she had been wearing regular pantyhose. Clothing that is tight at the waist, knees, ankles, shoulders, elbows or wrists can all cause problems.

Changes in You

Swelling during Pregnancy

You may notice, especially as you near the end of pregnancy, that if you take your shoes off and leave them off for a while, you may not be able to put them back on. This problem is related to swelling.

You may also notice that wearing nylon stockings that are tight at the knee (or tight socks) leaves an indentation in your legs. It may look like you still have clothing on.

Your body produces as much as 50% more blood and body fluids during pregnancy to meet baby's needs. Some of this extra fluid leaks into your body tissues. When your enlarging uterus pushes on pelvic veins, blood flow in the lower part of your body is partially blocked. This pushes fluid into your legs and feet, causing swelling.

The way you sit can also affect circulation of these body fluids. Crossing your legs, either at the knee or at the ankle, restricts blood flow to your legs. To improve circulation, don't cross your legs.

How Your Actions Affect Your Baby's Development

Sleeping Positions

We've already described the importance of resting on a regular basis and lying on your side when you sleep. (See Week 15.) Now is when

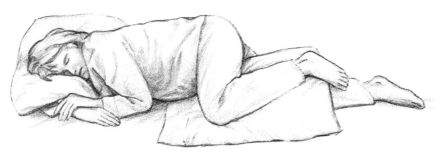

Use extra pillows to support your abdomen or your legs
as your pregnancy progresses.

it will pay off. You may notice you begin to retain water if you don't lie on your side when sleeping or resting. Lying on your side could help you feel better quickly.

Visiting Your Healthcare Provider

It's important to keep appointments with your caregiver. It may seem to you that not much happens at these visits, especially when everything is normal and going well. But the information your healthcare provider collects tells him or her a lot about your condition and your baby's.

> **It's important to keep appointments with your caregiver.**

Your caregiver is watching for signs that tell him or her you might have a problem, such as changes in your blood pressure, changes in your weight or the inadequate growth of the baby. If these problems are not discovered early, they may have serious consequences for you and your baby.

Your Nutrition

Pregnancy precautions can often be applied to everyday life, such as avoiding *Salmonella* poisoning. *Salmonella* bacteria can cause a range of problems, from mild gastric discomfort to severe, sometimes fatal, food poisoning. Any of these could be serious to you. *Salmonella* bacteria has many sources—there are over 1,400 different strains! They are found in raw eggs and raw poultry. The bacteria is destroyed when a food is cooked, but it's wise to take additional precautions. Keep in mind the following measures to ensure your safety.

Tip for Week 31

Wearing rings and watches can cause circulation problems. Sometimes a ring becomes so tight on a pregnant woman's finger that it must be cut off by a jeweler. You might not want to wear rings if swelling occurs. Some pregnant women purchase inexpensive rings in larger sizes to wear during pregnancy. Or you could put your rings on a pretty chain and wear them around your neck or as a bracelet.

- When preparing poultry or products made with raw eggs, clean your counters, utensils, dishes and pans with hot water and a disinfecting agent.
- Cook poultry thoroughly.
- Don't eat products made with raw eggs, such as Caesar salad, hollandaise sauce, homemade eggnog, homemade ice cream and so on. Don't taste cake batter, cookie dough or anything else that contains raw eggs before it is cooked.
- When you eat eggs, be sure they are cooked thoroughly. Boil eggs for at least 7 minutes. Poach eggs for 5 minutes. Fry them on each side for 3 minutes. Don't eat eggs that are cooked "sunnyside up."

You Should Also Know

Pregnancy-Induced Hypertension
Pregnancy-induced hypertension (high blood pressure) occurs only during pregnancy. With hypertension of pregnancy, the systolic pressure (the first number) increases to higher than 140ml of mercury or a rise of 30ml of mercury over your beginning blood pressure. A diastolic reading  (the second number) of over 90 or a rise of 15ml of mercury also indicates a problem. An example is a woman whose blood pressure at the beginning of pregnancy is 100/60. Later in pregnancy, it is

130/90. This indicates she may be developing high blood pressure or pre-eclampsia.

Your healthcare provider will be able to determine if your blood pressure is rising to a serious level by checking it at every prenatal appointment.

What Is Pre-eclampsia during Pregnancy?

Pre-eclampsia describes a variety of symptoms that occur only during pregnancy or shortly after delivery. Pre-eclampsia problems are characterized by a collection of symptoms:

- swelling (edema)
- protein in the urine (proteinuria)
- hypertension (high blood pressure)
- a change in reflexes (hyperreflexia)

Other nonspecific, important symptoms of pre-eclampsia include pain under the ribs on the right side, headache, seeing spots or other changes in vision. These are all warning signs. Report them to your healthcare provider immediately, particularly if you've had blood-pressure problems during pregnancy!

Pre-eclampsia can progress to *eclampsia*. Eclampsia refers to seizures or convulsions in a woman with pre-eclampsia. Seizures are not caused by a previous history of epilepsy or a seizure disorder.

Most pregnant women have some swelling during pregnancy; swelling in the legs does not mean you have pre-eclampsia. You must also have some of the other symptoms of pre-eclampsia. It is also possible to have hypertension during pregnancy without having pre-eclampsia.

What Causes Pre-eclampsia?

No one knows what causes pre-eclampsia or eclampsia. It occurs most often during a woman's first pregnancy. Women over 30 years old who are having their first baby are more likely to develop high blood pressure and pre-eclampsia. (See page 18 for more information on pregnancy after 30.)

Treating Pre-eclampsia

The goal in treating pre-eclampsia is to avoid eclampsia (seizures). That means keeping a close watch on you throughout pregnancy and checking your blood pressure and weight at every prenatal visit.

Weight gain can be a sign of pre-eclampsia or worsening pre-eclampsia. Pre-eclampsia affects weight gain because it increases water retention. If you notice any symptoms, call your healthcare provider's office.

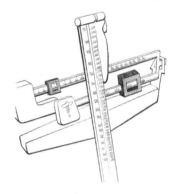

Treatment of pre-eclampsia begins with bed rest at home. You may not be able to work or to spend much time on your feet. Bed rest allows for the most efficient functioning of your kidneys and the greatest blood flow to the uterus.

Lie on your side, not on your back. Drink lots of water. Avoid salt, salty foods and foods that contain sodium, which make you retain fluid. Diuretics, which were used in the past, are not prescribed to treat pre-eclampsia today and are not recommended.

If you can't rest at home in bed or if symptoms do not improve, your healthcare provider may have to admit you to the hospital or deliver your baby. A baby is delivered for the following reasons:

- for your well-being
- to avoid seizures in you
- for the baby's well-being

During labor, pre-eclampsia may be treated with magnesium sulfate. It is given by I.V. to prevent seizures during and after delivery. High blood pressure may be treated with antihypertensive medication.

If you think you've had a seizure, call your healthcare provider immediately! Diagnosis may be difficult. If possible, someone who observed the possible seizure should describe it to your caregiver. Eclampsia is treated with medications similar to those prescribed for seizure disorders (see Week 26).

Dad Tip

Now's the time to begin discussing baby equipment, such as cribs, car seats or blankets, with your partner. You'll need to make some of these purchases before baby's birth. Most hospitals or birthing centers won't let you take baby home without a car seat.

Notes

Week 32

How Big Is Your Baby?

By this week, your baby weighs almost 4 pounds (1.8kg). Crown-to-rump length is over 11.6 inches (29cm), and total length is 18.9 inches (42cm).

How Big Are You?

Measurement to the top of the uterus from the pubic symphysis is about 12.8 inches (32cm). Measuring from your bellybutton to the top of the uterus now measures almost 5 inches (12cm).

How Your Baby Is Growing and Developing

Twins? Triplets? More?

When talking about pregnancies of more than one baby, in most cases we refer to twins. The chance of a twin pregnancy is more likely than pregnancy with triplets, quadruplets or quintuplets (or even more!).

You and your partner may be in shock if you learn you have more than one baby on the way. It's a normal reaction. Eventually the joy of expecting two babies may help offset the apprehension and responsibility you may feel. If you are expecting two or more babies, you will visit your healthcare provider more often. You will need to plan carefully for delivery and care of the babies after you go home. Read the following pages for detailed information on the many different issues surrounding multiples.

Multiples

Identical Twins and Fraternal Twins

Twin fetuses usually result from the fertilization of two separate eggs. These are called *dizygotic* twins or *fraternal twins*. With fraternal twins, you can have a boy and a girl.

About 33% of the time, twins come from a single egg that divides into two similar structures. Each has the potential of developing into a separate individual. These are known as *monozygotic twins* or *identical twins*. The two babies are almost always the same sex. Identical twins are not always identical. It is possible for fraternal twins to appear more alike than identical twins!

Either or both processes may be involved when more than two fetuses are formed. For example, quadruplets may result from fertilization of one, two, three or four eggs.

Division of the fertilized egg occurs between the first few days and about day 8. In this book, we refer to it as the third week of pregnancy. If division of the egg occurs after 8 days, the result can be twins that are connected, called *conjoined twins*. (Conjoined twins used to be called *Siamese twins*.) These babies may share important internal organs, such as the heart, lungs or liver. Fortunately this is a rare occurrence.

> It is possible for fraternal twins to appear more alike than identical twins!

Frequency of Multiple Births

The frequency of twins depends on the type of twins. Identical twins occur about once in every 250 births around the world. This type of twin formation appears to be uninfluenced by age, race, heredity, number of pregnancies or medications taken for infertility (fertility drugs). The incidence of fraternal twins, however, is influenced by race, heredity, maternal age, the number of previous pregnancies and the use of fertility drugs.

(continued)

Mother's abdomen

Placenta   Babies' heads

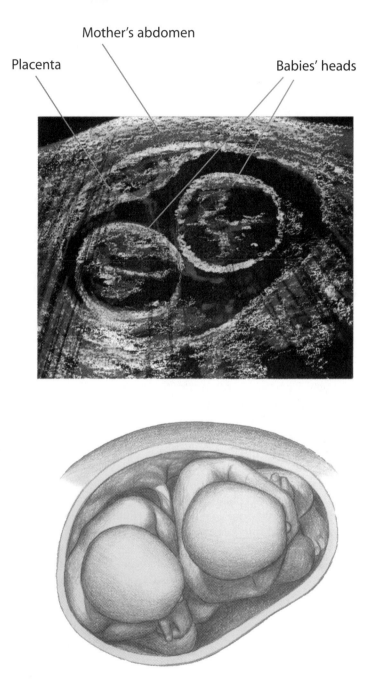

*Ultrasound of twins shows two babies in the uterus. If you
look closely, you can see the two heads. The interpretive
illustration shows how the babies are lying.*

The frequency of multiple fetuses varies significantly among different races. Twins occur in 1 out of every 100 pregnancies in white women compared to 1 out of every 79 pregnancies in black women. Certain areas of Africa have an incredibly high frequency of twins. In some places, twins occur once in every 20 births! Hispanic women also have a higher number of twin births than white women do. The occurrence of twins among Asians is less common: about 1 in every 150 births.

Heredity also plays a part in the occurrence of twins. In one study of fraternal twins, the chance of a female twin giving birth to a set of twins herself was about 1 in 58 births.

The occurrence of twins is probably more common than we know. Early ultrasound exams often reveal two sacs or two pregnancies. Later ultrasounds of the same woman may show that one sac (or one pregnancy) has disappeared, while the other pregnancy continues to grow and to develop normally. Some researchers believe ultrasound should not be done in the first 8 to 10 weeks of pregnancy. Parents who are informed of twins at this point may be distraught to learn later that one of the babies will not be born.

Triplets occur once in every 8,000 deliveries. Many doctors never deliver or participate in the delivery of triplets in their medical careers.

Some families are more blessed than others. In one case we know of, a woman had three single births. Her fourth pregnancy was twins, and her fifth pregnancy was triplets! She and her husband decided on another pregnancy— they were surprised (and probably relieved) when the sixth pregnancy resulted in only one baby.

Fertility Medication, In-Vitro Fertilization and Multiple Pregnancies

We have known for a long time that fertility drugs increase the chance of multiple pregnancies. Several different medications are used to treat infertility. Each one affects your chances of conceiving more than one fetus to a different degree. One of the more common medications is clomiphene (Clomid®). It increases the chance of multiple fetuses somewhat less than other medications. But an increased chance is still there.

Twins are more common in pregnancies that result from the use of fertility drugs or with the implantation of more than one embryo with in-vitro fertilization. The percentage of male fetuses decreases as the number of fetuses per pregnancy increases. This means more females are born in these multiple pregnancies.

Discovering You're Carrying More than One Baby

Diagnosis of twins was more difficult before ultrasound was available. The illustration on page 293 shows an ultrasound of twins. You can see parts of both fetuses.

It is uncommon to discover twin pregnancies just by hearing

> **Many people believe when only one heartbeat is heard, there could be no possibility of twins. This may not be the case. Two rapid heartbeats may have a similar or almost identical rate.**

two heartbeats. Many people believe when only one heartbeat is heard, there could be no possibility of twins. This may not be the case. Two rapid heartbeats may have a similar or almost identical rate. That could make it difficult to determine that there are two babies.

Measuring and examining your abdomen during pregnancy is important. Usually a twin pregnancy is noted during the second trimester because you are too big and growth seems too fast for a single pregnancy.

Ultrasound examination is the best way to tell if you are carrying more than one baby. Diagnosis can also be made by X-ray after 16 to 18 weeks of pregnancy, when fetal skeletons are visible. However, this method is used infrequently today.

Do Multiple Pregnancies Have More Problems?

With a multiple pregnancy, the possibility of problems goes up. Possible problems include the following:

- increased risk of miscarriage
- fetal death or mortality
- fetal malformations
- low birthweight or growth retardation
- pre-eclampsia
- problems with the placenta, including placental abruption and placenta previa
- maternal anemia
- maternal bleeding or hemorrhage
- problems with the umbilical cord, including entwinement or tangling of the babies' umbilical cords
- hydramnios or polyhydramnios
- labor complicated by abnormal fetal presentation, such as breech or transverse lie
- premature labor

One of the biggest problems with multiple pregnancies is premature delivery. As the number of fetuses increases, the length of gestation and the birthweight decreases, although this is not true in every case.

The average pregnancy for twins is about 37 weeks. For triplets it is about 35 weeks. For every week the babies remain in the uterus, their birthweights increase, along with the maturity of organs and systems.

Major malformations in multiple pregnancies are more common than they are in single pregnancies. The incidence of minor malformation is twice as high as it is in a single pregnancy. Malformations are more common among identical twins than fraternal twins.

One of the main goals in dealing with multiple fetuses is to continue the pregnancy as long as possible to avoid premature delivery. This may best be accomplished by bed rest. You may not be able to carry on with regular activities during your entire pregnancy. If your healthcare provider recommends bed rest, follow his or her advice.

Weight gain is important with a multiple pregnancy. You will gain more than the normal 25 to 35 pounds, depending on the number of fetuses you are carrying. Supplementation with iron is essential.

Some researchers believe use of a *tocolytic agent* (medication to stop labor), such as ritodrine, is critical in preventing premature delivery. (See Week 29.) These agents are used to relax the uterus to keep you from going into premature labor.

Follow your healthcare provider's instruction closely. Every day and every week you're able to keep the babies inside you are days or weeks you won't have to visit them in an intensive-care nursery while they grow, develop and finish maturing.

Delivering More than One Baby

How multiple fetuses are delivered often depends on how the babies are lying in your uterus. Possible complications of labor and delivery, in addition to prematurity, include the following:

• abnormal presentations (breech or transverse)
• prolapse of the umbilical cord (the umbilical cord comes out ahead of the babies)
• placental abruption
• fetal distress
• bleeding after delivery

These problems occur more often with multiple fetuses. Because there is higher risk during labor and delivery, precautions are taken before delivery and during labor. These include the need for an I.V., the presence of an anesthesiologist and the availability and possible presence of pediatricians or other medical personnel to take care of the babies.

With twins, all possible combinations of fetal positions can occur. Both babies may come head first (vertex). They may come *breech*, meaning bottom or feet first. They may come sideways or *oblique*, meaning at an angle that is neither breech nor vertex. Or they may come in any combination of the above. (See discussion of birth presentation in Week 38.)

When both twins are head first, a vaginal delivery may be attempted and may be accomplished safely. It may be possible for one baby to deliver normally. The second one could require a C-section if it turns, the cord comes out ahead of the baby or the baby is distressed following delivery of the first fetus. Some doctors believe delivery of two or more babies requires a C-section.

After delivery of two or more babies, doctors pay strict attention to maternal bleeding because of the rapid change in the size of the uterus. It is greatly overdistended with more than one baby. Medication, usually oxytocin (Pitocin®), is given by I.V. to contract the uterus to stop bleeding so the mother doesn't lose too much blood. A heavy blood loss could produce anemia and make a blood transfusion or long-term treatment with iron supplementation necessary.

Changes in You

Until this week, your visits to the doctor have probably been on a monthly basis, unless you've had

> **Now is a good time to ask questions and to discuss concerns about labor and delivery.**

complications or problems. At week 32, most doctors begin seeing a pregnant woman every 2 weeks. This will continue until you reach your last month of pregnancy; at that time, you'll probably switch to weekly visits.

By this time, you probably know your caregiver fairly well and feel comfortable talking about your concerns. Now is a good time to ask questions and to discuss concerns about labor and delivery. If there are complications or problems later in pregnancy or at delivery, you'll be able to communicate better with your caregiver and know what is going on. You'll feel comfortable with the care you're receiving.

Your healthcare provider may plan on talking to you about many things in the weeks to come, but you can't always assume this. You may be taking prenatal classes and hearing different things about labor and delivery, such as stories about enemas, I.V.s and complications. Don't be afraid to ask any questions you have. Most doctors and nurses are receptive to your queries. They want you to discuss things you're concerned about instead of worry about them unnecessarily.

A Visit with the Doctor

Jackie admitted to me that she wasn't taking her prenatal vitamins as regularly as she had early in pregnancy. She said she was tired of taking them and asked if it was OK to skip them now that she was in the third trimester. I told her it was a mistake not to take her prenatal vitamin every day.

How Your Actions Affect Your Baby's Development

Taking Prenatal Vitamins

The vitamins and iron in prenatal vitamins are essential to your well-being and the well-being of your baby. If you're anemic at the time of delivery, a low blood count could have a negative effect on you and your baby. Your chance of needing a blood transfusion could be higher. Keep taking your prenatal vitamins every day!

Your Nutrition

If you're expecting more than one baby, your nutrition and weight gain are extremely important during your pregnancy. Food is your best source of nutrients and calories, but it's also important for you to take your prenatal vitamin every day. If you don't gain weight early in pregnancy, you have a greater chance of developing pre-eclampsia. Your babies may be tiny, too.

If you're expecting twins, target weight gain (for a normal-weight woman) is about 45 pounds. Don't be alarmed when your healthcare provider discusses the amount of weight he or she wants you to gain. Studies show that if a woman gains the targeted amount of weight with a multiple pregnancy, her babies are often healthier.

> ### Tip for Week 32
>
> Your requirements for calories, protein, vitamins and minerals increase if you carry more than one baby. You'll need to eat about 300 calories a day more per baby than for a normal pregnancy. For ideas on how to add those 300 calories, see page 160.

How can you gain the amount of weight you need to? Just adding extra calories won't benefit you or your developing babies. Junk food, full of empty calories, doesn't add much. You can get your calories from specific sources. For example, it's important to eat an extra serving of a dairy product and an extra serving of a protein each day. These two servings provide you with the extra calcium, protein and iron you require to meet the needs of your growing babies. Discuss the situation with your healthcare provider; he or she may suggest you see a nutritionist.

You Should Also Know

Postpartum Bleeding and Hemorrhage

It is normal to lose blood during labor and delivery. However, a heavy postpartum hemorrhage is different and significant. Postpartum hemorrhage is a loss of blood in excess of 17 ounces (500ml) in the first 24 hours after your baby's birth.

There can be many reasons for postpartum hemorrhage. The most common causes include a uterus that will not contract and lacerations or tearing of the vagina or cervix during the birth process.

Other causes include trauma to the genital tract, such as a large or bleeding episiotomy, or a rupture, hole or tear in the uterus. Blood loss may be related to the failure of blood vessels inside the uterus (where the placenta was attached) to compress to stop bleeding. This may occur if the uterus fails to contract because of rapid labor, a long labor, several previous deliveries, a uterine infection, an overdistended uterus (with multiple fetuses) or certain agents used for general anesthesia.

Heavy bleeding may also result from retained placental tissue. In this situation, most of the placenta delivers, but part of it remains inside the uterus. Retained placental tissue may cause bleeding immediately, or bleeding may occur weeks or even months later.

Problems with blood clotting can cause hemorrhaging. This may be related to pregnancy, or it may be a congenital medical problem. Bleeding following delivery requires constant attention from your healthcare provider and the nurses caring for you.

> **Dad Tip**
>
> Together with your partner, make a list of important telephone numbers and keep it with you. Include numbers of your work, her work, the hospital, the doctor's office, a back-up driver, baby-sitter or others. You may also want to make a list of numbers of people you want to call after the delivery of your baby. Take this list to the hospital with you.

Notes

Week 33

How Big Is Your Baby?

Your baby weighs about 4.4 pounds (2kg) by this week. Its crown-to-rump length is about 12 inches (30cm) and total length is 19.4 inches (43cm).

How Big Are You?

Measuring from the pubic symphysis, it is now about 13.2 inches (33cm) to the top of the uterus. Measurement from your bellybutton to the top of your uterus is about 5.2 inches (13cm). Your total weight gain should be between 22 and 28 pounds (9.9 and 12.6kg).

How Your Baby Is Growing and Developing

Placental Abruption

The illustration on page 302 shows placental abruption, which is separation of the placenta from the wall of the uterus. Normally, the placenta does not separate from the uterus until after the baby is delivered. Separation before delivery can be very serious.

The frequency of placental abruption is estimated to be about 1 in every 80 deliveries. We do not have a more exact statistic because time of separation varies, altering risk to the fetus. If the placenta separates at the time of delivery and the infant is delivered without incident, it is not as significant as a placenta separating during pregnancy.

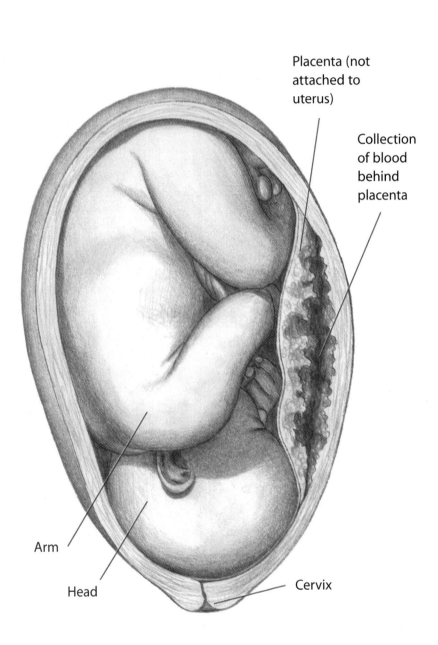

Placenta (not attached to uterus)

Collection of blood behind placenta

Arm

Head

Cervix

This illustration of placental abruption shows the placenta has separated from the wall of the uterus.

Causes of Placental Abruption

The cause of placental abruption is unknown. Certain conditions may increase its chance of occurring:

- physical injury to the mother, as from a car accident
- a short umbilical cord
- sudden change in the size of the uterus (from delivery or rupture of membranes)
- hypertension
- dietary deficiency
- a uterine abnormality, such as a band of tissue in the uterus where the placenta cannot attach properly
- previous surgery on the uterus (removal of fibroids) or D&C for abortion or miscarriage

Studies indicate that folic-acid deficiency can play a role in causing placental abruption. Others suggest maternal smoking and alcohol consumption may make a woman more likely to have placental abruption.

A woman who has had placental abruption in the past is at increased risk of having it recur. Rate of recurrence has been estimated to be as high as 10%. This can make a pregnancy following placental abruption a high-risk pregnancy.

Separation of the placenta may involve partial or total separation from the uterine wall. The situation is most severe when the placenta totally separates from the uterine wall. The fetus relies entirely on circulation from the placenta. With separation, it cannot receive blood from the umbilical cord, which is attached to the placenta.

Symptoms of placental abruption can vary a great deal. There may be heavy bleeding from the vagina, or you may experience no bleeding at all. The illustration on page 302 shows bleeding behind the placenta with complete separation. There is no apparent bleeding from the cervix and vagina. Other symptoms can include lower-back pain, tenderness of the uterus or abdomen, and contractions or tightening of the uterus.

Ultrasound may be helpful in diagnosing this problem, although it does not always provide an exact diagnosis. This is particularly true if the placenta is located on the back surface of the uterus where it cannot be seen easily with ultrasound examination.

Frequency of Placental Abruption Symptoms

Of the various symptoms associated with placental abruption, the following are the most common.

- Vaginal bleeding occurs in about 75% of all cases.
- Tenderness of the uterus occurs about 60% of the time.
- Fetal distress or problems with the fetal heart rate also occur about 60% of the time.
- Tightening or contraction of the uterus occurs about 34% of the time.
- Premature labor occurs in about 20% of the cases.
- Fetal death occurs about 15% of the time.

Serious problems, such as shock, may occur with separation of the placenta. Shock occurs because of the rapid loss of large quantities of blood. Intravascular coagulation, in which a large blood clot develops, can also be a problem. Factors that clot the blood may be used up, which can make bleeding a problem.

Can Placental Abruption Be Treated?
Treatment of placental abruption varies, based on the ability to diagnose the problem and the status of the mother and baby. With heavy bleeding, delivery of the baby may be necessary.

When bleeding is not heavy, the problem may be treated with a more conservative approach. This depends on whether the fetus is in distress and if it appears to be in immediate danger.

Placental abruption is one of the most serious problems related to the second and third trimesters of pregnancy. If you have any symptoms, call your healthcare provider immediately!

Changes in You

How Will You Know Your Membranes Have Ruptured?
How will you know when your water breaks? It isn't usually just one gush of water, with no further leakage. There is often a gush of amniotic fluid, usually followed by a leaking of small amounts of fluid. Women describe it as a constant wetness or water

running down their leg when they stand. *Continuous* leakage of water is a good clue that your water has broken.

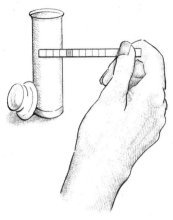

Amniotic fluid is usually clear and watery. Occasionally it may have a bloody appearance, or it may be yellow or green.

It isn't uncommon to have an increase in vaginal discharge or to lose urine in small amounts as your baby puts pressure on your bladder. But there are ways for your healthcare provider to tell if your water has broken. Two tests can be done on the amniotic fluid.

One is a *nitrazine test*. When amniotic fluid is placed on a small strip of paper, it changes the color of the paper. This test is based on the acidity or pH of the amniotic fluid. However, blood can also change the color of nitrazine paper, even if your water hasn't broken.

Another test that may be done is a *ferning test*. Amniotic fluid or fluid from the back of the vagina is taken with a swab and placed on a slide for examination under a microscope. Dried amniotic fluid has the appearance of a fern or branches of a pine tree. Ferning is often more helpful in diagnosing ruptured membranes than looking at color changes on nitrazine paper.

> ***Continuous* leakage of water is a good clue that your water has broken.**

What Do You Do When Your Water Breaks?

Your membranes may rupture at any point in pregnancy. Don't assume it will happen only around the time of labor.

If you think your water has broken, notify your healthcare provider. Avoid sexual intercourse at this time. Intercourse increases the possibility of introducing an infection into your uterus and thus to your baby.

How Your Actions Affect Your Baby's Development

Weight Gain Continues

You are continuing to gain weight as your pregnancy progresses. You may be gaining weight faster than at any other time during pregnancy. This is because your baby is going through a period of increased growth. It may be gaining as much as 8 ounces (1/2 lb; 224g) or more every week!

Continue to eat the right foods for you. Heartburn may be more of a problem now because your growing baby may not allow your stomach much room. You may find eating several small meals, rather than three large meals, makes you feel more comfortable.

Your Nutrition

You know the importance of eating a well-balanced diet during pregnancy. Eating fresh fruit and vegetables, dairy products, whole-grain products and protein all contribute to the healthful development of your baby. You may be concerned about what foods to avoid. Some foods may be OK to eat when you're not pregnant but should be avoided now.

When possible, avoid food additives. We aren't really sure how they can affect a developing baby, but if you can avoid them, do so. Be careful about pesticides, too. Thoroughly wash and wipe dry all fruits and vegetables before you eat or prepare them, even if you don't normally eat the peel. Contaminants could get on your hands if you don't wash them. Peel a fruit or vegetable after you wash it, if that's the way you normally eat it. It helps to remove even more of the fruit that might be contaminated.

> **Tip for Week 33**
>
> Don't stop eating or start skipping meals as your weight increases. Both you and your baby need the calories and nutrition you receive from a healthy diet.

Avoid fish that might be contaminated with PCBs. (See page 64 for further information.) Buy fish only from a reputable market or eat those caught only in areas free from contamination. Be vigilant about the foods you consume to protect your growing baby.

You Should Also Know

Will Your Doctor Perform an Episiotomy?
An *episiotomy* is an incision made from the vagina toward the rectum during delivery to avoid undue tearing as the baby's head passes

through the birth canal. It may be a cut directly in the midline toward the rectum, or it may be a cut to the side.

There is little you can do if you need an episiotomy. Some people practice, teach and believe in stretching the birth canal during labor and at the time of delivery to try to avoid an episiotomy. It may work for some, but it doesn't work for every woman. Others suggest an episiotomy to avoid stretching the vagina, bladder and rectum. Stretching the vagina can result in loss of control of your urine or bowels and can change sensations experienced during sexual intercourse.

The reason for an episiotomy usually becomes clear at delivery when the baby's head is in the vagina. The episiotomy substitutes a controlled, straight, clean cut for a tear or rip that could go in many directions. This may include tearing or ripping into the bladder, large blood vessels or rectum. An episiotomy heals better than a ragged tear.

Ask your healthcare provider if he or she thinks you may need an episiotomy. Discuss why an episiotomy is necessary. Find out whether it might be a cut in the middle or to the side of the vagina. You might also ask if there is anything you can do to prepare for the possibility of an episiotomy, such as having an enema or stretching the vagina. If a vacuum extractor or forceps are used for delivery, an episiotomy may be done before the device is placed on the baby's head.

Description of an episiotomy also includes a description of the depth of the incision.

- A first-degree episiotomy cuts only the skin.
- A second-degree episiotomy cuts the skin and underlying tissue.
- A third-degree episiotomy cuts the skin, underlying tissue and rectal sphincter, which is the muscle that goes around the anus.
- A fourth-degree episiotomy goes through the three layers and through the rectal mucosa.

After the baby is delivered, layers are closed separately with absorbable sutures that do not require removal after they heal.

After your baby is born, the most painful part of the entire birth experience might be the episiotomy. It may continue to cause some discomfort as it heals. Don't be afraid to ask for medication to ease any pain. You can take many safe medications, even if you are breastfeeding your baby, including acetaminophen (Tylenol). Tylenol with Codeine® or other medications may also be prescribed for pain.

Dad Tip

Is your home safe for your new baby? Things to consider when thinking about safety include pets, furniture, second-hand smoke, window coverings or anything else in your home that could pose a danger to your little one.

Week 34

How Big Is Your Baby?

Your baby weighs almost 5 pounds (2.28kg) by this week. Its crown-to-rump length is about 12.8 inches (32cm). Total length is 19.8 inches (44cm).

How Big Are You?

Measuring up from your bellybutton, it's about 5.6 inches (14cm) to the top of your uterus. From the pubic symphysis, you will measure about 13.6 inches (34cm).

It's not important that your measurements match any of your friends' at similar points in their pregnancies. What's important is that you're growing appropriately and that your uterus grows and gets larger at an appropriate rate. These are the signs of normal growth of your baby inside your uterus.

How Your Baby Is Growing and Developing

Testing Your Baby before Birth?

An ideal test done before delivery would determine if the fetus is healthy. It would be able to detect major fetal malformations or fetal stress, which could indicate an impending problem. Ultrasound accomplishes some of these goals by enabling doctors to observe the baby inside the uterus, as well as to evaluate the brain, heart and other organs of the fetal body. Along with ultrasound examinations, fetal monitoring in the form of a *nonstress test* and a *contraction stress test* can indicate fetal well-being or problems. (See page 317 for a discussion of the nonstress test and page 346 for a discussion of the contraction stress test.)

Biophysical Profile

A comprehensive test, called a *biophysical profile*, is used to examine the fetus while it is still

> **The amount of change and number of changes in the fetal heart rate differ, depending on who is doing the nonstress test and their definition of normal.**

in the uterus. The test helps determine fetal health and is done when there is concern about fetal well-being. It may also be done when a pregnancy passes the expected due date.

A biophysical profile uses a particular scoring system. The first four of the five tests listed below are made with ultrasound; the fifth is done with external fetal monitors. A score is given to each area. Following are the five areas of evaluation:

- fetal breathing movements
- fetal body movements
- fetal tone
- amount of amniotic fluid
- reactive fetal heart rate (nonstress test)

During the test, doctors evaluate fetal "breathing"—the movement or expansion of the baby's chest inside the uterus. This score is based on the amount of fetal breathing that occurs.

Movement of the baby's body is noted. A normal score indicates normal body movements. An abnormal score is applied when there are few or no body movements during the allotted time period.

Fetal tone is evaluated similarly. Movement, or lack of movement, of the arms and legs of the baby is noted.

Amniotic-fluid volume evaluation requires experience in ultrasound examination. A normal pregnancy has adequate fluid around the baby. An abnormal test indicates no amniotic fluid or decreased amniotic fluid around the baby.

Fetal heart-rate monitoring (nonstress test) is done with external monitors. It evaluates changes in the fetal heart rate associated with movement of the baby. The amount of change and number of changes in the fetal heart rate differ, depending on who is doing the test and their definition of normal.

A normal score is 2; an abnormal score is 0 for any of these tests. A score of 1 in any of the tests is a middle score. From these five scores, a total score is obtained by adding all the values together. Evaluation may vary depending on the sophistication of the equipment used and the expertise of the person doing the test. The higher the score, the better the baby's condition. A lower score may cause concern about the well-being of the fetus.

If the score is low, a recommendation may be made to deliver the baby immediately. If the score is reassuring, the test may be repeated at weekly or twice-weekly intervals. If results fall between these two values, the test may be repeated the following day. It depends on the circumstances of your pregnancy and the biophysical-profile findings. Your healthcare provider will evaluate all the information before making any decision.

A biophysical profile may be valuable in evaluating an infant with IUGR, pregnancy of a diabetic mother, a pregnancy in which the baby doesn't move much, high-risk pregnancies or overdue pregnancies. Because ultrasound is an important part of a biophysical profile, it may be useful in finding major congenital problems and evaluating the well-being of the infant inside the uterus.

> **Tip for Week 34**
>
> A strip of paper, tape or a bandage can cover a bellybutton that is sensitive or unsightly (poking through your clothing).

Changes in You

Will Your Baby Drop?

A few weeks before labor begins or at the beginning of labor, you may notice a change in your abdomen. When examined by your healthcare provider, measurement from your bellybutton or the pubic symphysis to the top of the uterus may be smaller than what you noticed on a previous visit. This phenomenon occurs as the head of the baby enters the birth canal. It can also be a part of the decrease in amniotic fluid that may occur without rupture of membranes or loss of fluid. This change is often called *lightening*.

Don't be concerned if you don't notice lightening or a drop of the fetus. This doesn't occur with every woman or with every pregnancy. It's common for your baby to drop during labor or just before labor begins.

With lightening, you may experience benefits and problems. One benefit may be more room in your upper abdomen. This gives you more room to breathe because there's more room for your lungs to expand. However, with the descent of the baby, you may notice more pressure in your pelvis, bladder and rectum, which can make you more uncomfortable.

In some instances, your caregiver may examine you and tell you your baby is "not in the pelvis" or "is high up." He or she is saying the baby has not yet descended into the birth canal. However, this situation can change quickly.

If your caregiver says your baby is "floating" or "ballotable," it means part of the baby is felt high in the birth canal. But the baby is not engaged (fixed) in the birth canal at this point. The baby may even bounce or move away from your doctor's fingers when you are examined.

Uncomfortable Feelings You May Experience
At this point in their pregnancies, some women have the uncomfortable feeling the baby is going to "fall out." This feeling is related to pressure the baby exerts because it has moved lower in the birth canal. Some women describe the feeling as an increase in pressure.

If you're concerned or worried about it, consult your healthcare provider. It may be a reason to perform a pelvic exam to see how low the baby's head is. In almost all cases, the baby will not be coming out. But because it is at a lower position than what you're used to, the baby will exert more pressure than you have noticed during recent weeks.

Another feeling associated with increased pressure may occur around this week. Some pregnant women have described it as a "pins-and-needles" sensation. The feeling is tingling, pressure or numbness in the pelvis or pelvic region from the pressure of the baby. It is a common symptom and shouldn't concern you.

These feelings may not be relieved until delivery occurs. You can lie on your side to help decrease pressure in your pelvis and on the nerves, vessels and arteries in the pelvic area. If the problem is severe, talk to your healthcare provider about it. Don't try to move the baby or push the baby out of the way. It could be dangerous for both of you.

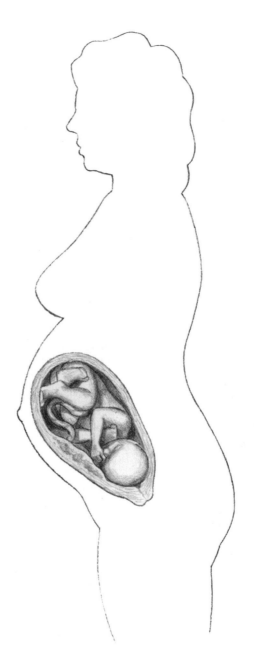

Comparative size of the uterus at 34 weeks of pregnancy
(fetal age—32 weeks). The uterus can be felt about 5.6 inches
(14cm) above your bellybutton.

Understanding Labor

It's important to know what to expect when labor occurs and what to do when it begins. What causes labor? Why does it happen?

We don't have good answers to these questions. The factors that cause labor to begin are unknown. There are many theories; one is that hormones made by the mother and fetus trigger labor. It could be that a hormone produced by the fetus makes the uterus contract.

Labor is the *dilatation* (stretching, expanding) of the cervix. This occurs because the uterus, which is a muscle, tightens to squeeze out its contents (the baby). As it pushes the baby out, the cervix stretches. It may be possible to feel tightening, contractions or cramps, but in the purest sense, it isn't labor until there is a change in the cervix.

Braxton-Hicks Contractions and False Labor

Braxton-Hicks contractions are painless, nonrhythmical contractions you may be able to feel when you place your hand on your abdomen. These contractions often begin early in pregnancy and are felt at irregular intervals. They may increase in number and strength when the uterus is massaged. Like false labor, they are not positive signs of true labor.

False labor often occurs before true labor begins. False labor contractions can be painful and may appear to be real labor to you.

In most instances, false-labor contractions are irregular. They usually last less than 45 seconds. The discomfort of the contraction

may occur in various parts of your body, such as the groin, lower abdomen or back. With true labor, uterine contractions produce pain that starts at the top of the uterus and radiates over the entire uterus, through the lower back into the pelvis.

False labor is usually seen in late pregnancy. It seems to occur more often in women who have been pregnant before and delivered more babies. It usually stops as quickly as it begins. There doesn't appear to be any danger to your baby.

What Is a "Bloody Show"?

Often following a vaginal examination or with the beginning of early labor and early contractions, you may bleed a small amount. This is called a *bloody show*; it can occur as the cervix stretches and dilates. You shouldn't lose a large amount of blood. If it causes you concern or appears

> In most instances, false-labor contractions are irregular. They usually last less than 45 seconds.

to be a large amount of blood, call your healthcare provider immediately.

Along with a bloody show, you may pass a mucus plug at the beginning of labor. This is different from your bag of waters breaking (ruptured membranes). Passing this mucus plug doesn't necessarily mean you'll have your baby soon or even that you'll go into labor in the next few hours. It poses no danger to you or your baby.

How Long Will Labor Last?

The length of the first and second stages of labor, from the beginning of cervical dilatation to delivery of the baby, can last 14 to 15 hours or more in a first pregnancy. Women have had faster labors than this, but don't count on it.

A woman who has already had one or two children will probably have a shorter labor, but don't count on that either! The average time for labor is usually decreased by a few hours for a second or third delivery.

> The average time for labor is usually decreased by a few hours for a second or third delivery.

Everyone's heard of women who barely make it to the hospital or had a 1-hour labor. For every one of those patients, there are many women who have labored 18, 20, 24 hours or longer.

It's almost impossible to predict the amount of time that will be required for labor. You may ask your healthcare provider about it, but his or her answer is only a guess.

Timing Contractions

Most women are instructed in prenatal classes or by their healthcare provider about how to time contractions during labor. To time how long a contraction lasts, begin timing when the contraction starts and end timing when the contraction lets up and goes away.

It's also important to know how often contractions occur. There is much confusion about this. You can choose from two methods.

1. Note the time period from when a contraction starts to the time the next contraction starts. This is the most commonly used method and the most reliable.

2. Note the time period from when a contraction *ends* to the time the next contraction starts.

Ask your healthcare provider which method he or she prefers.

It's helpful for you and your partner or labor coach to time your contractions before calling your healthcare provider or the hospital. Your caregiver will probably want to know how often contractions occur and how long each contraction lasts. With this information, your caregiver can decide when you should to go to the hospital.

(continued)

Three Stages of Labor

Stage one: The first stage of labor begins with uterine contractions of great enough intensity, duration and frequency to cause thinning (effacement) and dilatation of the cervix. The first stage of labor ends when the cervix is fully dilated (usually 10cm) and sufficiently open to allow the baby's head to come through it.

Stage two: The second stage of labor begins when the cervix is completely dilated at 10cm. This stage ends with the delivery of the baby.

Stage three: The third stage of labor begins after delivery of the baby. It ends with delivery of the placenta and the membranes that have surrounded the fetus.

Some doctors have even described a fourth stage of labor, referring to a time period after delivery of the placenta during which the uterus contracts. Contraction of the uterus is important in controlling bleeding that can occur after delivery of the baby and the placenta.

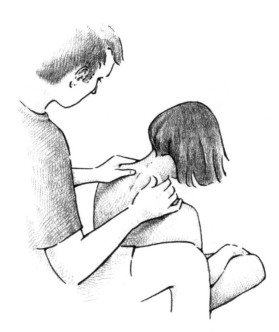

How Your Actions Affect Your Baby's Development

The end of your pregnancy begins with labor. One of the end results of labor is the birth of your baby.

Some women are concerned (or hope!) that their actions can cause labor to begin. The old wives' tales about going for a ride over a bumpy road or taking a long walk to start labor aren't true. We do know intercourse and stimulation of the nipples may cause labor to start in some cases, but this isn't true for every woman. Going about your daily activities (unless your caregiver has advised bed rest) will not cause labor to start before your baby is ready to be born. In the following weekly discussions, we continue to discuss what labor involves and the many issues surrounding this climactic event.

Your Nutrition

Cholesterol Check

It's a waste of time and effort to have your cholesterol level checked during your pregnancy. The level of cholesterol in your blood rises during pregnancy due to hormonal changes. Wait until after you have your baby or stop breastfeeding to check your cholesterol.

A Vitamin-Rich Snack

When you're looking for something to snack on, you might not think of a baked potato, but it's an excellent snack! You get protein, fiber, calcium, iron, B vitamins and vitamin C when you eat a potato. Bake up a few, and store them in the refrigerator. Heat one up when you're hungry. Broccoli is another food filled with vitamins. Add it to your baked potato and top both with some plain yogurt or nonfat sour cream for a delicious treat!

You Should Also Know

The Nonstress Test

The biophysical profile (discussed earlier in this chapter) evaluates the well-being of your baby inside your uterus. One part of the biophysical profile is fetal monitoring, commonly called a *nonstress test*.

A nonstress test is performed in your healthcare provider's office or in the labor and delivery department of a hospital. While you are lying down, a technician attaches a fetal monitor to your abdomen. Every time you feel your baby move, you push a button to make a mark on a strip of monitor paper. At the same time, the monitor records the baby's heartbeat.

Dad Tip

Preregister at the hospital to save you time and inconvenience when you finally get to the hospital for baby's birth. Ask your partner to inquire at the doctor's office, or ask about preregistering in your prenatal classes. If your doctor or prenatal instructor doesn't know, call the hospital and ask.

When the baby moves, its heart rate usually goes up. Doctors use the findings from fetal monitoring to help them evaluate how well a baby is tolerating life inside the uterus. Your healthcare provider will decide if further action is necessary.

Week 35

How Big Is Your Baby?

Your baby now weighs over 5.5 pounds (2.5kg). Crown-to-rump length by this week of pregnancy is about 13.2 inches (33cm). Its total length is 20.25 inches (45cm).

How Big Are You?

Measuring from the bellybutton, it is now about 6 inches (15cm) to the top of the uterus. Measuring from the pubic symphysis, the distance is about 14 inches (35cm). By this week, your total weight gain should be between 24 and 29 pounds (10.8 and 13kg).

How Your Baby Is Growing and Developing

How Much Does Your Baby Weigh?
You have probably asked your caregiver several times how big your baby is or how much your baby will weigh when it's born. Next to asking about the sex of a baby, this is the most frequently asked question.

As you can see by the illustration on page 320, you're getting larger. Your increasing size is due to the growth of baby and placenta as well as the increased amount of fluid around the baby. All these factors make estimating fetal weight more difficult.

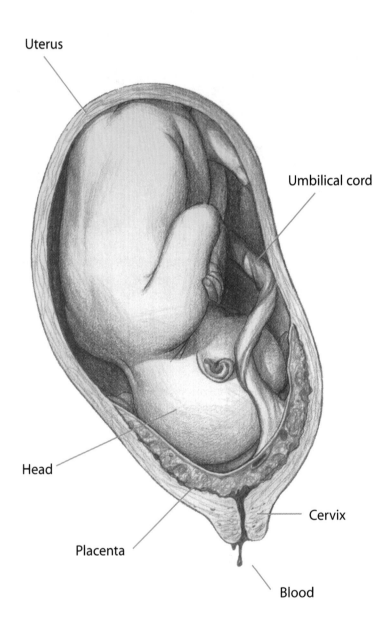

Uterus

Umbilical cord

Head

Cervix

Placenta

Blood

*In this illustration of placenta previa, note how the placenta
completely covers the cervical opening to the uterus. (See
page 325 for more information.)*

A Visit with the Doctor

It is difficult to guess the weight of the unborn baby. Studies have been done in which 1) the doctor, 2) the mother and 3) the ultrasound are used to estimate weight. All three methods are equally accurate (and equally inaccurate!) Claudia asked me to tell her how much her baby would weigh at birth. I guessed more than 8 pounds and was surprised when she delivered a 6-pound, 10-ounce baby!

Using Ultrasound to Estimate Fetal Weight

Ultrasound can be used to estimate fetal weight, but errors in weight estimates can and do occur. The accuracy of predicting fetal weight using ultrasound is improving. Making an accurate estimate can be valuable.

Several measurements are used in a formula or computer program to estimate a baby's weight. These include diameter of the baby's head, circumference of the baby's head, circumference of the baby's abdomen, length of the femur of the baby's leg and, in some instances, other fetal measurements.

Many feel that ultrasound is the method of choice to estimate fetal weight. But even with ultrasound, estimates may vary as much as half a pound (225g) or more in either direction.

Will Your Baby Fit through the Birth Canal?

Even with a fetal-weight estimate, whether by your caregiver or by ultrasound, your healthcare provider can't tell if the baby is too big for you or whether you'll need a C-section. Usually, it's necessary for you to labor to be able to see how the baby fits into your pelvis and if there is room for it to pass through the birth canal.

> The best test or method of evaluating whether your baby will deliver through your pelvis is labor itself.

In some women who appear to be average or better-than-average size, a 6- or 6.5-pound (2.7- to 2.9-kg) baby won't fit through the pelvis. Experience has also shown that women who may appear to be petite are sometimes able to deliver 7.5-pound (3.4-kg) or larger babies without much difficulty. The best test or method of evaluating whether your baby will deliver through your pelvis is labor itself.

Changes in You

Emotional Changes in Late Pregnancy
As you come closer to delivery, you and your partner may become more anxious about the events to come. You may have even more mood swings, which seem to occur for no reason. You may become more irritable, which can place a significant strain on your relationship. You may be concerned about insignificant or unimportant things. Your concern about the health and well-being of the baby may also increase during the last weeks of your pregnancy. This can include concern about how well you will tolerate labor and how you will get through delivery. You may be concerned about whether you'll be a good mother or be able to raise a baby properly.

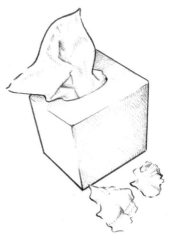

While these emotions rage inside you, you'll notice you're getting bigger and aren't able to do things you used to do. You may feel more uncomfortable, and you may not be sleeping well. These things can all work together to make your emotions swing wildly from highs to lows.

How Can You Deal with These Changes?
Emotional changes are normal; don't feel as though you're the "Lone Ranger." Other pregnant women and their partners have the same concerns.

Talk with your partner about your concerns. Tell him how you feel and what's going on. You may be surprised to discover the concerns your partner has about you, the baby and his role during labor and delivery. By talking about these things, your partner may find it easier to understand what you're experiencing, including mood swings and crying spells.

Discuss emotional problems with your healthcare provider. He or she may be able to reassure you that what you're going through is normal. Take advantage of prenatal classes and information available about pregnancy and delivery.

Emotional changes often occur, so be ready for them. Ask your partner, the nurse in the doctor's office and your doctor to help you understand what is normal and what can be done about mood swings.

How Your Actions Affect Your Baby's Development

Preparing for Baby's Birth

At this point, you may be feeling a little nervous about the birth. You might be afraid you won't know when it's time to call the doctor or go to the hospital. Don't hesitate to talk to your healthcare provider about it at one of your visits. He or she will tell you what signs to watch for. In prenatal classes, you learn to recognize the signs of labor and when you should call your healthcare provider or go to the hospital.

Tip for Week 35

Maternity bras are designed to provide extra support to your growing breasts. You may feel more comfortable wearing one during the day and at night while you sleep.

Ask your healthcare provider what the signs of labor contractions are. Labor contractions are usually regular. They increase in duration and strength over time. You'll notice a regular rhythm to real labor contractions. You'll want to time them so you know how frequently they occur and how long they last. (See Week 33.) When you go to the hospital depends in part on your contractions.

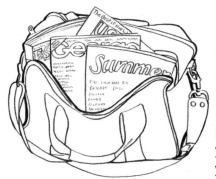

Your bag of waters may rupture before you go into labor. In most cases, you'll notice this as a gush of water followed by a steady leaking. (See Week 33.)

During the last few weeks of pregnancy, have your suitcase packed and ready to go. That way, you'll have the things you want with you in the hospital ready to go.

If you can, tour the hospital facilities a few weeks ahead of your scheduled due date. Find out where to go and what to do when you get there.

Talk with your partner about the best ways to reach him if you think you are in labor. You might have him check with you periodically. It's common for a partner to wear a pager if he is often away from a phone, especially during the last few weeks of pregnancy.

Ask your healthcare provider what you should do if you think you're in labor. Is it best to call the office? Should you go directly to the hospital? Should you call the answering service? By knowing what to do, and when, you'll be able to relax a little and not worry about the beginning of labor and delivery.

Preregistering at the Hospital
During pregnancy, your healthcare provider has recorded various things that have occurred during your pregnancy. A copy of this record is usually kept in the labor-and-delivery area.

> If you can, tour the hospital facilities a few weeks ahead of your scheduled due date. Find out where to go and what to do when you get there.

It may be helpful and save you time if you register at the hospital a few weeks before your due date. You will be able to do this with forms that you get at your healthcare provider's office or by getting forms from the hospital. It's wise to do this before you go to the hospital in labor because by then you may be in a hurry or concerned with other things.

You should know certain facts that may not be included in your chart:

- your blood type and Rh-factor
- when your last period was and when your due date is
- details of your past pregnancies, including any complications
- your doctor's name
- your pediatrician's name

Your Nutrition

Your body continues to need lots of vitamins and minerals for your developing

baby. And you'll need even more of them if you choose to breastfeed! Below is a chart showing your daily requirements during pregnancy and breastfeeding. It's important to realize how necessary your continued good nutrition is for you and your baby.

Nutrient Requirements during Pregnancy and Breastfeeding

Vitamins & Minerals	During Pregnancy	During Breastfeeding
A	800mcg	1,300mcg
B_1 (thiamine)	1.5mg	1.6mg
B_2 (riboflavin)	1.6mg	1.8mg
B_3 (niacin)	17mg	20mg
B_6	2.2mg	2.2mg
B_{12}	2.2mcg	2.6mcg
C	70mg	95mg
Calcium	1,200mg	1,200mg
D	10mcg	10mcg
E	10mg	12mg
Folic acid (B_9)	400mcg	280mcg
Iron	30mg	15mg
Magnesium	320mg	355mg
Phosphorous	1,200mg	1,200mg
Zinc	15mg	19mg

You Should Also Know

What Is Placenta Previa?

With *placenta previa*, the placenta lies close to the cervix or covers the cervix. The illustration on page 320 shows placenta previa.

Placenta previa is serious because of the chance of heavy bleeding. Bleeding may occur during pregnancy or during labor.

This problem is not common; it happens about once in every 170 pregnancies.

The cause of placenta previa is not completely understood. Risk factors for an increased chance of placenta previa include previous Cesarean delivery, many pregnancies and increased maternal age.

Symptoms of Placenta Previa

The most characteristic symptom of placenta previa is painless bleeding without any contractions of the uterus. This doesn't usually occur until close to the end of your second trimester or later when the cervix thins out, stretches and tears the placenta loose.

Bleeding with placenta previa may occur without warning and may be extremely heavy. It occurs when the cervix begins to dilate with early labor, and blood escapes.

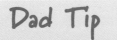

Dad Tip

At a prenatal visit, ask the doctor about your part in the delivery. There may be some things you'd like to do, such as cutting the cord or videotaping your baby's birth. It's easier to talk about these things ahead of time. Not every new father wants an active role in the delivery. That's OK.

Placenta previa should be suspected when a woman experiences vaginal bleeding during the latter half of pregnancy. The problem cannot be diagnosed with a physical exam because a pelvic examination may cause heavier bleeding. Doctors use ultrasound to identify placenta previa. Ultrasound is particularly accurate in the second half of pregnancy as the uterus and placenta get bigger.

If you know you have placenta previa, your healthcare provider may tell you not to have a pelvic exam. This is important to remember if you see another caregiver or when you go to the hospital.

The baby is more likely to be in a breech position with placenta previa. For this reason, and to control bleeding, a Cesarean delivery is usually performed. Cesarean delivery with placenta previa offers the healthcare provider the advantage of delivering the baby, then removing the placenta so the uterus can contract. Bleeding can be kept to a minimum.

Week 36

How Big Is Your Baby?

By this week, your baby weighs about 6 pounds (2.75kg). Its crown-to-rump length is over 13.5 inches (34cm), and total length is 20.7 inches (46cm).

How Big Are You?

Measuring from the pubic symphysis, it's about 14.5 inches (36cm) to the top of your uterus. If you measure from your bellybutton, it's more than 5.5 inches (14cm) to the top of your uterus.

You may feel as though you've run out of room! Your uterus has grown bigger in the past few weeks as the baby has grown inside of it. Now the uterus is probably up under your ribs.

How Your Baby Is Growing and Developing

Maturity of Your Baby's Lungs and Respiratory System
An important part of your baby's development is maturation of the lungs and respiratory system. When a baby is born prematurely, a common problem is development of *respiratory-distress syndrome* in the newborn fetus. This problem is also called *hyaline membrane disease*. In this situation, lungs are not completely mature, and the baby can't breathe on its own without help. Oxygen is necessary. The baby may require a machine, such as a ventilator, to breathe for it.

In the early 1970s, scientists developed a couple of methods for evaluating the maturity of fetal lungs. An amniocentesis test must be done at this point in pregnancy for either test. The first method, the *L/S ratio,* enables doctors to determine in advance if a baby can breathe on its own after delivery.

The L/S-ratio test doesn't usually indicate that a baby's lungs are mature until at least 34 weeks of pregnancy. At that time, the relationship between two blood factors in the amniotic fluid changes. Levels of lecithin go up, and levels of sphingomyelin go down. The ratio between these two levels indicates if a baby's lungs are mature.

The *phosphatidyl glycerol* (PG) test is another way doctors can evaluate the maturity of the baby's lungs. This test is either positive or negative. If phosphatidyl glycerol is present in the amniotic fluid (positive result), doctors are reassured; the infant will probably not suffer respiratory distress upon delivery.

Specific cells in the lungs produce chemicals that are essential for respiration immediately after birth. An important part of a newborn baby's breathing is determined by the chemical *surfactant.* A baby born prematurely may not have surfactant in its lungs. Surfactant can be introduced directly into the lungs of the newborn to prevent respiratory-distress syndrome. The chemical is available for immediate use by the baby. Many premature babies who receive surfactant do not have to be put on respirators—they can breathe on their own!

Changes in You

You have only 4 to 5 weeks to go until your due date. It's easy to get anxious for your baby to be delivered. However, don't ask your doctor to induce labor at this point.

> It isn't unusual for your weight to stay the same at each of your weekly visits after this point.

You may have gained 25 to 30 pounds (11.25 to 13.5kg), and you still have a month to go. It isn't unusual for your weight to stay the same at each of your weekly visits after this point.

The maximum amount of amniotic fluid surrounds the baby now. In the weeks to come, the baby continues to grow. However, some amniotic fluid is reabsorbed by your body, which decreases the amount of fluid around the baby and decreases the amount of room in which the baby has to move. You may notice a difference in sensation of fetal movements. For some women, it feels as if the baby is not moving as much as it had been.

How Your Actions Affect Your Baby's Development

Vaginal Birth after Cesarean
Should you attempt a vaginal delivery after having had a C-section? Vaginal birth after Cesarean (VBAC) is becoming more common. Medically speaking, the method of delivery is not as important as the well-being of you and your baby!

Before you and your healthcare provider make a final decision, you need to weigh the risks and the benefits to you and your baby with both types of delivery. In some cases, you won't have any choice in the matter. In other cases, you and your caregiver may decide to let you labor for a while to see if you can deliver vaginally.

Some women like having a repeat Cesarean section. They request one because they don't want to go through labor only to end up with a Cesarean delivery anyway.

Advantages and Risks of VBAC
Advantages of a vaginal delivery include a decreased risk of problems associated with major surgery, which Cesarean birth is. Recovery after a vaginal delivery is shorter. You can be up and about in the hospital and at home in a much shorter amount of time.

If you are small and the baby is large, you may need a C-section. Multiple fetuses may make vaginal delivery difficult or impossible without danger to the babies. Problems, such as high blood pressure or diabetes, may require a repeat C-section.

If you want to attempt VBAC, discuss it with your healthcare provider in advance so plans can be made. During labor, you will probably be monitored more closely with fetal monitors. You may be attached to I.V.s in case a Cesarean section becomes necessary.

Consider the benefits and risks in deciding whether to attempt a vaginal delivery after a previous Cesarean section. Discuss advantages and disadvantages at length with your healthcare provider and your partner before making a final decision. Don't be afraid to ask your caregiver his or her opinion of your chances of a successful vaginal delivery. He or she knows your health and pregnancy history.

A Visit with the Doctor

The type of incision previously performed on the uterus dictates if labor can be attempted. One of my new patients, Carol, wanted a VBAC but didn't know what kind of uterine incision she'd had previously. When I got her records from Rhode Island, I discovered she'd had a classical incision. Labor is not permitted after a classical incision that goes high up on the uterus. This is a vertical incision in the uterus and is more likely to rupture or open during labor—a serious complication. (You can't see this incision; your doctor must provide you with this information.) Carol was disappointed she couldn't try a vaginal birth, but she understood the reason for another C-section.

Your Nutrition

Eating fish can be healthy for you during pregnancy. Omega-3 fatty acids, found in fish, may help prevent high blood pressure and pre-eclampsia. They also help enhance baby's brain development.

Don't overdo it, though. You don't need more than 2.4mg of omega-3 fatty acids a day. Fish rich in these oils include salmon, mackerel, herring and tuna.

Research has shown that women who eat a variety of fish during their pregnancy have longer pregnancies and give birth to babies with higher birthweights. The longer a baby stays in the uterus, the better its chances of being healthy at delivery.

Unfortunately, because of environmental pollution, some fish are contaminated with methyl mercury. If a person eats too much fish containing this poison, he or she is at risk of methyl-mercury poisoning. We know it can cross the placenta

> **Research has shown that women who eat a variety of fish during their pregnancy have longer pregnancies and give birth to babies with higher birthweights.**

to the baby. During pregnancy, keep your consumption of shark, swordfish and tuna (fresh or frozen) to a minimum of once a month. Canned tuna is safer, but don't eat more than two 6-ounce cans a week.

There are many fish to choose from that provide you with essential nutrients, vitamins and minerals. Most fish is low in fat and high in vitamin B, copper, iron, selenium and zinc. The list below contains the types of fish and shellfish you can eat at any time in your pregnancy—you can have them as often as you want! If you need to watch your calories, have them baked, broiled or steamed. Avoid lots of butter and deep frying.

bass • catfish • clams • cod • crab • croaker • flounder • freshwater perch • haddock • herring • lobster • mackerel • marlin • ocean perch • orange roughy • oysters • Pacific halibut • pollack • red snapper • salmon • scallops • scrod • shrimp • sole

You Should Also Know

Cesarean Delivery
Most women plan on a normal vaginal birth, but a Cesarean delivery is always a possibility. With a Cesarean, the baby is delivered through an incision made in the mother's abdominal wall and uterus. The illustration on page 333 shows a Cesarean delivery. Common names for this type of surgery are *C-section, Cesarean section* and *Cesarean delivery.*

Reasons for a C-Section
C-sections are done for many reasons. The most common reason for having a C-section is a previous Cesarean delivery. However, some women who have had C-sections can have a vaginal delivery with later pregnancies; this is called vaginal birth after Cesarean (VBAC). See the discussion on page 329. Discuss the matter with your healthcare provider if you've had a C-section and would like to attempt a vaginal delivery this time.

There is some risk that the internal surgical scar from an earlier C-section could stretch and pull apart during subsequent labor and delivery, with serious consequences. In this case, a repeat C-section may be advised to avoid rupture of the uterus. However, if pregnancy and labor are closely monitored, a woman may be able to have a normal vaginal delivery (VBAC).

A Cesarean delivery may be necessary if your baby is too big to fit through the birth canal. This condition is called *cephalo-pelvic disproportion* (CPD). CPD may be suspected during pregnancy, but usually labor must begin before it can be confirmed.

Fetal distress is another reason for a Cesarean section. Doctors use fetal monitors during labor to watch the fetal heartbeat and its response to labor. If the heartbeat indicates the baby is having trouble with labor contractions, a C-section may be necessary for the baby's well-being.

If the umbilical cord is compressed, a C-section may be necessary. The cord may come into the vagina ahead of the baby's head or the baby can press on part of the cord. This is a dangerous situation because a compressed umbilical cord can cut off the blood supply to the baby.

A C-section is necessary if the baby is in a *breech presentation,* which means the baby's feet or buttocks enter the birth canal first. Delivering the shoulders and the head after the baby's body may damage the baby's head or neck, especially with a first baby.

Placental abruption or placenta previa are also reasons for a Cesarean delivery. If the placenta separates from the uterus before delivery (placental abruption), the baby loses its supply of oxygen and nutrients. This is usually diagnosed when a woman has heavy vaginal bleeding. If the placenta blocks the birth canal (placenta previa), the baby cannot be delivered any other way.

Rising Rate of Cesarean Deliveries

In 1965, only 4% of all deliveries were by C-section. Today, in the United States, Cesarean deliveries account for about 20% of all deliveries. In some areas, this percentage is even higher. In Canada, Cesarean deliveries account for almost 18% of all deliveries. This increase is related in part to more stringent monitoring during labor and safer procedures for C-sections. Another reason for more Cesarean deliveries is bigger babies. With bigger babies, a C-section is sometimes the only way to deliver. Researchers believe this

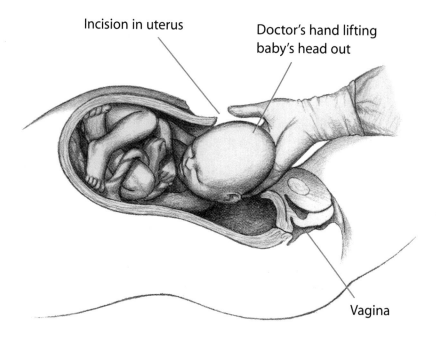

Incision in uterus

Doctor's hand lifting
baby's head out

Vagina

*Delivery of a baby by
Cesarean section.*

increase in the size of babies is due to pregnant women eating a
better diet and not smoking during pregnancy. The rising rate may
also be related to the pressure on doctors to deliver a baby safely.

How Is a C-Section Performed?

You may be awake when a C-section is done. An anesthesiologist usually gives you an epidural or spinal anesthetic. (Types of anesthesia are discussed in Week 39.) If you're awake for the procedure, you may be able to see your baby immediately after delivery!

With a C-section, an incision is made through the skin of the abdominal wall to the uterus. The wall of the uterus is cut, then the amniotic sac containing the baby and placenta is cut. The baby is removed through the incision. Next, the placenta is removed. The uterus is closed in layers with sutures that absorb and do not have to be removed. The remainder of the abdomen is sewn together with absorbable sutures.

Dad Tip

Pack for yourself, too! Some essential items you might need include magazines, phone numbers, a change of clothes and something to sleep in, a camera, snacks, a telephone calling card or lots of change, insurance information, a comfortable pillow and extra cash.

Most Cesarean deliveries done today are *low-cervical* Cesareans or *low-transverse* Cesareans. This means the incision is made low in the uterus.

In the past, a Cesarean was often done with a classical incision, in which the uterus is cut down the midline. This incision doesn't heal as well as a low-cervical incision. Because the incision is made in the muscular part of the uterus, it is more likely to pull apart with contractions (as in a vaginal birth after Cesarean). This can cause heavy bleeding and injure the baby. If you have had a classical Cesarean section in the past, you must have a C-section every time you have a baby.

A T-incision is another type of C-section incision. This incision goes across and up the uterus in the shape of an inverted T. It provides more room to get the baby out. If you have had this type of incision, you will need to have a Cesarean delivery with all subsequent pregnancies. It too is more likely to rupture than other types of incisions.

Advantages and Disadvantages of Having a C-Section

There are advantages to having a C-section. The most important advantage is delivery of a healthy infant. The baby you are carrying may be too large to fit through your pelvis. The only safe method of delivery might be a C-section. Usually a woman needs to experience labor before her doctor will know if the baby will fit. It may be impossible to predict ahead of time.

The disadvantage is that a Cesarean section is a major operation and carries with it all the risks of surgery. Risks include infection, bleeding, shock due to blood loss, and the possibility of blood clots and injury to other organs, such as the bladder or rectum. You will probably stay in the hospital an extra couple of days.

> **There are advantages to having a C-section.**

Recovery at home from a Cesarean section takes longer than recovery from a regular delivery. The normal time for full recovery from a C-section is usually 4 to 6 weeks.

In most areas, an obstetrician performs a C-section. In small communities, a general surgeon or a family practitioner may perform C-sections.

Will You Need a Cesarean?

It would be nice to know you're going to need a C-section before delivery so you wouldn't have to go through labor. Unfortunately, it's usually necessary to wait for labor contractions for a couple of reasons. You won't know ahead of time if your baby is stressed by labor contractions. And it is often hard to predict if the baby will fit through your birth canal.

Some women believe that if they have a Cesarean, "it won't be like having a baby." They falsely believe they won't experience the entire birth process. That's not true. If you deliver by C-section, try not to feel this way. You haven't failed in any way!

> **Remember, having a baby has taken 9 long months. Even with a C-section, you have accomplished an amazing feat.**

Remember, having a baby has taken 9 long months. Even with a C-section, you have accomplished an amazing feat. After a C-section, you can hold the baby and perhaps even nurse.

Notes

Week 37

How Big Is Your Baby?

Your baby weighs almost 6.5 pounds (2.95kg). Crown-to-rump length is 14 inches (35cm). Its total length is 21 inches (47cm).

How Big Are You?

Your uterus may stay the same size as measured in the last week or two. Measuring from the pubic symphysis, the top of the uterus is about 14.8 inches (37cm). From the bellybutton, it is 6.4 to 6.8 inches (16 to 17cm). Your total weight gain by this time should be about as high as it will go at 25 to 35 pounds (11.3 to 15.9kg).

How Your Baby Is Growing and Developing

Is Your Baby's Head Down in Your Pelvis?
Your baby is continuing to grow and to gain weight, even during these last few weeks of pregnancy. As the illustration on page 338 shows, the baby's head is usually directed down into the pelvis around this time. However, in about 3% of all pregnancies, the baby's bottom or legs come into the pelvis first. This is called a *breech presentation*, which we discuss in Week 38.

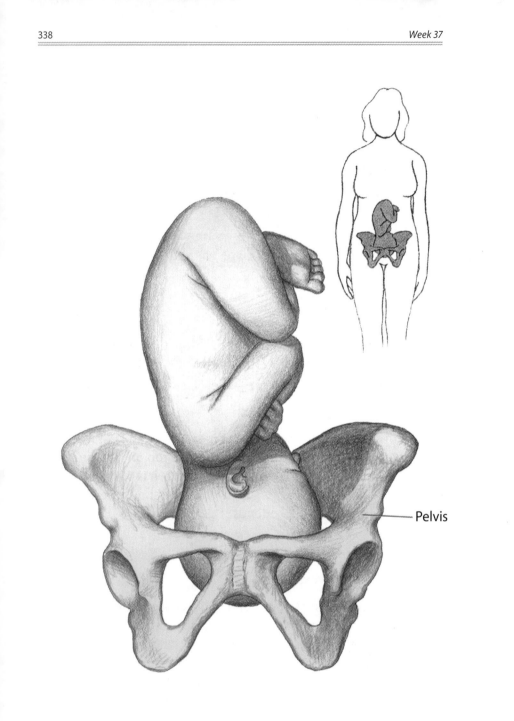

Alignment of baby with head in pelvis before delivery. This is the preferable presentation.

Pelvis

Changes in You

Pelvic Exam in Late Pregnancy

About this time in your pregnancy, your healthcare provider may do a pelvic exam. This pelvic exam helps your caregiver evaluate the progress of your pregnancy. One of the first things he or she will observe is whether you are leaking amniotic fluid. If you think you are, it's important to tell your caregiver.

Your healthcare provider will examine your cervix at the pelvic exam. During labor, the cervix usually becomes softer and thins out. This process is called *effacement*. Your caregiver will evaluate the cervix for its softness or firmness and the amount of thinning.

Before labor begins, the cervix is thick and is "0% effaced." When you're in active labor, the cervix thins out; when it is half-thinned, it is "50% effaced." Immediately before delivery, the cervix is "100% effaced" or "completely effaced."

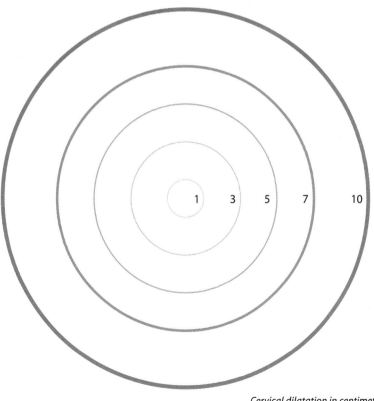

Cervical dilatation in centimeters
(shown actual size).

The dilatation (amount of opening) of the cervix is also important. This is usually measured in centimeters. The cervix is fully open when the diameter of the cervical opening measures 10cm. The goal is to be a 10! Before labor begins, the cervix may be closed. Or it may be open a little way, such as 1cm (0.4 inch). The goal of labor is the stretching and opening of the cervix so the baby fits through it and can pass out of the uterus.

Your caregiver also evaluates whether the baby's head, bottom or legs are coming first. (He or she may refer to a "presenting part.") The shape of your pelvic bones is also noted.

The station is then determined. Station describes the degree to which the presenting part of the baby has descended into the birth canal. If the baby's head is at a -2 station, it means the head is higher inside you than if it were at a +2 station. The 0 point is a bony landmark in the pelvis, the starting place of the birth canal.

Think of the birth canal as a tube going from the pelvic girdle down through the pelvis and out the vagina. The baby travels through this tube from the uterus. It's possible that you may dilate during labor but the baby doesn't move down through the pelvis. In this case, a C-section may be called for because the baby's head doesn't fit through the pelvic girdle.

What Can Your Doctor Tell from a Pelvic Exam?

When your doctor examines you, he or she may describe your situation in medical terms. You might hear you are "2cm, 50% and a -2 station." This means the cervix is open 2cm (about 1 inch), it is halfway thinned out (50% effaced) and the presenting part (baby's head, feet or buttocks) is at a -2 station.

Try to remember this information. It's helpful when you go to the hospital and are checked there by a nurse or doctor. You can tell the medical personnel in labor and delivery what your dilatation and effacement were at your last checkup so they can know if your situation has changed.

How Your Actions Affect Your Baby's Development

Choosing Your Baby's Doctor

At this point in your pregnancy, it's time to choose a doctor for your baby. You might choose a pediatrician—a doctor who specializes in treating children. Or you might choose a family practitioner. If the doctor you are seeing during pregnancy is a family practitioner, and you want him or her to care for your baby, you probably don't need to consider this at all.

It's good to meet this doctor before the birth of your baby. Many pediatricians welcome it. This gives you the opportunity to discuss matters that are important to you with this new caregiver. You might want to talk to him or her about a circumcision for your baby if it's a boy. You may want to ask questions about breastfeeding, exams, immunizations and vaccinations, emergencies and other things that concern you. It's also good to find out whether a particular doctor shares your views on child rearing.

By choosing someone to care for your baby before it's born, you have a chance to take part in deciding who will have that important task. If you don't, the doctor who delivers your baby, or the hospital personnel, will select someone. Another good reason for choosing someone ahead of time is if your baby has complications.

After your baby is born, the pediatrician will visit him or her in the hospital and give the baby a physical exam within 24 hours after birth. Then he or she will visit you in the hospital, let you know how things are going for the baby and arrange for follow-up care after you leave the hospital.

> By choosing someone to care for your baby before it's born, you have a chance to take part in deciding who will have that important task. If you don't, the doctor who delivers your baby, or the hospital personnel, will select someone.

Your Nutrition

You and your partner have been invited to a big party. You've been diligent about your nutrition, and your pregnancy is almost over. Should you let yourself go, and eat and drink whatever you want? It's probably a good idea to maintain your good eating habits. You *can* party healthfully. Below are some suggestions to help you have a good time.

- Eat food when it's fresh and hot—at the beginning of the party. As the party goes on, the food may not be chilled or heated enough to prevent bacteria from growing. So eat early or when dishes are refilled.
- Eat something before you go to take the edge off your appetite. Or drink a large glass of water. It may be easier to avoid high-fat and high-calorie foods if you're not ravenous.
- Avoid alcohol. Drink fruit juice "spiked" with ginger ale or lemon-lime soda. If it's the holiday season and they're serving eggnog, have a glass if it's alcohol-free and has been pasteurized.
- Raw fruits and vegetables can be satisfying. Avoid raw seafood and meat and soft cheeses, such as Brie, Camembert and feta. They may contain listeriosis.
- Stay away from the refreshment table if you can't resist the goods. It may feel better to sit down (away from food), relax and talk with friends.

You Should Also Know

Will You Have an Enema?
Will you be required to have an enema when you arrive at labor and delivery? Most hospitals offer an enema at the beginning of labor, but it is not always mandatory. However, there are certain advantages to having an enema before labor. You may not want to have a bowel movement soon after your baby's delivery because of discomfort with an episiotomy. Having an enema before labor can prevent this discomfort.

An enema before labor can also make the birth of your baby a more pleasant experience. When the baby's head comes out through the birth canal, anything in the rectum comes out, too. An enema decreases the amount of contamination by bowel movement or feces at the time of delivery and during labor, preventing possible infection.

Ask your healthcare provider if an enema is routine or considered helpful. Tell him or her you'd like to know about the benefits of an enema and the reason for giving an enema in early labor. It isn't required by all doctors or all hospitals.

What Is Back Labor?

Some women experience back labor. Back labor refers to a baby that is coming through the birth canal looking straight up. With this type of labor, you will probably experience lower-back pain.

The mechanics of labor work better if the baby is looking down at the ground so it can extend its head as it comes out through the birth canal. If the baby can't extend its head, its chin points toward its chest. This can cause pain in your lower back during labor.

This type of labor can also last longer. Your doctor may need to rotate the baby so it comes out looking down at the ground rather than up at the sky.

How Is Your Baby Presenting?

At what point in your pregnancy can your healthcare provider tell how baby is presenting for delivery—for example, if the baby's head is down or if you are carrying the baby breech? At what point will the baby stay in the position it is in?

Usually between 32 and 34 weeks of pregnancy, you can feel the baby's head in the lower abdomen below your umbilicus. Some women can feel different parts of the baby earlier than this. But the baby's head may not be hard enough yet to identify as the head.

The head gradually becomes harder as calcium is deposited in the fetal skull. Your baby's head has a distinct feeling. It is different from the feeling your doctor gets with a breech. A breech position has a soft, round feeling.

Beginning at 32 to 34 weeks, your caregiver will probably feel your abdomen to determine how the baby is lying inside you. This position may have changed many times during pregnancy.

At 34 to 36 weeks of pregnancy, the baby usually gets into the position it's going to stay in. If you have a breech at 37 weeks, it's possible the baby can still turn to be head-down. But it becomes less likely the closer you get to the end of your pregnancy.

Tip for Week 37

Now is the time to find a pediatrician for your baby. Ask for referrals; your healthcare provider can give you a reference. Or ask family, friends or people in your childbirth-education classes for names of doctors they like.

It may be difficult at times to tell the exact location of different parts of the baby. You may have a good idea according to where you feel kicks and punches. Ask your caregiver to show you on your tummy how the baby is lying. Some doctors even take a marking pen and draw on your stomach to show you. You can leave it so you can show your partner how your baby was lying when you were seen in the office that day.

Will Your Doctor Have to Use Forceps?

The use of forceps—metal instruments used in the delivery of babies—has decreased in recent years for a couple of reasons. One is the more frequent use of Cesarean delivery to deliver a baby that might be high up in the pelvis. A C-section may be much safer for the baby if it's not close to delivering on its own.

Another reason for the decrease in the use of forceps is the use of a vacuum extractor. There are two types of vacuum extractors. One has a plastic cup that fits on the baby's head by suction. The other has a metal cup. The doctor is able to pull on the vacuum cup to deliver the baby's head. The vacuum easily releases from the baby's head, so the baby can't be pulled as hard through the birth canal as with forceps.

The goal with every birth is to deliver the baby as safely as possible. If a large amount of traction with forceps is needed to deliver the baby, a Cesarean section might be a better choice.

If the possible use of a vacuum extractor or forceps causes you concern, discuss it with your physician. It's important to establish good communication with your healthcare provider so you can communicate before and during labor about these concerns.

Dad Tip

Let your partner know how she can get hold of you at work or when you're out. You may not understand how nervous she can be about getting in touch with you when she needs you. Carry a cell phone or a beeper with you all the time. This can provide her with comfort and peace of mind.

Week 38

How Big Is Your Baby?

At this time, your baby weighs about 6.8 pounds (3.1kg). Crown-to-rump length hasn't changed much; it's still about 14 inches (35cm). Total length is 21 inches (47cm).

How Big Are You?

Many women don't grow larger during the last several weeks of pregnancy, but they feel very uncomfortable. The distance between your uterus and the pubic symphysis is 14.4 to 15.2 inches (36 to 38cm). From your bellybutton to the top of your uterus is about 6.4 to 7.2 inches (16 to 18cm).

How Your Baby Is Growing and Developing

Fetal Monitoring during Labor

You may wonder how your doctor can tell your baby is all right, especially during labor. In many hospitals, the baby's heart rate is monitored throughout labor. Being able to detect problems early is important so they can be resolved.

Every time the uterus contracts during labor, less oxygenated blood flows from you to the placenta. Most babies are able to handle this stress without any problem. However, some are affected; this is called *fetal distress*.

> In many hospitals, the baby's heart rate is monitored throughout labor.

There are two ways to monitor the baby's heartbeat during labor. External fetal monitoring can be used before your membranes rupture. A belt with a receiver is strapped to your abdomen. It uses a principle similar to ultrasound to detect the baby's heartbeat.

An internal fetal monitor monitors the baby's heartbeat more precisely. An electrode is placed on the baby's scalp and is connected by wires to a machine that records the fetal heart rate. Only women whose membranes are broken and who are dilated at least 1cm can be attached to an internal fetal monitor.

The Contraction Stress Test
In evaluating a fetal heart rate, a doctor looks at a large portion of the fetal monitoring strip, not just a small section. He or she also looks for other information. For example, if you are having contractions, it's important to know how your baby is affected. Fetal monitoring can help determine this.

A contraction stress test (CST) gives an indication of how well the baby will tolerate contractions and labor. If the baby doesn't respond well to contractions, it can be a sign of fetal distress. Some believe this test is more accurate than the nonstress test (discussed in Week 34) in evaluating the baby's well-being. A monitor is placed on your abdomen to monitor the baby. You are attached to an I.V. that dispenses small amounts of the hormone oxytocin to make your uterus contract.

If you've had problem pregnancies before, such as a stillbirth, or medical problems during pregnancy, such as diabetes, your healthcare provider may have you tested as you go through pregnancy. You may be tested weekly or biweekly to determine if the baby is doing well inside your uterus.

Fetal Blood Sampling
Doctors can also test your baby's blood pH to see how well your baby is tolerating the stress of labor. Before this test can be done, your membranes must be ruptured, and you must be dilated at least 2cm.

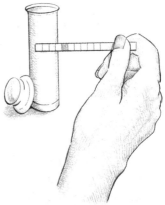

An instrument is applied to the scalp of the baby to make a small nick in the skin. The baby's blood is collected in a small tube or pipette, and its pH (acidity)

is checked. If the baby is having trouble with labor and is under stress, the pH level can help determine this. This test may be useful in making a decision as to whether labor can continue or if a C-section needs to be done.

Changes in You

Postpartum Distress Syndrome

After your baby is born, you may feel emotional. You may even wonder if having a baby was a good idea. This

> **Baby blues are temporary and usually leave as quickly as they come.**

is called *postpartum distress*. Many women experience some degree of postpartum distress; in fact, up to 80% of all women have "baby blues." It usually appears between 2 days and 2 weeks after the baby is born. Baby blues are temporary and usually leave as quickly as they come.

Many experts consider some degree of postpartum distress to be normal. Symptoms vary:

- anxiety
- exhaustion
- irritability
- lack of feeling for the baby
- oversensitivity

- crying for no reason
- impatience
- lack of confidence
- low self-esteem
- restlessness

If you believe you may be suffering from some form of postpartum distress, contact your healthcare provider. Every postpartum reaction, whether mild or severe, is usually temporary and treatable.

The mildest form of postpartum distress is baby blues. This situation lasts only a couple of weeks, and symptoms do not worsen.

A more serious version of postpartum distress is called *postpartum depression* (PPD). It affects about 10% of all new mothers. The difference between baby blues and postpartum depression lies in the frequency, intensity and duration of the symptoms.

PPD can occur from 2 weeks to 1 year after the birth. A mother may have feelings of anger, confusion, panic and hopelessness. She may experience changes in her eating and sleeping patterns. She may fear she will hurt her baby or feel as if she is going crazy. Anxiety is one of the major symptoms of PPD.

Handling the Blues

There is no single treatment for baby blues, but there are ways you can help relieve the symptoms.

- Ask for help.
- Rest when your baby sleeps.
- Find other mothers who are in the same situation; it helps to share your feelings and experiences.
- Don't try to be perfect.
- Pamper yourself.
- Do some form of moderate exercise every day.
- Eat nutritiously and drink plenty of fluids.
- Go out every day.
- Consider using antidepressants temporarily if the above steps don't work for you. About 85% of all women who suffer from postpartum depression require medication for up to 1 year.

The most serious form of postpartum distress is postpartum psychosis. The woman may have hallucinations, think about suicide or try to harm the baby.

We don't really know what causes postpartum distress; not all women experience it. We believe a woman's individual sensitivity to hormonal changes may be the cause, but hormones are only part of it.

One of the most important ways you can help yourself is to have a good support system. Ask family members and friends to help. Ask your mother or mother-in-law to stay for a while. Ask your husband to take some work leave, or hire someone to come in and help each day.

How Your Actions Affect Your Baby's Development

Breech Presentation

As we've mentioned already, it's common for your baby to be in the breech presentation early in pregnancy. However, when labor starts, only 3 to 5% of all babies, not including multiple pregnancies, present as a breech. Do your actions determine how your baby presents?

Certain factors make a breech presentation more likely. One of the main causes is the baby's prematurity. Near the end of the second trimester, a baby may be in a breech presentation. By taking care of yourself, you can more easily avoid going into premature labor. That gives your baby the best opportunity to change its position naturally.

Other factors that may result in a breech presentation include relaxation of the uterus because of previous pregnancies and multiple fetuses. Certain conditions, such as polyhydramnios, hydrocephalus and uterine abnormalities or tumors, may also increase the chance of a breech presentation.

There are different kinds of breech presentations. A *frank breech* occurs when the lower legs are flexed at the hips and extended at the knees. This is the most common type of breech found at term or the end of pregnancy; feet are up by the face or head.

With a *complete breech presentation,* one or both knees are flexed, not extended. See the illustration on page 350.

Delivering a Breech Baby

There is some controversy in obstetrics over the best method of delivering a breech baby. For many years, breech deliveries were performed vaginally. Then it was believed the safest method was to deliver the breech by C-section, especially if it was a first baby.

Many doctors believe a Cesarean section is still the safest method of delivering a breech baby. However, some doctors believe a woman can deliver a breech without difficulty if the situation is right. This usually includes a frank breech in a mature fetus of a woman who has had previous normal deliveries. Most agree a *footling breech presentation* (one leg extended, one knee flexed) should be delivered by Cesarean section.

Most doctors believe a baby in the breech position can probably be delivered more safely by a Cesarean section performed during early labor or before labor begins. Ask your healthcare provider what he or she normally does in this situation.

Attempts may be made to turn the baby from a breech to a head-down (vertex) presentation. It is more difficult to do this after your water breaks or when you are in labor.

If your baby is breech, it's important to discuss it with your healthcare provider. When you get to the hospital, tell the nurses and hospital personnel you have a breech presentation. If you call

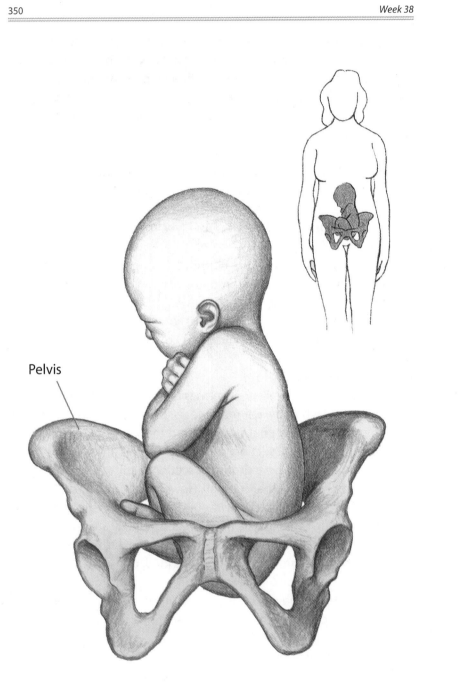

Pelvis

Baby aligned in the pelvis bottom-first, with knees flexed, is called a complete breech presentation.

with a question about labor and you have a breech presentation, mention this information to the person you talk with.

Other Types of Presentations

Another unusual presentation is a *face presentation*. The baby's head is hyperextended so the face comes into the birth canal first. This type of presentation is most often delivered by C-section if it does not convert to a regular presentation during labor.

In a *shoulder presentation*, the shoulder presents first. In a *transverse lie*, the baby is lying almost as if in a cradle in the pelvis. The baby's head is on one side of your abdomen, and its bottom is on the other side. There is only one way to deliver this type of presentation, and that is by Cesarean section.

Tip for Week 38

If your healthcare provider suspects your baby is in a breech position, he or she may order an ultrasound to confirm it. It helps identify how the baby is lying in your uterus.

Your Nutrition

You may not feel much like eating about this time, but it's important to keep eating a healthful diet. Snacks might be the answer. Instead of eating large meals, eat small snacks throughout the day to keep your energy levels up and to help avoid heartburn. You may be tired of the foods you've been eating. The list below offers some smart snacks for your healthy nutrition:

- bananas, raisins, dried fruit and mangoes to satisfy your sweet tooth and to provide you with iron, potassium and magnesium
- string cheese; it's high in calcium and protein
- fruit shakes made with skim milk and yogurt or ice cream for calcium, vitamins and minerals
- crackers that are high in fiber; spread with a little peanut butter for taste and protein
- cottage cheese and fruit, flavored with a little sugar and some cinnamon, for a tasty milk serving
- salt-free chips or tortillas with salsa or bean dip for fiber and good taste

- hummus and pita slices for fiber and good taste
- fresh tomatoes, flavored with some olive oil and fresh basil; eat with a few thin slices of Parmesan cheese for a dairy serving and vegetable serving
- chicken or tuna salad (made from fresh chicken or tuna packed in water) and crackers or tortilla pieces for protein and fiber

You Should Also Know

What Is a Retained Placenta?

In most instances, the placenta is delivered within 30 minutes after the birth of your baby and is a routine part of the delivery. In some cases, a piece of placenta remains inside the uterus and does not deliver spontaneously. When this happens, the uterus cannot contract adequately, resulting in vaginal bleeding that can be heavy.

In other cases, the placenta does not separate because it's still attached to the wall of the uterus. This can be a very serious situation. However, this complication is rare.

Bleeding is usually severe after delivery, and surgery may be necessary to stop it. An attempt may be made to remove the placenta by D&C.

Reasons for an abnormally adherent placenta are many. It is believed a placenta may attach over a previous Cesarean-section scar or other previous incisions on the uterus. The placenta may attach over an area that has been scraped, such as with a D&C, or over an area of the uterus that was infected at one time.

Your healthcare provider will pay attention to the delivery of your placenta while you are paying attention to your baby. Some people ask to see the placenta after delivery; you may wish to have your caregiver show it to you.

Dad Tip

Ask your partner if there are things she would like you to bring to the hospital for her, such as tapes or CDs and a player for the music. Discuss it ahead of time and have things ready. If you take a tour of the hospital or birthing center, you might get other ideas of things you can do to help control the environment your new baby enters.

Week 39

How Big Is Your Baby?

Your baby weighs a little more than 7 pounds (3.25kg). By this point in your pregnancy, crown-to-rump length is about 14.4 inches (36cm). The baby's total length is 21.5 inches (48cm).

How Big Are You?

The illustration on page 355 shows a side view of a woman with a large uterus and her baby inside it. As you can see, she's about as big as she can get. You probably are, too!

If you measure from the pubic symphysis to the top of the uterus, the distance is 14.4 to 16 inches (36 to 40cm). Measuring from the bellybutton, the distance is 6.4 to 8 inches (16 to 20cm).

You're almost at the end of your pregnancy. Your weight should not increase much from this point. It should remain between 25 and 35 pounds (11.4 and 15.9kg) until delivery.

How Your Baby Is Growing and Developing

Your baby continues to gain weight, even up to the last week or two of pregnancy. It doesn't have much room to move inside your uterus. At this point, all the organ systems are developed and in place. The last organ to mature is the lungs.

Can Your Baby Get Tangled in the Cord?

You may have been told by friends not to raise your arms over your head or reach high to get things because it can cause the cord to wrap around the baby's neck. There doesn't seem to be any truth to this theory.

Some babies do get tangled in their umbilical cord and can get the cord tied in a knot or wrapped around their neck. However, nothing you do during pregnancy causes or prevents this from happening.

A tangled umbilical cord isn't necessarily a problem during labor. It only becomes a problem if the cord is stretched tight around the baby's neck or is in a knot.

Changes in You

It would be unusual for you *not* to be uncomfortable and feel huge at this time. Your uterus has filled your pelvis and most of your abdomen. It has pushed everything else out of the way.

At this point in pregnancy, you may think you'll never want to be pregnant again because you're so uncomfortable. Or you may be sure your family is complete. At this point, some women consider permanent sterilization, such as tubal ligation.

Tubal Ligation after Delivery?

Some women choose to have a tubal ligation done while they are in the hospital after having their baby. Now is *not* the time to make the decision about having a tubal ligation if you haven't seriously considered it before.

Being sterilized following delivery of a baby has some advantages. You're in the hospital and won't need another hospitalization. However, there are disadvantages to having a sterilization at this time. Consider the procedure permanent and not reversible. If you have your tubes tied within a few hours or a day after having your baby, then change your mind, you may regret the tubal ligation.

Tip for Week 39

Don't take tags off shower gifts and other gifts until after your baby is born. You may need to exchange the gift if its size, color or "sex" isn't correct.

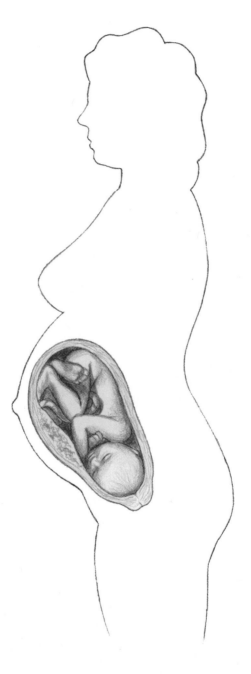

Comparative size of the uterus at 39 weeks of pregnancy (fetal age—37 weeks) with a baby that is close to full term.

If you have an epidural, it's possible to use the epidural as anesthesia for a tubal ligation. If you didn't have an epidural, it's necessary to put you to sleep. This is often done the morning after you've had your baby. This procedure does not usually lengthen the time you're in the hospital.

Different kinds of procedures are performed for permanent sterilization. Most common is a small incision underneath your bellybutton. The Fallopian tubes can be seen through this incision.

A piece of the tube can be removed, or a ring or clip can be placed on the tube to block it. This type of surgery usually requires 30 to 45 minutes to perform.

If you have second thoughts or are unsure about having it done, don't have the surgery performed. Consider the procedure permanent. Tubal ligations can be reversed, but it's expensive and requires a longer hospital stay—3 to 4 days. Reversals are about 50% effective, but pregnancy cannot be guaranteed.

How Your Actions Affect Your Baby's Development

The discussion on the following pages actually concerns your actions after your baby is born—whether or not to breastfeed your baby.

Is Breastfeeding Right for You and Your Baby?

Your decision about breastfeeding is a personal one. One of the more compelling reasons to breastfeed is the bonding that occurs between mother and baby. This close relationship can begin as soon as the baby is born—some women breastfeed on the delivery table. It helps stimulate uterine contractions, which can prevent hemorrhage.

Breastfeeding encourages the natural intimacy of a newborn baby with its mother and the mother with her baby. The opportunity to breastfeed may be a relaxing time for you. It may give you a chance to spend some wonderful time with your new baby. However, if it doesn't work out, it's all right to stop and switch to formula.

Benefits of Breastfeeding

Both you and your baby benefit if you breastfeed. Mother's milk is good for your baby because it contains all the nutrients your baby needs during the first months of life. Commercial formulas have good mixtures of vitamins, protein, sugar, fat and minerals, but none can match your breast milk.

Another advantage of breastfeeding is you pass protection against infection (through antibodies) to your baby in your breast milk. Many people believe a breastfed baby is less likely to get colds and infections than a bottlefed baby.

Breastfeeding is also good for the baby because the baby will probably have to nurse more vigorously than is necessary with some bottle nipples. This encourages good tooth and jaw development.

Advantages for you include decreased cost as compared to buying formula. It's convenient to breastfeed; you don't have to carry bottles and formula with you for the baby. Some women find breastfeeding makes it easier for them to regain their figure.

You may have noticed during pregnancy that your breasts got larger and were probably tender at times. This happens because increased hormonal activity makes the alveoli in the breasts get larger. Milk in the breast is stored in small sacs of these alveoli.

The first milk that comes from the breasts usually arrives 2 or 3 days after delivery. Its arrival is initiated by stimulation from the baby suckling at your breast. The sucking sends a message to your brain to produce prolactin, a hormone that stimulates milk production in the alveoli.

Learning to Breastfeed

You may want to learn how to breastfeed while you're in the hospital. Ask the nurses to show you some of the tricks they've

(continued)

A Visit with the Doctor

Laura called the office because she was concerned about discharge from her nipples —was it an infection? I explained to her that late in pregnancy, a woman's breasts may begin to secrete *colostrum*. Colostrum is rich in antibodies that provide the baby with protection against various infections. I told her colostrum is normal and should not cause her concern.

learned to help your baby catch on to breastfeeding. Ask them any questions you have. What you learn may make the difference in keeping your baby happy with breastfeeding.

Breastfeeding requires a healthful nutrition plan for you, similar to the one you followed during pregnancy. You'll need at least 500 extra calories each day (compared to the extra 300 during pregnancy). Some doctors recommend you continue taking your prenatal vitamins after pregnancy, while you are nursing.

Be careful about what you eat and drink because things you eat can pass into your breast milk. Certain foods may not "sit" well with you or your baby. Spicy foods and chocolate you eat may cause an upset stomach in your baby! Caffeine can also pass to your baby. Any alcohol you drink passes to your baby through your breast milk, so be careful about your consumption of alcoholic beverages. The longer you breastfeed, the more you'll realize what you can and cannot eat and drink.

There may be times when you are away from the baby but you want to continue to breastfeed. You can do this by using a pump. You can pump your breasts with battery-operated pumps, electrical pumps, or manual pumps. Ask for suggestions before you leave the hospital.

Find Out about Breastfeeding

Talk with your caregiver during pregnancy about breastfeeding. Ask friends about their experiences and how much they enjoyed it. You may also want to contact the local La Leche League, an organization that encourages and promotes breastfeeding. It offers help to women who may be having trouble getting started with breastfeeding. Give them a call if you need information or support.

Breastfeeding Problems

A common breastfeeding problem for some women is breast engorgement. The breasts become swollen, tender and filled with breast milk. What can you do to relieve this problem?

- The best cure is to drain the breasts, if possible, as you do when breastfeeding. Some women take a hot shower and empty their breasts in the warm water.
- Ice packs may also help.
- Feed your baby from both breasts each time you feed. Don't feed on only one side.
- When you're away from your baby, try to express some breast milk to keep your milk flowing and breast ducts open. You'll feel more comfortable.
- Mild pain medicines, such as acetaminophen (Tylenol), are often useful in relieving the pain of engorgement. Acetaminophen is recommended by the American Academy of Pediatrics as safe to use while you're breastfeeding.
- You might need to use stronger medications, such as Tylenol with Codeine, a prescription medication.
- Call your healthcare provider if engorgement is especially painful. He or she will decide on treatment.

It is possible to get an infection in your breast while breastfeeding. If you think you have an infection, call your healthcare provider. An infection may cause pain in the breast, and the breast may turn red and become swollen. You may have

Sore Nipples

Most nursing mothers have sore nipples at some point, particularly at first. You can take steps to lessen or relieve the soreness.

- Keep your breasts dry and clean.
- Do not air dry—it encourages scab formation and can take quite a while for a sore breast to heal.
- Moist healing is best: A new kind of lanolin, called *Lansinoh*, does not contain pesticides or allergens. Cover the entire nipple area with lanolin every time baby finishes nursing.

Good news! Before too long—a few days to a few weeks—your breasts will become accustomed to breastfeeding.

streaks of red discoloration on the breast; you may also feel as though you have the flu.

Inverted Nipples

Some women have trouble breastfeeding because of inverted nipples. This happens when the nipple retracts inward instead of pointing outward. If you have inverted nipples, it is possible to breastfeed. Plastic breast shields are available to wear under clothing to help bring out an inverted nipple.

(continued)

Some doctors also recommend pulling on the nipple and rolling it between the thumb and index finger.

Nursing with Silicone Breast Implants

Women have nursed with breast implants; however, implants may make nursing more difficult. Doctors don't agree as to whether it is safe or possibly harmful to nurse with implants. If you are concerned, discuss the matter with your healthcare provider; ask him or her for the latest information.

Silicone Breast Disease

Research continues into silicone breast implants and how they affect women. In 1995, the American College of Rheumatology issued a statement that there was no demonstrable risk between silicone breast implants and connective-tissue diseases or rheumatic disease. In contrast, other studies have shown a small but significant risk of developing a connective-tissue disorder with silicone breast implants.

Some labs in the United States offer diagnostic tests to screen for silicone breast disease. However, none of these tests have been approved by the Food and Drug Administration. Check with your physician if you are concerned.

Support Bras

Some women find wearing a support bra helpful in the last few weeks of pregnancy. A nursing bra is useful while nursing. Many doctors suggest wearing a nursing bra all the time, even when you sleep, to make you more comfortable.

To prepare your breasts for nursing, however, expose them regularly to the air. Not wearing a bra now and then while you are wearing clothes allows your nipples to toughen slightly when they rub against the fabric of your clothes.

Your Nutrition

If you're going to breastfeed your baby, you need to begin thinking about nutritional needs for the time you will nurse. You will probably be advised to eat about 500 extra calories each day during this time. A breastfeeding mother secretes 425 to 700 calories into her breast milk every day! The extra calories you take in will help you maintain good health. These calories should also be nutritious and healthy, like the ones you've been eating during pregnancy.

> You need to drink at least 2 quarts of fluid every day to make enough milk for your baby and for you to stay hydrated.

As previously discussed, you may have to avoid some foods because they can pass into breast milk and cause your baby some stomach distress. Avoid chocolate, foods that produce gas in you, such as Brussels sprouts and cauliflower, highly spiced foods and other foods you have problems with. Discuss the situation with your healthcare provider and your pediatrician if you have questions and concerns.

In addition to the food you eat, you need to continue to drink lots of fluids. You need to drink at least 2 quarts of fluid every day to make enough milk for your baby and for you to stay hydrated. You'll need more in hot weather. Avoid caffeine-containing drinks because caffeine can act as a diuretic. It can also pass to your baby through your breast milk. Although caffeine is out of your bloodstream in 3 to 5 hours, it can remain in a baby's bloodstream for up to 96 hours!

Keep up your calcium intake. It's important if you breastfeed. You might ask your healthcare provider what kind of vitamin supplement you should take. Some mothers take their prenatal vitamin as long as they breastfeed.

You Should Also Know

Pain Relief during Labor

Pain relief during labor is approached in many ways. When you take pain medication, remember there are two patients to consider—you and your unborn baby. It is best to find out in advance what is available for pain control. Then see how your labor goes for you before making a final decision.

A valuable part of your experience in labor and delivery is your preparation for it. This includes being aware of things that are happening to you, and why, and not being frightened by the pain you feel. You should have confidence in those taking care of you, including the staff at the hospital and your healthcare provider.

When contractions are regular and the cervix is beginning to dilate, uterine contractions may be uncomfortable. For pain in this early stage of labor, many hospitals use a mixture of a narcotic analgesic drug, such as meperidine (Demerol), and a tranquilizer, such as

> A valuable part of your experience in labor and delivery is your preparation for it.

promethazine (Phenergen®). This decreases pain and causes some sleepiness or sedation. Medication may be given through an I.V. or by injection into a muscle.

Narcotic analgesics pass to your baby through the placenta and may decrease respiratory function in the newborn infant. It can also affect your baby's Apgar scores. These medications should not be given close to the time of delivery.

In many places, anesthesia for delivery is given by an injection of a particular medication to affect a particular area of the body. This is called a block, such as a *pudendal block,* an *epidural block* or a *cervical block*. Medication is similar to the type used to block pain when you have a tooth filled. The agents are xylocaine or xylocaine-like medications.

Occasionally, it is necessary to use general anesthesia for delivery of a baby, usually for an emergency Cesarean section. A pediatrician attends the birth because it is possible the baby will be asleep following delivery.

What Is an Epidural Block?
The epidural block is a frequently used regional block. It provides relief from the pain of uterine contractions and delivery. It should be administered only by someone trained and experienced in this type of anesthesia. Some obstetricians have this experience, but in most areas an anesthesiologist must administer it.

A continuous epidural block can be started when you are sitting up or lying on your side. The anesthesiologist numbs an area of skin over your lower back in the middle of your spinal cord. He or she then introduces a needle through the numbed area of the skin;

anesthetic is placed around the spinal cord but not into the spinal canal. A plastic catheter is left in place.

Epidural pain medication may be given during labor with a pump. The anesthesiologist uses the pump to inject a small amount of medication at regular intervals or as needed. An epidural provides excellent relief from labor pain.

A problem with an epidural block is that it can make your blood pressure drop. Low blood pressure may affect blood flow to the baby. Fortunately, I.V. fluids administered with the epidural help reduce the risk of hypotension (low blood pressure). You may also have problems pushing during delivery.

Other Pain Blocks

Spinal anesthesia may be used for a Cesarean section. With this anesthesia, pain relief lasts long enough for the Cesarean section to be performed. Epidural anesthesia is used more often than spinal anesthesia for labor.

Other types of blocks used occasionally include a pudendal block. It is given through the vaginal canal and decreases pain in the birth canal itself. You still feel the contraction and tightening with pain in the uterus. Some hospitals use a paracervical block. It provides pain relief for the dilating cervix, but doesn't relieve the pain of contractions.

There is no perfect method for pain relief during labor and delivery. Discuss the possibilities with your healthcare provider, and mention your concerns. Find out what types of anesthesia are available and the risks and benefits of each.

Anesthesia Complications

There are other possible complications from use of anesthesia. These include increased sedation of the baby with use of narcotics, such as Demerol. The newborn may have lower Apgar scores and depressed breathing. The baby may require resuscitation or it may need to receive another drug, such as naloxone (Narcan®), to reverse the effects of the first drug.

Increased sedation, slower respiration and a slower heartbeat may also be observed in a baby whose mother is given general anesthesia. The mother is usually "out" for more than an hour and is unable to see her newborn infant until later.

It may be impossible to determine before you go into labor which anesthesia will be best for you. But it's helpful to know what's available and what types of pain relief you might be able to count on during your labor and delivery.

Contraction of the Uterus after Delivery

After you deliver your baby, your uterus shrinks from about the size of a watermelon to the size of a volleyball. When this happens, the placenta detaches from the uterine wall. At this time, there may be a gush of blood from inside the uterus signaling delivery of the placenta.

After the placenta is delivered, you may be given oxytocin (Pitocin). This helps the uterus contract and clamp down so it won't bleed. Extremely heavy bleeding after vaginal delivery is called *postpartum hemorrhage,* which is bleeding more than 17 ounces (500ml). It can often be prevented by massaging the uterus and using medications to help the uterus contract.

The main reason a woman experiences heavy bleeding after delivering a baby is her uterus does not contract, called an *atonic* uterus. Your doctor, midwife or the nurse attending you may massage your uterus after delivery. They may show you how to do it so your uterus will stay firm and contracted. This is important so you won't lose more blood and become anemic.

Cord-Blood Banking

Cord blood is blood left in the umbilical cord and placenta after a baby is born. In the past, the placenta and the umbilical cord were usually discarded following delivery. There is a great deal of interest now about saving cord blood after delivery. Cord-blood banking was called one of the top 10 medical advances of 1996 by the *Harvard Health Letter.*

Umbilical-cord blood can be used to treat cancer and genetic diseases that are now treated by bone-marrow transplants. Cord blood has been used successfully to treat childhood leukemia, some immune diseases and other blood diseases. At present, research is being conducted in the United States and Europe to use cord blood for gene therapy in a number of diseases, including sickle cell anemia, diabetes and AIDS.

Cord blood contains the same valuable cells that are found in bone marrow. These "stem cells" are the building blocks of the blood and immune systems. These special cells are undeveloped in cord blood. Because they are undeveloped, cord blood does not need to be matched as closely for a transplant as bone-marrow blood does. This feature can be especially important for members of ethnic minority groups or people with rare blood types. These groups traditionally have had more difficulty finding acceptable donor "matches."

> **Dad Tip**
>
> Who do you and your partner want in the delivery room? Having a baby is a unique and wonderful experience. Some couples choose the intimacy and privacy of being alone during the birth. If you talk about it ahead of time, you can decide what the two of you want. After all, it's your baby's birth.

Before their baby's birth, parents may request that the baby's cord blood be collected and "banked" for future use. The blood can be used by the child from whom it was collected, his siblings or parents. You also may donate your baby's cord blood at no cost to you, similar to blood banking.

Blood is collected directly from the umbilical cord immediately after delivery. There is no risk or pain to the mother or baby. The blood is transported to a banking facility where it is frozen and cryogenically stored.

The cost of cord-blood banking includes an initial fee of about $1,000, with about a $100-a-year storage fee. As more is learned about blood banking and its use becomes more common, the cost may go down. Some health-insurance companies pay the fees for families at high risk of cancer or genetically based diseases. Cord-blood banking services may waive fees for at-risk families who are unable to afford them. For more information about cord-blood banking services, contact the International Cord Blood Foundation at (415) 635-1456.

Notes

Week 40

How Big Is Your Baby?

Your baby weighs about 7.5 pounds (3.4kg). Its crown-to-rump length is about 14.8 to 15.2 inches (37 to 38cm). Total length is 21.5 inches (48cm). Your baby fills your uterus and has little room to move. See the illustration on page 370.

How Big Are You?

From the pubic symphysis to the top of the uterus, you probably measure 14.4 to 16 inches (36 to 40cm). From your bellybutton to the top of your uterus is 6.4 to 8 inches (16 to 20cm).

By this time, you probably don't care an awful lot about how much you measure. You feel you're as big as you could ever be, and you're ready to have your baby. You may continue to grow and even to get a little bit bigger until you have your baby. But don't be discouraged—you'll have your baby soon.

How Your Baby Is Growing and Developing

Bilirubin is a breakdown product from red blood cells. Before your baby is born, bilirubin is transferred easily across the placenta from the fetus to the maternal circulation. Through this process, your body is able to get rid of the bilirubin from the baby. Once your baby is delivered and the umbilical cord is clamped, the baby is on its own to handle the bilirubin produced in its body.

367

Jaundice in a Newborn

After birth, if your baby has problems dealing with bilirubin, it may develop high levels of it in the blood. Your baby may develop jaundice—yellowing of the skin and the whites of the eyes. Bilirubin levels typically increase for 3 or 4 days after the baby's delivery, then decrease.

Your pediatrician and the nurses in the nursery check for jaundice by observing your baby's color. Your baby may have a test to measure his or her bilirubin levels at the hospital or at your pediatrician's office.

A baby is treated for jaundice with *phototherapy*. The baby is placed under special lights; the light penetrates the skin and destroys the bilirubin. If high levels of bilirubin are present, the baby may undergo an exchange blood transfusion.

Kernicterus in a Newborn

Extremely high levels of bilirubin (hyperbilirubinemia) in a newborn infant cause doctors concern because a serious condition called *kernicterus* can develop. Kernicterus is seen more frequently in premature infants than in babies delivered at full term. If the baby survives the kernicterus, it may have neurological problems— spasticity, lack of muscle coordination and varying degrees of mental retardation. However, kernicterus in a newborn is a rare occurrence.

Changes in You

What Happens When You're Overdue?

By now you're anticipating the delivery of your baby. You're probably counting the days to your due date. As we've mentioned, not every woman delivers by her due date. A pregnancy is considered to be overdue (postdate) when it exceeds 42 weeks or 294 days from the first day of the last menstrual period.

While the fetus is growing and developing inside your uterus, it depends on two important functions performed by the placenta— respiration and nutrition. The baby relies on these functions for continued growth and development.

When a pregnancy is postdate, the placenta may fail to provide the respiratory function and essential nutrients the baby needs to grow, and an infant may begin to suffer nutritional deprivation. The baby is called *postmature*.

A Visit with the Doctor

At Jill's office visit, she wearily asked me, "How much longer?" She was 39 weeks pregnant, so I explained to her that most doctors agree that once a woman reaches 42 weeks of pregnancy, the baby should be delivered if the cervix is beginning to dilate and to thin, and the baby is in the proper presentation, with the head down.

She was disappointed that her baby wasn't coming yet. But when I explained that it's best for the baby to wait until it is ready to deliver, she agreed it was worth the wait for a healthy baby.

At birth, a postmature baby has dry, cracked, peeling, wrinkled skin, long fingernails and abundant hair. It also has less vernix covering its body. The baby appears almost malnourished, with decreased amounts of subcutaneous fat.

Because the postmature infant is in danger of losing nutritional support from the placenta, it's important to know the true dating of your pregnancy. This is one reason it's important to go to all of your prenatal visits.

Inducing Labor

If your caregiver must induce labor, you will receive oxytocin (Pitocin) intravenously. Medication is gradually increased until contractions begin. The amount of oxytocin you receive is controlled by a pump, so you can't receive too much of it. While you receive oxytocin, you are monitored for the baby's reaction to your labor.

Ripening the Cervix for Induction

It is estimated that obstetricians in the United States induce labor in about 450,000 women a year. Prepidil Gel® (dinoprostone cervical gel; 0.5mg) is a drug used to ripen the cervix and induce labor. *Ripening the cervix* means softening, thinning and dilating the cervix.

Prepidil Gel is most often used to ripen a cervix in a pregnant woman at or near term with a medical or obstetric need for labor

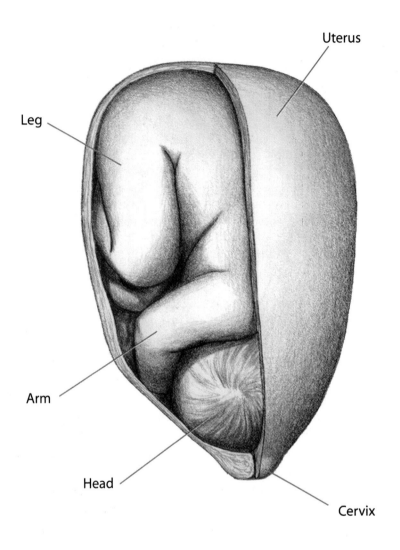

A full-term baby in the uterus has little room to move.
This is one reason fetal movements may slow down in
the last few weeks of pregnancy.

induction. These conditions include postmaturity (overdue baby), hypertension, pre-eclampsia or other problems.

Cervidil™ (dinoprostone, 10mg) is another preparation that ripens the cervix. It uses a controlled-release system.

In most cases, doctors use Prepidil Gel and Cervidil to prepare the cervix the day before induction. Both preparations are placed in the top of the vagina, behind the cervix. Medication is released directly onto the cervix, which causes it to ripen for induction of labor. Doctors do this procedure in the labor-and-delivery area of the hospital, so the baby can be monitored.

> You need to decide who you want with you during delivery. Sometimes, family members assume they're invited to the delivery.

How Your Actions Affect Your Baby's Development

The delivery of your baby is the event you've been planning for! If this is your first baby, you may be excited and a little apprehensive. Delivery of your baby is something you'll remember for a long time.

You need to decide who you want with you during delivery. Sometimes, family members assume they're invited to the delivery. Some couples choose to bring young children into the delivery room to see the birth of a new brother or sister. Discuss this with your healthcare provider ahead of time, and get his or her opinion. The delivery of the baby might be exciting and special to you and your partner, but it may be frightening to a young child.

Many places offer special classes for brothers- and sisters-to-be to help prepare them for the new baby. This is a good way to help older children feel they are part of the birth experience.

Your Nutrition

You won't be allowed to eat or drink anything during your labor. A woman often gets nauseated when she's in labor, which may cause vomiting. For your health and comfort, your caregiver wants to avoid this problem, so you will be advised to keep your stomach empty during labor for your own safety.

Eating probably won't be of interest to you, but you may be thirsty. However, understand that you won't be allowed to drink anything during labor for the same reasons as stated above. You will be allowed sips of water or ice chips to suck on. You may even be offered a wet face cloth to suck on. If your labor is long, your body may be hydrated with fluids through an I.V. After your baby's birth, if everything is OK, you will be able to eat and drink.

You Should Also Know

What Happens When You Arrive at the Hospital?
Don't be embarrassed if you have to go to the hospital to be checked for labor. This isn't a nuisance to hospital personnel or your doctor—that's why they're there! If you're concerned you might be in labor and you aren't sure, talk with your doctor or the nurses at labor-and-delivery. They'll tell you if you should come in to be evaluated.

When you go to the hospital, you'll be evaluated. A copy of your office record is kept in the labor-and-delivery area. Those seeing you in the hospital should know about any problems or complications that have occurred during your pregnancy and any other information that is important.

If you think you're in labor, don't eat. Even something light in your stomach can cause nausea. You may have to ask for an antacid for relief of stomach upset.

> If you think you're in labor, don't eat.

After you check in, you will be put in a labor room or an evaluation room to determine if you're actually in labor. It's important to know whether you're having contractions, how often they occur, how long they last and how strong they are. This is normally done with an external fetal monitor (discussed in Week 38). The monitor is placed on your abdomen; it shows the frequency and duration of contractions.

Check-in at the Hospital

You will probably be asked many questions when you arrive at the hospital to check in. They may include the following.

- Have your membranes ruptured? At what time?
- Are you bleeding?
- Are you having contractions? How often do they occur? How long do they last?
- When did you last eat and what did you eat?

Other important information for you to share includes medical problems you have and any medications you take or have taken during pregnancy. If you've had complications, such as placenta previa, tell medical personnel when you first come to labor-and-delivery.

It's important to know whether your membranes have ruptured (your water has broken). Ruptured membranes can be confirmed in any of several ways:

- by your description of what happened, such as a large gush of fluid
- with the nitrazine paper test
- with a ferning test

You will also be checked to see if you are dilated. It's helpful to know if you were dilated (and how much) when last checked by your healthcare provider. A nurse or doctor performs this exam.

You will be asked to give a brief history of your pregnancy. Mention any other medical problems you have. If you've had any complications during pregnancy, such as bleeding, or if you know your baby is breech, tell them. Don't assume they know. They will note your vital signs, including your blood pressure, pulse and temperature.

Evaluation and determination of whether you're in labor is usually not a 5-minute experience. It takes time to check everything out.

If you are in labor and remain at the hospital, other things will happen. Your partner may have to admit you to the hospital if you haven't filled out pre-admittance papers. You may be asked to sign a release form or a permission slip from the hospital, your doctor or the anesthesiologist. This is done to ensure you are informed and aware of the procedures that will be done for you and any risks that are involved.

After you have been admitted, you may receive an enema, or an I.V. may be started. Your doctor may want to discuss pain relief, or you may have an epidural put in place.

Blood will probably be drawn to be tested for hematocrit and complete blood count (CBC). Other things that are done at the hospital vary depending on where you go, your doctor's preferences and arrangements you have made ahead of time.

> Don't force your partner or labor coach to watch the delivery if he or she doesn't want to.

Your Labor Coach

In most instances, your partner is your labor coach. However, this isn't an absolute requirement. A close friend or relative, such as your mother or sister, can also serve as your labor coach. Ask someone ahead of time; don't wait until the last minute. Give the person time to prepare for the experience and to make sure he or she will be able to be there with you.

Not everyone feels comfortable watching the entire labor and delivery. This may include your partner. Don't force your partner or labor coach to watch the delivery if he or she doesn't want to. It's not unusual for a labor coach to get lightheaded, dizzy or pass out during labor and delivery. On more than one occasion, coaches or partners have fainted or become extremely lightheaded just from talking about plans for labor and delivery or a C-section!

Preparing ahead of time, as with prenatal classes, helps avoid some problems. In the past, you would have been alone with the nurses and doctor while your partner paced in the waiting room. Things have changed!

> Many couples do different things to distract themselves and to help pass time during labor. These include picking names for the baby, playing games, watching TV or listening to music.

The most important thing about the labor coach is the support he or she gives you during pregnancy, labor, delivery and recovery following the birth of the baby. Choose this person carefully.

What Can a Partner or Labor Coach Do?

Your partner or labor coach may be one of the most valuable assets you have during labor and delivery. He (or she) can help you prepare for labor and delivery in many ways. He can be there to support you as you go through the experience of labor together. He can share with you the joy of the delivery of your baby.

An important role of the labor coach is to make sure you get to the hospital! Work out a plan during the last 4 to 6 weeks of pregnancy so you know how to reach your coach. It's helpful to have an alternate driver, such as a neighbor or friend, who is available in case you are unable to reach your labor coach immediately and need to be taken to the hospital. Before going to the hospital, your labor coach can time your contractions so you are aware of the progress of your labor.

It's all right for your labor coach to rest or to take a break during labor. This is especially true if labor lasts a long time. It's better if your coach eats in the lounge or hospital cafeteria.

Many couples do different things to distract themselves and to help pass time during labor. These include picking names for the baby, playing games, watching TV or listening to music. A labor

Coaching Tips

Once you arrive at the hospital, both of you may be nervous. Your coach can do the following to help you both relax:

- talk to you while you're in labor to distract you and to help you relax
- encourage and reassure you during labor and when it comes time for you to push
- keep a watch on the door and protect your privacy
- help relieve tension during labor
- touch, hug and kiss (If you don't want to be touched during labor, tell your coach.)
- reassure you it's OK for you to deal vocally with your pain
- wipe your face or your mouth with a washcloth
- rub your abdomen or your back
- support your back while you're pushing
- help create a mood in the labor room, including music and lighting (Discuss it ahead of time; bring things with you that you would like to have available during labor.)
- take pictures (Many couples find still pictures taken of the baby after the delivery help them best remember these wonderful moments of joy.)

coach shouldn't bring work to the labor room. Talking on the phone to clients or doing work is inappropriate and shows little support for the laboring woman.

Talk to your healthcare provider about your coach's participation in the delivery, such as cutting the umbilical cord or bathing the baby after birth. Things like this vary from one place to another. Understand that the responsibility of your healthcare provider is the well-being of you and your baby—don't make requests or demands that could cause complications.

Talk ahead of time about who needs to be called. Bring a list of names and phone numbers with you. There are some people you may want to call yourself. In most places, a telephone is available in labor and delivery rooms.

Talk to your labor coach about showing the baby to those who are waiting. If you want to be with your partner when friends or relatives first see the baby, make it clear. Don't allow your baby to be taken out of the room unless that's what you want. In most instances, you need some cleaning up. Take 10 or 15 minutes for yourselves. After that you can show the baby to friends and relatives and share the joy with them.

What Happens to You after the Birth?

What happens to you after the birth of your baby depends on the hospital or birthing-center facilities where you have your baby. Hospitals vary in the arrangements and accommodations they have available.

LDRP

With LDRP (labor, delivery, recovery and postpartum), the room you are admitted to at the beginning of your labor is the room you labor in, deliver in, recover in and remain in for your entire hospital stay. This isn't available everywhere, but these facilities are becoming more popular.

The concept of LDRP has evolved because many women don't want to be moved from the labor area to recovery to another part of the hospital after delivery. The nursery is usually close to labor-and-delivery and the recovery area. This enables you to see your baby as often as you like and to have your baby in your room for longer periods.

Choosing Where to Give Birth

Whatever birthing setup you choose, the most important considerations are the health of your baby and the welfare of you both. When you decide where to have your baby, be sure you have answered the following questions, if you can.

- What facilities and staff do you have available?
- What is the availability of anesthesia? Is an anesthesiologist available 24 hours a day?
- How long does it take them to respond to and perform a Cesarean delivery, if necessary? (This should be 30 minutes or less.)
- Is a pediatrician available 24 hours a day for an emergency or problems?
- Is the nursery staffed at all times?
- In the event of an emergency or a premature baby that needs to be transported to a high-risk nursery, how is it done? By ambulance? By helicopter? How close is the nearest high-risk nursery, if not at this hospital?

These may seem like a lot of questions to ask, but the answers can help put your mind at ease. When it's your baby and your health, it's nice to know emergency measures can be employed in an efficient, timely manner when necessary.

Labor and Delivery Suite

In many places, you will labor in the labor-and-delivery suite, then be moved to a delivery room at the time of delivery. Following this, you may go to a postpartum floor, which is an area in the hospital where you will spend the remainder of your hospital stay.

Most hospitals allow you to have your baby in your room as much as you want. This is called rooming in or boarding in. Some hospitals also have a cot, couch or chair that makes into a bed in your room so your partner can stay with you after delivery. Check the availability of various facilities in the hospitals in your area.

Birthing Room

Another concept is the birthing room; this generally refers to delivering your baby in the same room you labor in. You don't have to be moved from the room you're laboring in to another place to have the baby. Even if you use a birthing room, you may have to move to another area of the hospital for recovery.

What Happens to Your Baby after It's Born?

When your baby is delivered, the healthcare provider clamps and cuts the umbilical cord, then the baby's mouth and throat are suctioned out. The baby may be placed on your abdomen in clean blankets. Or the baby may be passed to a nurse or pediatrician for initial evaluation and attention. The Apgar scores (see page 379) are recorded at 1- and 5-minute intervals. An identification band is placed on the baby so there's no mix-up in the nursery.

It's important to keep the baby warm immediately after birth. To do this, the nurse will dry the baby and wrap it in warm blankets. This is done whether the baby is on your chest or attended to by a nurse or doctor.

If your labor is complicated, the baby may need to be evaluated more thoroughly in the nursery. The baby's well-being and health are of primary concern. You'll be able to hold and to nurse the baby, but if your child is having trouble breathing or needs special attention, such as monitors, immediate evaluation is the most appropriate procedure at this time.

Your baby will be taken to the nursery by a nurse and your partner or labor coach. In the nursery, the baby is weighed, measured and footprinted (in some places). Drops to prevent infection are placed in the baby's eyes. A vitamin-K shot is given to help with the baby's blood-clotting factors. Your baby may receive the hepatitis vaccine if you request it. Then the baby is put in a heated bassinet for 30 minutes to 2 hours. The time period varies, depending on how stable the baby is.

Your pediatrician is notified immediately if there are problems or concerns. Otherwise, he or she will be notified soon after birth, and a physical exam will be performed within 24 hours.

Tip for Week 40

If you want to use a different labor position, massage, relaxation techniques or hypnotherapy to relieve labor pain, discuss it with your healthcare provider at one of your prenatal visits.

Your Baby's Apgar Score

After a baby is born, it is examined and evaluated at 1 minute and 5 minutes after delivery. The system of evaluation is called the Apgar score. This scoring system is a method of evaluating the overall well-being of the newborn infant.

In general, the higher the score, the better the infant's condition. The baby is scored in five areas. Each area is scored 0, 1 or 2; 2 points is the highest score for each category. The top total score is 10. Areas scored include the following.

- **Heart rate of the baby.** If the heart rate is absent, a score of 0 is given. If it is slow, less than 100 beats per minute (bpm), a score of 1 is given. If it's over 100 bpm, 2 points are scored.

- **Respiratory effort of the baby.** Respiratory effort indicates the newborn's attempts at breathing. If the baby isn't breathing, the score is 0. If breathing is slow and irregular, the score is 1. If the baby is crying and breathing well, the score is 2.

- **Baby's muscle tone.** Muscle tone evaluates how well the baby moves. If arms and legs are limp and flabby, the score is 0. If some movement is observed and the arms and legs bend a little, the score is 1. If the baby is active and moving, the score is 2.

- **Reflex irritability of the baby.** Reflex irritability is scored 0 if the baby doesn't respond to stimulus, such as rubbing his or her back or arms. If there is a small movement or a grimace when the baby is stimulated, the score is 1. A baby who responds vigorously is scored with 2 points.

- **Baby's color.** The baby's color is rated 0 if the baby is blue or pale. A score of 1 is given if the baby's body is pink and arms and legs are blue. A completely pink baby is scored at 2.

A perfect score of 10 is unusual. Most babies receive scores of 7, 8 or 9 in a normal healthy delivery. A baby with a low 1-minute Apgar may need to be resuscitated. This means a pediatrician or nurse must help stimulate the baby to breathe and to recover from the delivery. In most cases, the 5-minute Apgar is higher than the 1-minute score because the baby becomes more active and more accustomed to being outside the uterus.

Keep Your Options Open during Labor and Delivery

An important consideration in planning for your labor and delivery is the method(s) you may use to get through the process. Will you have epidural anesthesia? Are you going to attempt a drug-free delivery? Will you need an episiotomy?

Every woman is different, and every labor is different. It's difficult to anticipate what will happen and what you will need during labor and delivery for pain relief. It's impossible to know how long labor will last—3 hours or 20 hours. It's best to adopt a flexible plan. Understand what's available and what options you can choose during labor.

During the last 2 months of your pregnancy, discuss these concerns with your healthcare provider and become familiar with his or her philosophy about labor. Know what can be provided for you at the hospital you're going to. Some medications may not be available in some areas.

> A woman who chooses natural childbirth usually needs some advance instruction to prepare for it.

What Is Natural Childbirth?

Some women decide before the birth of their baby that they are going to labor and deliver with *natural childbirth*. What does this mean? The description or definition of natural childbirth varies from one couple to another.

Many people equate natural childbirth with drug-free labor and delivery. Others equate natural childbirth with the use of mild pain medications or local pain medications, such as numbing medications in the area of the vagina for delivery, or for an episiotomy and repair of episiotomy. Most agree that natural childbirth is birth with as few artificial procedures as possible. A woman who chooses natural childbirth usually needs some advance instruction to prepare for it.

Natural childbirth isn't for every woman. If you arrive at the hospital dilated 1cm, with strong contractions and in pain, natural childbirth may be hard for you. In this situation, an epidural might be appropriate.

Dad Tip

Discuss your role in labor and delivery. Learn what you can do to assist your partner. You may be able to help maintain privacy. When people visit during or after labor, be sure they don't get too loud or it doesn't become too crowded. Let your partner rest and recuperate; be her gatekeeper.

Natural Childbirth Techniques

There are three major philosophies of natural childbirth: Lamaze, Bradley and Grantly Dick-Read.

- **Lamaze** is the oldest technique of childbirth preparation. It conditions mothers, through training, to replace unproductive laboring efforts with fruitful ones and emphasizes relaxation and breathing during labor and delivery.
- **Bradley classes** teach the Bradley method of relaxation and inward focus; many types of relaxation are used. Strong emphasis is put on relaxation and deep abdominal breathing to make labor more comfortable. Classes begin when pregnancy is confirmed and continue until after the birth.
- **Grantly Dick-Read** is a method that attempts to break the fear-tension-pain cycle of labor and delivery. These classes were the first to include fathers in the birth experience.

On the other hand, if you arrive at the hospital dilated 4 or 5cm and contractions are OK, natural childbirth might be a reasonable choice. It's impossible to know what will happen ahead of time, but it helps to be aware of, and ready for, everything.

It's important to keep an open mind during the unpredictable process of labor and delivery. Don't feel guilty or disappointed if you can't do all the things you planned before labor. You may need an epidural. Or the birth may not be accomplished without an episiotomy. Don't let anyone make you feel guilty or make you feel as though you've accomplished less if you end up needing a C-section, an epidural or an episiotomy.

Beware of instruction that tells you labor is free of pain, no one really needs a C-section, I.V.s are unnecessary or an episiotomy is foolish. This can create unrealistic expectations for you. If you do need any of the above procedures, you may feel as though you failed during your labor.

The goal in labor and delivery is a healthy baby. If this means you end up with a C-section, you haven't failed. Be grateful a Cesarean delivery can be performed safely. Babies that would not have survived birth in the past can be delivered safely. This is a wonderful accomplishment!

Birth Journal

Baby's name: _____   **ID Bracelet**

Hospital: _____

City & state: _____

Date: _____

Time: _____

Sex: _____

Weight: _____

Length: _____

Doctor: _____

Photographs

My Birth Experience

Where I was when labor began, where dad was, how long it lasted, who was there, our first reactions when our baby was born.

_____

_____

_____

_____

_____

_____

_____

_____

_____

_____

_____

_____

_____

_____

_____

_____

Love at First Sight

What our baby looks like.

Eye color: _____

Hair: _____

Skin: _____

Birthmarks: _____

Other features: _____

_____

_____

_____

_____

Photographs, lock of hair, footprint

First 24 Hours with Baby

People Who Came to See Us

Name   Special notes

_____   _____

_____   _____

_____   _____

_____   _____

_____   _____

_____   _____

_____   _____

_____   _____

_____   _____

_____   _____

_____   _____

_____   _____

_____   _____

_____   _____

_____   _____

_____   _____

Photographs

Resources

Breastfeeding and Nutrition

Avent
800-542-8368
www.aventamerica.com
Gives information to parents on breastfeeding, bottlefeeding or a combination of the two.

Beechnut Nutrition Hotline
800-523-6633

Best Start
3500 E. Fletcher Ave., Suite 519
Tampa, FL 33613
800-277-4975
e-mail:
beststart@beststartinc.org

Breastfeeding National Network
800-TELL-YOU

International Lactation Consultant Association
919-787-5181

La Leche League
1400 North Meacham Road
Schaumburg, IL 60173-4048
847-519-7730
www.lalecheleague.org/

Medela, Inc.
1101 Corporate Drive
McHenry, IL 60050
815-363-1166, 800-435-8316
www.medela.com

National Center for Education & Maternal Child Health
Arlington, VA
703-524-7802
www.nce.mch.org

National Center for Nutrition and Dietetics' Consumer-Nutrition Hotline
800-366-1655
To speak with a dietitian.

Wellstart
4062 First Avenue
San Diego, CA 92103
619-295-5192

Dads

Boot Camp for New Dads
www.newdads.com
Information and resources for new dads. Experienced dads teach new dads; men learn from each other.

Father's World
www.fathersworld.com
Promotes and celebrates fatherhood and family. Good source of information for resources, support and education for any father.

Full-Time Dads
193 Shelley Ave.
Elizabeth, NJ 07208
908-355-9722; Fax 908-355-9723
www.fathersworld.com/
fulltimedad
Information for fathers, with open forums, to enhance and to promote the role of fathers in family and society. (Linked from Father's World.)

Health and Safety for Baby

American Academy of Pediatrics (AAP)
141 Northwest Point Blvd.
Elk Grove Village, IL 60007-1098
847-434-4000
www.aap.org

Auto Safety Hotline
888-327-4236

SafetyBeltSafe U.S.A.
P.O. Box 553
Altadena, CA 91003
www.carseat.org
Provides accurate, authoritative information about car seats for infants and children.

U.S. Consumer Products Safety Commission
800-638-2772
www.cpsc.gov
Provides information on keeping American families safe by reducing risk or death from use of consumer products.

Multiples

Center for Loss in Multiple Birth (C.L.I.M.B.)
P.O. Box 91377
Anchorage, AK 99509
907-222-5321
www.climb-support.org
e-mail: climb@pobox.alaska.net

Center for Study of Multiple Births
333 E. Superior St., Rm. 464
Chicago, IL 60611
312-266-9093

National Organization of Mothers of Twins Clubs, Inc.
P.O. Box 438
Thompson Station, TN 37179
877-540-2200
www.nomotc.org

The Twins Foundation
P.O. Box 6043
Providence, RI 02940-6043
401-729-1000

Triplet Connection
P.O. Box 99571
Stockton, CA 95209
209-474-0885
www.tripletconnection.org

Twin Services
P.O. Box 10066
Berkeley, CA 94709
510-524-0863
www.twinservices.org

Twinnet
www.ghg.net/4dee/index.html

Twins Magazine
5350 S. Roslyn St., Suite 400
Englewood, CO 80111
800-328-3211
www.twinsmagazine.com

Miscellaneous

*National Organization of Single
Mothers*
P.O. Box 68
Midland, NC 28107-0068
704-888-5437
singlemothers.org

On-line announcements
www.senada.com
Place to send on-line
announcements and invitations
for almost every occasion.

Social Security Administration
800-772-1213
www.ssa.gov

Some useful websites

- **www.babycenter.com** includes a catalog of baby products
  for shopping online, chat rooms for the expectant mother-
  to-be and information on various topics of interest.
- **www.babytalkandshop.com** helps parents create a baby-
  registry page.
- **www.parenttime.com** contains articles from current
  magazines, interviews with celebrity parents, advice from
  an OB-GYN or nurse-midwife, and chat rooms.
- **www.storksite.com** is a fun site for expectant parents
  that includes information on stages of development,
  help choosing a baby's name and a place to announce
  baby's arrival.
- **www.maternity.org** is an organization committed to
  improving the maternity-care system in the United States.

Due Date Calendar

In the following pages, find the month and day of your last menstrual period (the larger number). Your approximate due date is the month and day in the upper right triangle.

First day of your last menstrual period

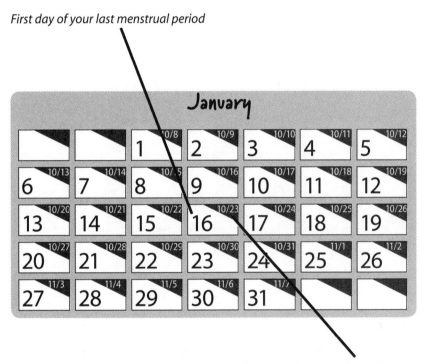

Your approximate due date

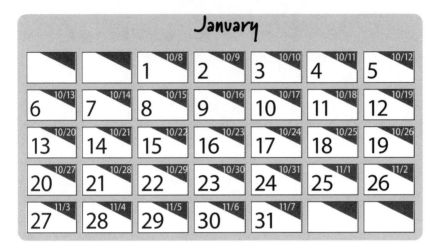

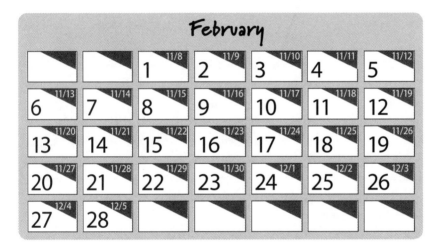

April

		1 ¹ᐟ⁶	2 ¹ᐟ⁷	3 ¹ᐟ⁸	4 ¹ᐟ⁹	5 ¹ᐟ¹⁰
6 ¹ᐟ¹¹	7 ¹ᐟ¹²	8 ¹ᐟ¹³	9 ¹ᐟ¹⁴	10 ¹ᐟ¹⁵	11 ¹ᐟ¹⁶	12 ¹ᐟ¹⁷
13 ¹ᐟ¹⁸	14 ¹ᐟ¹⁹	15 ¹ᐟ²⁰	16 ¹ᐟ²¹	17 ¹ᐟ²²	18 ¹ᐟ²³	19 ¹ᐟ²⁴
20 ¹ᐟ²⁵	21 ¹ᐟ²⁶	22 ¹ᐟ²⁷	23 ¹ᐟ²⁸	24 ¹ᐟ²⁹	25 ¹ᐟ³⁰	26 ¹ᐟ³¹
27 ²ᐟ¹	28 ²ᐟ²	29 ²ᐟ³	30 ²ᐟ⁴			

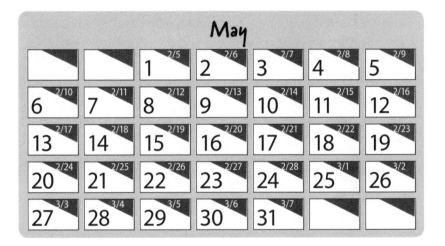

May

		1 ²ᐟ⁵	2 ²ᐟ⁶	3 ²ᐟ⁷	4 ²ᐟ⁸	5 ²ᐟ⁹
6 ²ᐟ¹⁰	7 ²ᐟ¹¹	8 ²ᐟ¹²	9 ²ᐟ¹³	10 ²ᐟ¹⁴	11 ²ᐟ¹⁵	12 ²ᐟ¹⁶
13 ²ᐟ¹⁷	14 ²ᐟ¹⁸	15 ²ᐟ¹⁹	16 ²ᐟ²⁰	17 ²ᐟ²¹	18 ²ᐟ²²	19 ²ᐟ²³
20 ²ᐟ²⁴	21 ²ᐟ²⁵	22 ²ᐟ²⁶	23 ²ᐟ²⁷	24 ²ᐟ²⁸	25 ³ᐟ¹	26 ³ᐟ²
27 ³ᐟ³	28 ³ᐟ⁴	29 ³ᐟ⁵	30 ³ᐟ⁶	31 ³ᐟ⁷		

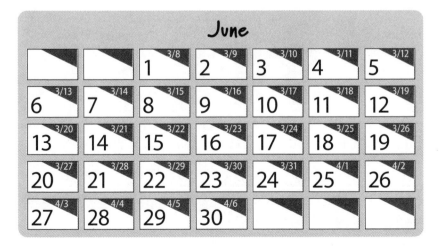

June

		1 ³ᐟ⁸	2 ³ᐟ⁹	3 ³ᐟ¹⁰	4 ³ᐟ¹¹	5 ³ᐟ¹²
6 ³ᐟ¹³	7 ³ᐟ¹⁴	8 ³ᐟ¹⁵	9 ³ᐟ¹⁶	10 ³ᐟ¹⁷	11 ³ᐟ¹⁸	12 ³ᐟ¹⁹
13 ³ᐟ²⁰	14 ³ᐟ²¹	15 ³ᐟ²²	16 ³ᐟ²³	17 ³ᐟ²⁴	18 ³ᐟ²⁵	19 ³ᐟ²⁶
20 ³ᐟ²⁷	21 ³ᐟ²⁸	22 ³ᐟ²⁹	23 ³ᐟ³⁰	24 ³ᐟ³¹	25 ⁴ᐟ¹	26 ⁴ᐟ²
27 ⁴ᐟ³	28 ⁴ᐟ⁴	29 ⁴ᐟ⁵	30 ⁴ᐟ⁶			

July

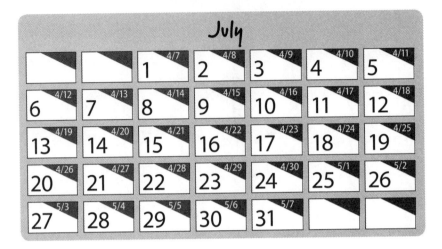

		1 4/7	2 4/8	3 4/9	4 4/10	5 4/11
6 4/12	7 4/13	8 4/14	9 4/15	10 4/16	11 4/17	12 4/18
13 4/19	14 4/20	15 4/21	16 4/22	17 4/23	18 4/24	19 4/25
20 4/26	21 4/27	22 4/28	23 4/29	24 4/30	25 5/1	26 5/2
27 5/3	28 5/4	29 5/5	30 5/6	31 5/7		

August

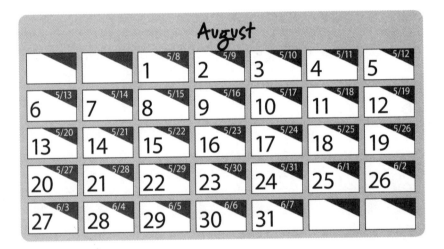

		1 5/8	2 5/9	3 5/10	4 5/11	5 5/12
6 5/13	7 5/14	8 5/15	9 5/16	10 5/17	11 5/18	12 5/19
13 5/20	14 5/21	15 5/22	16 5/23	17 5/24	18 5/25	19 5/26
20 5/27	21 5/28	22 5/29	23 5/30	24 5/31	25 6/1	26 6/2
27 6/3	28 6/4	29 6/5	30 6/6	31 6/7		

September

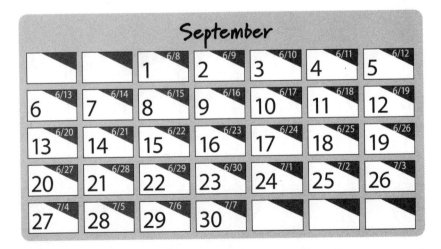

		1 6/8	2 6/9	3 6/10	4 6/11	5 6/12
6 6/13	7 6/14	8 6/15	9 6/16	10 6/17	11 6/18	12 6/19
13 6/20	14 6/21	15 6/22	16 6/23	17 6/24	18 6/25	19 6/26
20 6/27	21 6/28	22 6/29	23 6/30	24 7/1	25 7/2	26 7/3
27 7/4	28 7/5	29 7/6	30 7/7			

October

		1 ^7/8	2 ^7/9	3 ^7/10	4 ^7/11	5 ^7/12
6 ^7/13	7 ^7/14	8 ^7/15	9 ^7/16	10 ^7/17	11 ^7/18	12 ^7/19
13 ^7/20	14 ^7/21	15 ^7/22	16 ^7/23	17 ^7/24	18 ^7/25	19 ^7/26
20 ^7/27	21 ^7/28	22 ^7/29	23 ^7/30	24 ^7/31	25 ^8/1	26 ^8/2
27 ^8/3	28 ^8/4	29 ^8/5	30 ^8/6	31 ^8/7		

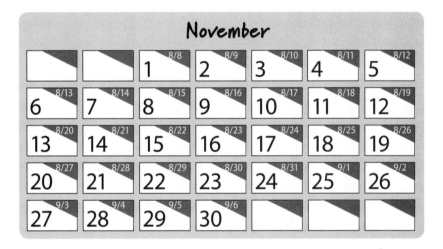

November

		1 ^8/8	2 ^8/9	3 ^8/10	4 ^8/11	5 ^8/12
6 ^8/13	7 ^8/14	8 ^8/15	9 ^8/16	10 ^8/17	11 ^8/18	12 ^8/19
13 ^8/20	14 ^8/21	15 ^8/22	16 ^8/23	17 ^8/24	18 ^8/25	19 ^8/26
20 ^8/27	21 ^8/28	22 ^8/29	23 ^8/30	24 ^8/31	25 ^9/1	26 ^9/2
27 ^9/3	28 ^9/4	29 ^9/5	30 ^9/6			

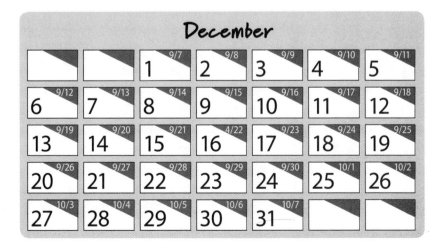

December

		1 ^9/7	2 ^9/8	3 ^9/9	4 ^9/10	5 ^9/11
6 ^9/12	7 ^9/13	8 ^9/14	9 ^9/15	10 ^9/16	11 ^9/17	12 ^9/18
13 ^9/19	14 ^9/20	15 ^9/21	16 ^4/22	17 ^9/23	18 ^9/24	19 ^9/25
20 ^9/26	21 ^9/27	22 ^9/28	23 ^9/29	24 ^9/30	25 ^10/1	26 ^10/2
27 ^10/3	28 ^10/4	29 ^10/5	30 ^10/6	31 ^10/7		

Glossary

A

abruptio placenta. See *placental abruption*.

acquired immune deficiency syndrome (AIDS). Debilitating and frequently fatal illness that affects the body's ability to respond to infection. Caused by the human immune deficiency virus (HIV).

aerobic exercise. Exercise that increases your heart rate and causes you to consume oxygen.

afterbirth. See *placenta*.

alpha-fetoprotein (AFP). Substance produced by the unborn baby as it grows inside the uterus. Large amounts of AFP are found in the amniotic fluid. Larger-than-normal amounts are found in the maternal bloodstream if neural-tube defects are present in the fetus.

alveoli. Ends of the ducts of the lung.

amino acids. Substances that act as building blocks in the developing embryo and fetus.

amniocentesis. Removal of amniotic fluid from the amniotic sac. Fluid is tested for some genetic defects.

amnion. Membrane around the fetus. It surrounds the amniotic cavity.

amniotic fluid. Liquid surrounding the baby inside the amniotic sac.

amniotic sac. Sac that surrounds baby inside the uterus. It contains the baby, the placenta and the amniotic fluid.

ampulla. Dilated opening of a tube or duct.

anemia. Any condition in which the number of red blood cells is less than normal. Term usually applies to the concentration of the oxygen-transporting material in the blood, which is the red blood cell.

anencephaly. Defective development of the brain combined with the absence of the bones normally surrounding the brain.

angioma. Tumor, usually benign, or swelling composed of lymph and blood vessels.

anovulatory. Lack of or cessation of ovulation.

anti-inflammatory medications. Drugs to relieve pain or inflammation.

areola. Pigmented or colored ring surrounding the nipple of the breast.

arrhythmia. Irregular or missed heartbeat.

aspiration. Swallowing or sucking a foreign body or fluid, such as vomit, into an airway.

asthma. Disease marked by recurrent attacks of shortness of breath and difficulty breathing. Often caused by an allergic reaction.

atonic uterus. Flaccid; relaxed; lacking tone.

autoantibodies. Antibodies that attack parts of your body or your own tissues.

B

back labor. Pain of labor felt in lower back.

beta-adrenergics. Substances that interfere with transmission of stimuli. They affect the autonomic nervous system.

bilirubin. Breakdown product of pigment formed in the liver from hemoglobin during the destruction of red blood cells.

biophysical profile. Method of evaluating a fetus before birth.

biopsy. Removal of a small piece of tissue for microscopic study.

birthing center. Facility in which a woman labors, delivers and recovers in the same room. It may be part of a hospital or a freestanding unit.

blastomere. One of the cells the egg divides into after it has been fertilized.

bloody show. Small amount of vaginal bleeding late in pregnancy; often precedes labor.

board certification. Doctor has had additional training and testing in a particular specialty. In the area of obstetrics, the American College of Obstetricians and Gynecologists offers this training. Certification requires expertise in care of a pregnant woman.

Braxton-Hicks contractions. Irregular, painless tightening of uterus during pregnancy.

breech presentation. Abnormal position of the fetus. Buttocks or legs come into the birth canal ahead of the head.

C

cataract, congenital. Cloudiness of the eye lens present at birth.

cell antibodies. See *autoantibodies.*

Cesarean section (delivery). Delivery of a baby through an abdominal incision rather than through the vagina.

Chadwick's sign. Dark-blue or purple discoloration of the mucosa of the vagina and cervix during pregnancy.

chemotherapy. Treatment of disease by chemical substances or drugs.

Chlamydia. Sexually transmitted venereal infection.

chloasma. Extensive brown patches of irregular shape and size on the face or other parts of the body.

chorion. Outermost fetal membrane found around the amnion.

chorionic villus sampling. Diagnostic test done early in pregnancy. A biopsy of tissue is taken from inside the uterus through the cervical opening to determine abnormalities of pregnancy.

cleft palate. Defect in the palate, a part of the upper jaw or mouth.

colostrum. Thin yellow fluid, which is the first milk to come from the breast. Most often seen toward the end of pregnancy. It is different in content from milk produced later during nursing.

condyloma acuminatum. Skin tags or warts that are sexually transmitted. Also called *venereal warts*.

congenital problem. Problem present at birth.

conization of the cervix. Surgical procedure performed on premalignant and malignant conditions of the cervix. A large biopsy of the cervix is taken in the shape of a cone.

conjoined twins. Twins connected at the body; they may share vital organs. Also called *Siamese twins*.

constipation. Bowel movements are infrequent or incomplete.

contraction stress test. Test of fetal response to uterine contractions to evaluate fetal well-being.

corpus luteum. Area in the ovary where the egg is released at ovulation. A cyst may form in this area after ovulation. Called a *corpus luteum cyst*.

crown-to-rump length. Measurement from the top of the baby's head (crown) to the buttocks of the baby (rump).

cystitis. Inflammation of the bladder.

cytomegalovirus (CMV) infection. Group of viruses from the herpes virus family.

D

D&C (dilatation and curettage). Surgical procedure in which the cervix is dilated and the lining of the uterus is scraped.

developmental delay. Condition in which the development of the baby or child is slower than normal.

diastasis recti. Separation of abdominal muscles.

diethylstilbestrol (DES). Non-steroidal synthetic estrogen. Used in the past to try to prevent miscarriage.

dizygotic twins. Twins derived from two different eggs. Often called fraternal twins.

dysuria. Difficulty or pain urinating.

E

eclampsia. Convulsions and coma in a woman with pre-eclampsia. Not related to epilepsy. See *pre-eclampsia*.

ectodermal germ layer. Layer in the developing embryo that gives rise to developing structures in the fetus. These include skin, teeth and glands of the mouth, the nervous system and the pituitary gland.

ectopic pregnancy. Pregnancy that occurs outside the uterine cavity.

EDC (estimated date of confinement). Anticipated due date for delivery of the baby. Calculated from the first day of the last period counting forward 280 days.

effacement. Thinning of cervix.

electroencephalogram. Recording of the electrical activity of the brain.

embryo. Organism in the early stages of development.

embryonic period. First 10 weeks of gestation.

endodermal germ layer. Area of tissue in early development of the embryo that gives rise to other structures. These include the digestive tract, respiratory organs, vagina, bladder and urethra. Also called *endoderm* or *entoderm*.

endometrial cycle. Regular development of the mucous membrane that lines the inside of the uterus. It begins with the preparation for acceptance of a pregnancy and ends with the shedding of the lining during a menstrual period.

endometrium. Mucous membrane that lines inside of the uterine wall.

enema. Fluid injected into the rectum for the purpose of clearing out the bowel.

engorgement. Congested; filled with fluid.

enzyme. Protein made by cells. It acts as a catalyst to improve or cause chemical changes in other substances.

epidural block. Type of anesthesia. Medication is injected around the spinal cord during labor or other types of surgery.

episiotomy. Surgical incision of the *vulva* (area behind the vagina, above the rectum). Used during delivery to avoid tearing or laceration of the vaginal opening and rectum.

estimated date of confinement. See *EDC*.

exotoxin. Poison or toxin from a source outside the body.

F

face presentation. Baby comes into the birth canal face first.

Fallopian tube. Tube that leads from the cavity of the uterus to the area of the ovary. Also called *uterine tube*.

false labor. Tightening of uterus without dilatation of the cervix.

fasting blood sugar. Blood test to evaluate the amount of sugar in the blood following a period of fasting.

ferrous gluconate. Iron supplement.

ferrous sulfate. Iron supplement.

fertilization. Joining of the sperm and egg.

fertilization age. Dating a pregnancy from the time of fertilization. 2 weeks shorter than the gestational age.

fetal anomaly. Fetal malformation or abnormal development.

fetal arrhythmia. See *arrhythmia*.

fetal goiter. Enlargement of the thyroid in the fetus.

fetal monitor. Device used before or during labor to listen to and record the fetal heartbeat. Can be external monitoring (through maternal abdomen) or internal monitoring (through maternal vagina) of the baby inside the uterus.

fetal period. Time period following the embryonic period (first 10 weeks of gestation) until birth.

fetus. Refers to the unborn baby after 10 weeks of gestation until birth.

fibrin. Elastic protein important in the coagulation of blood.

forceps. Instrument used to help remove baby from the birth canal during delivery.

frank breech. Baby presenting buttocks first. Legs are flexed and knees extended.

fraternal twins. See *dizygotic twins*.

G

genetic counseling. Consultation between a couple and a specialist about the possibility of genetic defects and genetic problems in a pregnancy.

genital herpes simplex. Herpes simplex infection involving the genital area. It can be significant during pregnancy because of the danger to a newborn fetus becoming infected with herpes simplex.

genitourinary problems. Defects or problems involving genital organs and the bladder or kidneys.

germ layers. Layers or areas of tissue important in the development of the baby.

gestational age. Dating a pregnancy from the first day of the last menstrual period; 2 weeks longer than fertilization age. See *fertilization age.*

gestational diabetes. Occurrence or worsening of diabetes during pregnancy (gestation).

gestational trophoblastic disease (GTN). Abnormal pregnancy with cystic growth of the placenta. Characterized by bleeding during early and middle pregnancy.

globulin. Family of proteins from plasma or serum of the blood.

glucose-tolerance test (GTT). Blood test done to evaluate the body's response to sugar. Blood is drawn at intervals following ingestion of a sugary substance.

glucosuria. Glucose in the urine.

gonorrhea. Contagious venereal infection, transmitted primarily by intercourse.

grand mal seizure. Loss of control of body functions. Seizure activity of a major form.

group-B streptococcal infection. Serious infection occurring in the mother's vagina and throat.

H

habitual abortion. Occurrence of three or more spontaneous miscarriages.

heartburn. Discomfort or pain that occurs in the chest. Often occurs after eating.

hematocrit. Determines the proportion of blood cells to plasma. Important in diagnosing anemia.

hemoglobin. Pigment in red blood cell that carries oxygen to body tissues.

hemolytic disease. Destruction of red blood cells. See *anemia.*

hemorrhoids. Dilated blood vessels in the rectum or rectal canal.

heparin. Medication used to thin the blood.

Homan's sign. Pain caused by flexing the toes when a person has a blood clot in the lower leg.

human chorionic gonadatropin. Hormone produced in early pregnancy; measured in a pregnancy test.

human placental lactogen. Hormone of pregnancy produced by the placenta and found in the bloodstream.

hyaline membrane disease. Respiratory disease of the newborn.

hydatidiform mole. See *gestational trophoblastic disease.*

hydramnios. Increased amniotic fluid.

hydrocephalus. Excessive accumulation of fluid around the brain of the baby. Sometimes called *water on the brain.*

hyperbilirubinemia. Extremely high level of bilirubin in the blood.

hyperemesis gravidarum. Severe nausea, dehydration and vomiting during pregnancy. Occurs most frequently during the first trimester.

hyperglycemia. Increased blood sugar.

hypertension, pregnancy-induced. High blood pressure that occurs during pregnancy. Defined by an increase in the diastolic or systolic blood pressure.

hyperthyroidism. Elevation of the thyroid hormone in the bloodstream.

hypoplasia. Defective or incomplete development or formation of tissue.

hypotension. Low blood pressure.

hypothyroidism. Low or inadequate levels of thyroid hormone in the bloodstream.

I

identical twins. See *monozygotic twins.*

immune globulin preparation. Substance used to protect against infection with certain diseases, such as hepatitis or measles.

in utero. Within the uterus.

incompetent cervix. Cervix that dilates painlessly, without contractions.

incomplete miscarriage. Miscarriage in which part, but not all, of the uterine contents are expelled.

inevitable miscarriage. Pregnancy complicated with bleeding and cramping. Usually results in miscarriage.

insulin. Peptide hormone made by the pancreas. It promotes the use of glucose.

intrauterine-growth retardation (IUGR). Inadequate growth of the fetus during the last stages of pregnancy.

iodides. Medications made up of negative ion of iodine.

iron-deficiency anemia. Anemia produced by lack of iron in the diet. Often seen in pregnancy. See *anemia.*

isoimmunization. Development of specific antibody directed at the red blood cells of another individual, such as a baby in utero. Often occurs when an Rh-negative woman carries an Rh-positive baby or is given Rh-positive blood.

J

jaundice. Yellow staining of the skin, sclera (eyes) and deeper tissues of the body. Caused by excessive amounts of bilirubin. Treated with phototherapy.

K

ketones. Breakdown product of metabolism found in the blood, particularly from starvation or uncontrolled diabetes.

kidney stones. Small mass or lesion found in the kidney or urinary tract. Can block the flow of urine.

L

labor. Process of expelling a fetus from the uterus.

laparoscopy. Minor surgical procedure performed for tubal ligation, diagnosis of pelvic pain or diagnosis of ectopic pregnancy.

leukorrhea. Vaginal discharge characterized by a white or yellowish color. Primarily composed of mucus.

lightening. Change in the shape of the pregnant uterus a few weeks before labor. Often described as the baby "dropping."

linea nigra. Line of increased pigmentation running down the abdomen from the bellybutton to the pubic area during pregnancy.

M

malignant GTN. Cancerous change of gestational trophoblastic disease. See *gestational trophoblastic disease.*

mammogram. X-ray study of the breasts to identify normal and abnormal breast tissue.

mask of pregnancy. Increased pigmentation over the area of the face under each eye. Commonly has the appearance of a butterfly.

McDonald cerclage. Surgical procedure performed on an incompetent cervix. A drawstring-type suture holds the cervical opening closed during pregnancy. See *incompetent cervix.*

meconium. First intestinal discharge of the newborn; green or yellow in color. It consists of epithelial or surface cells, mucus and bile. Discharge may occur before or during labor or soon after birth.

melanoma. Pigmented mole or tumor. It may or may not be cancerous.

meningomyelocele. Congenital defect of the central nervous system of the baby. Membranes and the spinal cord protrude through an opening or defect in the vertebral column.

menstrual age. See *gestational age.*

menstruation. Regular or periodic discharge of a bloody fluid from the uterus.

mesodermal germ layer. Tissue of the embryo that forms connective tissue, muscles, kidneys, ureters and other organs.

metaplasia. Change in the structure of a tissue into another type that is not normal for that tissue.

microcephaly. Abnormally small development of the head in the developing fetus.

microphthalmia. Abnormally small eyeballs.

miscarriage. Termination or end of pregnancy. Giving birth to an embryo or fetus before it can live outside the womb, usually defined as before 20 weeks of gestation.

missed miscarriage. Failed pregnancy without bleeding or cramping. Often diagnosed by ultrasound weeks or months after a pregnancy fails.

mittelschmerz. Pain that coincides with release of an egg from the ovary.

molar pregnancy. See *gestational trophoblastic disease.*

monilial vulvovaginitis. Infection caused by yeast or monilia. Usually affects the vagina and vulva.

monozygotic twins. Twins conceived from one egg. Often called *identical twins.*

morning sickness. Nausea and vomiting, with ill health, found primarily during the first trimester of pregnancy. Also see *hyperemesis gravidarum.*

morula. Cells resulting from the early division of the fertilized egg at the beginning of pregnancy.

mucus plug. Secretions in cervix; often released just before labor.

mutations. Change in the character of a gene. Passed from one cell division to another.

N

neural-tube defects. Abnormalities in the development of the spinal cord and brain in a fetus. See *anencephaly; hydrocephalus; spina bifida.*

nurse-midwife. Nurse who has received extra training in the care of pregnant patients and the delivery of babies.

O

obstetrician. Physician who specializes in the care of pregnant women and the delivery of babies.

oligohydramnios. Lack or deficiency of amniotic fluid.

omphalocele. Presence of congenital outpouching of the umbilicus containing internal organs in the fetus or newborn infant.

opioids. Synthetic compounds with effects similar to those of opium.

organogenesis. Development of the organ systems in the embryo.

ossification. Bone formation.

ovarian cycle. Regular production of hormones from the ovary in response to hormonal messages from the brain. The ovarian cycle governs the endometrial cycle.

ovulation. Cyclic production of an egg from the ovary.

ovulatory age. See *fertilization age.*

oxytocin. Medication that causes uterine contractions.

P

palmar erythema. Redness of palms of the hands.

Pap smear. Routine screening test that evaluates presence of premalignant or cancerous conditions of the cervix.

paracervical block. Local anesthetic for cervical dilatation.

pediatrician. Physician who specializes in the care of babies and children.

pelvimetry. Evaluation of the size of the birth canal or pelvis. Performed by X-ray.

perinatologist. Physician who specializes in the care of high-risk pregnancies.

petit mal seizure. Attack of a brief nature with possible short impairment of consciousness. Often associated with blinking or flickering of the eyelids and a mild twitching of the mouth.

phosphatidyl glycerol.
Lipoprotein present when fetal
lungs are mature.

phospholipids. Fat-containing
phosphorous. The most
important are lecithins and
sphingomyelin, which are
important in the maturation of
fetal lungs before birth.

phototherapy. Treatment for
jaundice in a newborn infant.
See *jaundice.*

**physiologic anemia of
pregnancy.** Anemia during
pregnancy caused by an
increase in the amount of
plasma (fluid) in the blood
compared to the number of
cells in the blood. See *anemia.*

placenta. Organ inside the
uterus that is attached to the
baby by the umbilical cord.
Essential during pregnancy for
growth and development
of the embryo and fetus. Also
called *afterbirth.*

placenta previa. Low
attachment of the placenta,
covering or very close
to the cervix.

placental abruption. Premature
separation of the placenta
from the uterus.

placentamegaly. Abnormally
large growth of the placenta
during pregnancy.

pneumonitis. Inflammation of
the lungs.

polyhydramnios. See
hydramnios.

postmature baby. Pregnancy of
42+ weeks' gestation.

postpartum blues. Mild
depression after delivery.

postpartum distress. A range
of symptoms including baby
blues, postpartum depression
and postpartum psychosis.

postpartum hemorrhage.
Bleeding greater than 15
ounces (450ml) at time
of delivery.

pre-eclampsia. Combination of
symptoms significant to
pregnancy, including high
blood pressure, edema,
swelling and changes in
reflexes.

pregnancy diabetes. See
gestational diabetes.

premature delivery. Delivery
before 38 weeks' gestation.

presentation. Describes which
part of the baby comes into
the birth canal first.

propylthiouracil. Medication
used to treat thyroid disease.

proteinuria. Protein in urine.

pruritis gravidarum. Itching
during pregnancy.

pubic symphysis. Bony
prominence in the pelvic bone
found in the midline.
Landmark from which the
doctor often measures during
pregnancy to follow growth of
the uterus.

pudendal block. Local
anesthesia during labor.

pulmonary embolism. Blood clot from another part of the body that travels to the lungs. Can cause closed passages in the lungs and decrease oxygen exchange.

pyelonephritis. Serious kidney infection.

Q

quickening. Feeling the baby move inside the uterus.

R

radiation therapy. Method of treatment for various cancers.

radioactive scan. Diagnostic test in which radioactive material is injected into the body and scanned to find a problem within a particular part of the body.

Rh-negative. Absence of rhesus antibody in the blood.

RhoGAM®. Medication given during pregnancy and following delivery to prevent isoimmunization. See *isoimmunization.*

Rh-sensitivity. See *isoimmunization.*

round-ligament pain. Pain caused by stretching ligament on the sides of the uterus during pregnancy.

rupture of membranes. Loss of fluid from the amniotic sac. Also called *breaking of waters.*

S

seizure. Sudden onset of a convulsion.

sexually transmitted disease (STD). Infection transmitted through sexual intercourse.

sickle cell anemia. Anemia caused by abnormal red blood cells shaped like a sickle or a cylinder.

sickle cell trait. Presence of the trait for sickle cell anemia. Not sickle cell disease itself.

sickle crisis. Painful episode caused by sickle cell disease.

skin tag. Flap or extra buildup of skin.

sodium. Element found in many foods, particularly salt. Ingestion of too much sodium may cause fluid retention.

spina bifida. Congenital abnormality characterized by a defect in the vertebral column. Membranes of the spinal cord and the spinal cord itself protrude outside the protective bony canal of the spine.

spinal anesthesia. Anesthesia given in the spinal canal.

spontaneous miscarriage. Loss of pregnancy during the first 20 weeks of gestation.

stasis. Decreased flow.

station. Estimation of the descent of the baby.

steroids. Group of medications of hormone origin. Often used to treat various diseases. Includes estrogen, testosterone, progesterone, prednisone.

stigma. Area on the ovary where the egg has been released at the time of ovulation.

stillbirth. Death of a fetus before birth, usually defined as after 20 weeks of gestation.

stretch marks. Areas of the skin that are torn or stretched. Often found on the abdomen, breasts, buttocks and legs.

striae distensa. See *stretch marks.*

sulci. Groove or furrow on the surface of the brain.

surfactant. Phospholipid present in the lungs. Controls surface tension of lungs. Premature babies often lack sufficient amounts of surfactant to breathe without assistance.

syphilis. Sexually transmitted venereal infection caused by *treponema pallidum.*

systemic lupus erythematosus (SLE). Connective-tissue disorder common in women in the reproductive ages. Antibodies made by the person act against his or her own tissues.

T

Tay-Sachs disease. Inherited disease characterized by mental and physcial retardation, convulsions, enlargement of the head and eventually death. Trait is usually carried by Ashkenazi Jews.

telangiectasias. Dilatation or swelling of a small blood vessel. Sometimes called an angioma. During pregnancy, another common name is a *spider angioma.*

teratogen. Anything that causes abnormal development in an embryo.

teratogenic. Causes abnormal development.

teratology. Branch of science that deals with substances that cause abnormal development.

thalassemia. Group of inherited disorders of hemoglobin metabolism, which results in a decrease in the amount of hemoglobin formed. Found most commonly in people of Mediterranean descent.

threatened miscarriage. Bleeding during the first trimester of pregnancy without cramping or contractions.

thrombosis. Formation of a blood clot (thrombus).

thrush. Monilial or yeast infection occurring in the mouth or mucous membranes of a newborn infant.

thyroid disease. Abnormality of the thyroid gland and its production of thyroid hormone. See *hyperthyroidism; hypothyroidism.*

thyroid hormone. Chemical made in the thyroid that affects the entire body.

thyroid panel. Series of blood tests done to evaluate the function of the thyroid gland.

thyroid-stimulating hormone (TSH). Hormone made in the brain that stimulates the thyroid to produce thyroid hormone.

tocolysis. Stopping contractions during premature labor.

tocolytic agents. Medications to stop labor. See *beta-adrenergics.*

toxoplasmosis. Infection caused by *toxoplasma gondii.*

transverse lie. Fetus is turned sideways in uterus.

trichomonal vaginitis. Venereal infection caused by *trichomonas.*

trimester. Method of dividing pregnancy into three equal time periods of about 13 weeks each.

trophoblast. Cell layer important in early development of the embryo and fetus. It provides nourishment from the mother to the fetus and participates in the formation of the placenta.

U

umbilical cord. Cord that connects the placenta to the developing baby. It removes waste products and carbon dioxide from the baby and brings oxygenated blood and nutrients from the mother through the placenta to the baby.

umbilicus. Bellybutton.

ureters. Tubes from the kidneys to the bladder that drain urine.

urinary calculi. See *kidney stones.*

uterine atony. Lack of tone of uterus.

uterus. Organ an embryo/fetus grows in. Also called a *womb.*

V

vaccine. Mild infection given to cause production of antibodies to protect against subsequent infections.

vacuum extractor. Device used to provide traction on fetal head during delivery.

varicose veins. Blood (veins) that are dilated enlarged.

vascular spiders. See
  telangiectasias.

vena cava. Major vein in the
  body that empties into the
  right atrium of the heart. It
  returns unoxygenated blood
  to the heart for transport to
  the lungs.

venereal warts. See *condyloma
  acuminatum.*

vernix. Fatty substance made up
  of epithelial cells that covers
  fetal skin inside the uterus.

vertex. Head first.

villi. Projection from a mucous
  membrane. Most important
  within the placenta in the
  exchange of nutrients from
  maternal blood to the
  placenta and fetus.

W

womb. See *uterus.*

Y

yeast infection. See *monilial
  vulvovaginitis; thrush.*

Z

zygote. Cell that results from the
  union of a sperm and egg at
  fertilization.

Index